Evelyn Abbott

Pericles and the golden Age of Athens

Evelyn Abbott

Pericles and the golden Age of Athens

ISBN/EAN: 9783743316270

Manufactured in Europe, USA, Canada, Australia, Japa

Cover: Foto ©ninafisch / pixelio.de

Manufactured and distributed by brebook publishing software (www.brebook.com)

Evelyn Abbott

Pericles and the golden Age of Athens

Heroes of the Nations

Nelson, and the Naval Supremacy of England. By W. CLARK RUSSELL, author of "The Wreck of the Grosvenor," etc.

Gustavus Adolphus, and the Struggle of Protestantism for Existence. By C. R. L. FLETCHER, M.A., late Fellow of All Souls College, Oxford.

Pericles, and the Golden Age of Athens. By EVELYN ABBOTT, M.A., Fellow of Balliol College, Oxford.

Theodoric the Goth, the Barbarian Champion of Civilisation. By THOMAS HODGKIN, author of "Italy and Her Invaders," etc.

Alexander the Great, and the Extension of Greek Rule and of Greek Ideas. By Prof. BENJAMIN J. WHEELER, Cornell University.

(For fuller details of this Series see prospectus at end of volume.)

G. P. PUTNAM'S SONS, PUBLISHERS,
NEW YORK AND LONDON.

Heroes of the Nations

EDITED BY

Evelyn Abbott, M.A.

FELLOW OF BALLIOL COLLEGE, OXFORD

FACTA DUCIS VIVENT, OPEROSAQUE
GLORIA RERUM.—OVID, IN LIVIAM, 265.

THE HERO'S DEEDS AND HARD-WON
FAME SHALL LIVE.

PERICLES

PERICLES.

From a Bust in the Vatican

(*Boetticher's "Akropolis."*)

PERICLES

AND

THE GOLDEN AGE OF ATHENS

BY

EVELYN ABBOTT, M.A.

FELLOW OF BALLIOL COLLEGE, OXFORD. AUTHOR OF
" A HISTORY OF GREECE," ETC.

G. P. PUTNAM'S SONS

NEW YORK   LONDON
27 WEST TWENTY-THIRD ST.   27 KING WILLIAM ST., STRAND
The Knickerbocker Press
1891

THIS sketch of the Age of Pericles consists of two parts: in the first and larger part I have endeavoured to trace the growth of the Athenian empire and the causes which alienated Athens and Sparta; in the second I have given a brief account of the government, the art and literature, the society and manners of the Periclean Athens.

It will be seen that I have ventured to form an opinion about the part which Pericles played as a practical statesman widely different from the estimate presented by Grote and Curtius. It is, so far as I can judge, impossible to deny that he destroyed a form of government under which his city attained to the height of her prosperity and that he plunged her into a hopeless and demoralising war. These are not the achievements of a great statesman. And so far as legislation goes, the Age of Pericles is a blank in the history of Athens.

In what then did his greatness lie? The answer is, that it lay in the ideals which he cherished. He saw what a city might do for her citizens; and what citizens might do for their city. In the years of peace his dreams took shape, and the result is before us in the Parthenon and the great Funeral Speech : but against the hard obstinacy of facts, which followed the outbreak of the war, he struggled in vain. His visions of empire faded away, and he lived long enough to see the treasury impoverished, the people more than decimated, the most faithful of Athenian allies shut up to certain destruction.

I am, of course, under great obligations to previous writers. More especially I am bound to mention the recent German histories of Greece by Duncker, Busolt, and Holm. All are admirable, but in different ways : Duncker, for his political insight ; Busolt, for his inexhaustible learning ; Holm, for his fresh and suggestive criticism. In the description of Athens I have mainly followed Curtius (vol. ii., sixth edition), and the article *Athen* in Baumeister's " Denkmaeler "; in what I have said about the Acropolis I have used Boetticher's work on the subject. Of Miss Harrison's very interesting book, which appeared after my pages were written, I have spoken in a note on p. 303.

I have also to thank Dr. Leaf and Mr. Clark for permission to use photographs out of their series for the purpose of illustration.

Contents. ix

CHAPTER VII.

PAGE

THE FIRST WAR BETWEEN ATHENS AND SPARTA, 459-453 B.C.) 89

Athens renounces her alliance with Sparta, and forms alliances with Argos and Thessaly—End of the revolt of the Helots—Athens and Megara—Renewal of the war in the East — The Egyptian expedition — Outbreak of war in Hellas— Halieis—Cecryphalea— Ægina— Building of the long walls at Athens— The Spartans in Phocis— Battle of Tanagra—Battle of Œnophyta—Athens at the height of her power—Cimon recalled—Disastrous failure of the Egyptian expedition.

CHAPTER VIII.

CONTINUATION OF THE WAR BETWEEN ATHENS AND SPARTA—A TRUCE FOR FIVE YEARS—CIMON'S LAST EXPEDITION—HIS DEATH AND CHARACTER (456 -449 B.C.) 108

War with Sparta—Athenian expeditions round the Peloponnesus—Disasters in Egypt—Cleruchs—Truce with Sparta for five years—Expedition to Cyprus—Death of Cimon— Battles off Salamis—Character of Cimon.

CHAPTER IX.

THE YEARS OF PEACE AND THE SECOND WAR BETWEEN ATHENS AND SPARTA (449-445 B.C.) . 118

Results of the death of Cimon—Difficulties with the allied cities—Miletus—Erythræ—The colony at Brea—The voyage into the Pontus—The "Sacred war"—Revolt of Bœotia— Battle of Coronea—Revolt of Megara and Eubœa—Critical position of Athens—Pericles and Plistoanax—Reduction of Eubœa—The thirty years' peace.

CHAPTER X.

CHAPTER XI.

CHAPTER XII.

CHAPTER XIII.

ILLUSTRATIONS.

Most of these illustrations have been reproduced from, or have been based upon, designs from the following sources : Müller's " *Denkmäler der alten Kunst,*" Boetticher's " *Die Akropolis von Athen,*" Baumeister's " *Denkmäler des klassischen Altertums,*" Curtius and Kaupert's " *Atlas von Athen,*" and Van Kampen's " *Orbis Terrarum Antiquus.*"

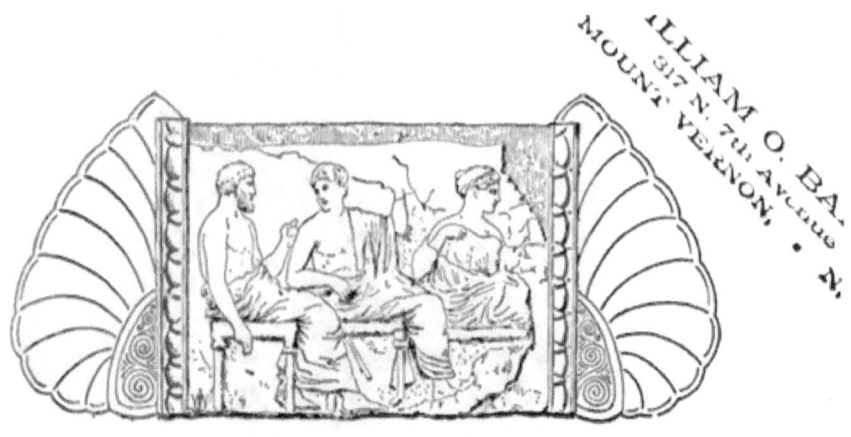

PERICLES

AND THE

GOLDEN AGE OF ATHENS.

CHAPTER I.

THE ALCMÆONIDÆ.

Sicyon—Clisthenes, the Tyrant—The wedding of Agariste—The "Accursed"—Parties at Athens—The Tyrants and their expulsion—The return of the Alcmæonidæ—Attempts at restoration—Clisthenes, the reformer—Effect of reform.

ABOUT two miles from the shore, at the southeast corner of the Corinthian Gulf, an elevated platform of triangular shape rises steeply between two streams, the Asopus on the east, and the Helisson on the west. The elevation is not great, but the sides of the tableland are so precipitous that only a few narrow paths lead up to it, and for this reason it forms the natural acropolis of the surrounding district. This was the site of the ancient Sicyon, and though the splendid city which once crowned the height has been swept away, the natural features of the place are what they ever were. Looking northward, we see the waters of the Corinthian Gulf, and beyond this the "summits old in story": Parnassus, sheltering the sacred Delphi ; Helicon, the home of the Muses and of Hesiod ; and Cithæron, the great rampart which divides Attica from Bœotia. On the east, beyond the Asopus, rises the lofty Acrocorinthus, the most imposing perhaps of all the mountains of Greece ; on the west stretches a fair and fertile plain, covered with the olive gardens for which Sicyon was famous. Behind the city, to the south, runs the valley of the Asopus, penetrating into the hills which form the northern rampart of Peloponnesus. Here were the mines of copper, whose produce enabled Sicyon at an early time to win a high place in the history of Grecian art.

In the beginning of the sixth century, B.C., this city was ruled by a Tyrant named Clisthenes, of the race of Orthagoras. In the ears of a Greek, who cherished his freedom above all things, the name of a Tyrant was at all times odious, but the knowledge that they would incur the deadly hatred of their citizens did not prevent ambitious men from aspiring to the sole command of their cities. "Only let me become Tyrant of my city," cried a contemporary of Solon, "and I will give my body to be flayed, my skin for a bottle." For seventy years or more before the accession of Clisthenes, Sicyon had been governed by the Orthagoridæ. Their origin was humble, but they had attained to wealth and distinction ; the second or third of the family had won an Olympian victory with his four-horse chariot, a distinction coveted beyond all others by a wealthy Greek. Clisthenes outshone all his predecessors ; he was one of the foremost of the Tyrants of his time, and under his rule the city enjoyed a prosperity which perhaps was never exceeded before or after.

Unhappily, his greatness was destined to die with him. His only child was a daughter, who could not inherit the position which her father held. But if she could not be Queen of Sicyon, she was at least the greatest heiress of her time, and in seeking a husband for her Clisthenes might choose from the best and richest families in Greece. Herodotus has told, in his inimitable way, the story of the wooing of Agariste. At the festival of Olympia, at which he was victorious in a four-horse chariot, Clisthenes caused a proclamation to be made, that anyone who held himself worthy to become the son-in-law of the King of Sicyon should repair to that city by the sixtieth day after the festival ; in a year from the sixtieth day, Clisthenes would betroth his daughter.

"Upon which notification, all such Grecians as thought highly of themselves and their country, went to Sicyon, where Clisthenes had made preparations for races and wrestling. From Italy arrived Smindyrides, the son of Hippocrates, a man plunged in voluptuousness beyond most examples, and born at Sybaris, which was then at the height of its prosperity ; with Damasus of Siris, the son of Amyris,

surnamed the Wise. From the Gulf of Ionia came
Amphimnestus, the son of Epistrophus of Epidamnus; and from Ætolia, Males, the brother of Titor-
mus, who surpassed all the Grecians in strength, and
had retired to the extremities of Ætolia. From
Peloponnesus arrived Leocedes, the son of Phidon,
Tyrant of Argos: of that Phidon, I say, who
prescribed measures to the Peloponnesians; and
exceeding all the Grecians in arrogance, removed
the Elean judges, and assumed to himself the power
of appointing the Olympian exercises; Amiantus,
an Arcadian of Trapezus, and son to Lycurgus;
with Laphanes, the Azanian of Pæus, son of that
Euphorion, who, according to a common report, entertained Castor and Pollux in his house, and from
that time received all strangers with great hospitality. These, with Onomastus of Elis, the son of
Agæus, came from Peloponnesus. From Athens
came Megacles, the son of that Alcmæon who visited
Crœsus; and Hippoclides, the son of Tisander, in
riches and beauty surpassing all the Athenians of
his time. From Eubœa, Lysanias alone, a native
of Eretria, which was then in a flourishing condition.
From Thessaly, Diactorides of Crannon; and from
the Molossians, Alcon. All these were pretenders
to the daughter of Clisthenes, and arrived in Sicyon
before the sixty days were expired. Clisthenes, in
pursuance of his design, first examined every one
touching his country and descent; after which he
detained them a whole year in order to inform
himself fully of their fortitude, temperance, institution, and manners; conversing with them frequently,

apart and together, and conducting the youngest to the gymnastic exercises. Above all, he endeavoured to discover their inclinations, when he entertained them with feasting; for he tried all experiments, and treated them with great magnificence, during the whole time they stayed with him. But among the several candidates he principally favoured the Athenians, especially Hippoclides, the son of Tisander, because he was esteemed for his courage, and derived his descent from the Corinthian Cypselidæ. When the day was come, which Clisthenes had appointed for the naming of the person he should choose, he sacrificed a hecatomb, and invited the pretenders, with all the Sicyonians, to the feast. After supper they entered into a dispute concerning music and other things that occasionally fell into discourse at that time; and as the wine went warmly about, Hippoclides, with an assuming air, commanded the musician to play a tune called 'Emmelia,' in which, being readily obeyed, he danced with much satisfaction to himself, though Clisthenes, observing all that passed, began to suspect the event. When Hippoclides had finished his dance, and rested some time, he commanded a table to be brought in, which was no sooner done than, mounting upon it, he first imitated the Laconian measures, then danced after the Athenian manner, and, last of all, setting his head upon the table, and erecting his feet, he moved his legs in such postures as he had already practised with his hands. Though the first and second of these dances had sufficiently dissuaded Clisthenes from choosing a son-in-law of

so much profligate impudence, yet he contained himself, and would not break out into an open passion.
But when he saw him endeavouring with his legs to
imitate the actions of his hands, he lost all patience,
and cried out : ' O son of Tisander, thou hast danced
away thy marriage.'   The other answered : ' That is
nought to Hippoclides,' which saying afterwards
obtained the authority of a proverb.   Then Clisthenes, having commanded silence, spoke to those
who pretended to his daughter in these words: ' I
commend you all, and am willing to gratify you all,
if I could, without distinguishing any one in particular, to the disadvantage of the rest.   But because I
have no more than one daughter, and consequently
cannot comply with the desires of so many persons, I
give a talent of silver to every one of those who shall
be excluded, as well in acknowledgment of your
readiness to enter into my family by this match, as
of the time you have spent in a long absence from
your habitations ; and I give my daughter Agariste
to Megacles, the son of Alcmæon, to be his wife
under the conditions and usages of the Athenians.'
Megacles immediately declared his consent, and the
nuptials were celebrated in the house of Clisthenes." *

The man thus distinguished was the heir of the
great house of the Alcmæonidæ, a family well known
for good and evil in the annals of Athens.   They
traced their lineage to Alcmæon, the grandson of
Nestor, the aged king of Pylus, whose figure is one
of the most striking in Homeric story.   Driven from

* Herod., vi., 126 *ff.*, Littlebury's translation.

the Peloponnesus at the time of the Dorian invasion,
they came to Athens, and established themselves as
one of the first families of the city.   Their kinsmen,
the Medontidæ, were for many generations the royal
race of Athens, and in the seventh century B.C.,
when the archonship was still closely restricted to
the noble families (the Eupatridæ), Megacles, the
grandfather of the youth now chosen by Clisthenes,
held the office.   In his archonship a distinguished
Athenian, named Cylon, attempted to make himself
Tyrant of Athens, and seized the Acropolis with a
number of followers.   The attempt was quickly
crushed, but not without fixing a lasting stain on the
city.   A number of Cylon's adherents, who had taken
refuge at the altars of the gods were induced to leave
the sanctuaries by promises of safety, and then
treacherously murdered (620? or 612? B.C.).   The
guilt of their death was laid upon the Alcmæonidæ,
who, it was said, had persuaded them to leave the
altars.   Henceforth the family was known as the
" Accursed "; and they were sentenced to banishment from Athens.   But either the sentence was
revoked, or it was not strictly enforced, for soon
afterwards we find Alcmæon, the son of Megacles,
leading the Athenian forces in the First Sacred War
(595–586 B.C.).   Many years later, after the marriage
of his son with Agariste, Alcmæon paid a visit to
Crœsus, the wealthy King of Lydia, who allowed him
to enter his treasure-house and carry away as much
gold as he could.   Alcmæon made the most of the opportunity.   He arrayed himself in the largest and
loosest attire he could procure, put on the widest

and tallest of top-boots, and thus equipped, entered
the chamber. Not content with stuffing his robe and
filling his boots to overflowing, he sprinkled gold-
dust on his hair, and crammed it into his mouth, till
nothing more could be added to his load. Then he
staggered from the room, looking " like anything
rather than a man," greatly to the amusement of
Crœsus. The gain thus strangely gotten added
largely to the wealth of the family, already increased
by the inheritance of Clisthenes. In the troubles
which overtook Athens in the second half of the
sixth century, the Alcmæonidæ made a not ignoble
use of their riches and power, but men did not forget that the curse was still upon them, and that their
wealth was derived, in a considerable degree, from
their connection with tyrants.

When next we hear of Megacles he is one of the
leaders in the party struggles, which disturbed
Athens in the middle of the sixth century B.C.
The reforms of Solon had failed to produce the
harmony, which their great author had expected;
and in twenty or thirty years after Solon's archonship, the parties of the Shore, the Plain, and the
Mountain were again arrayed against each other,
each seeking for the foremost place in the city.
Megacles, as the head of the house of the Alcmæonidæ, led the party of the Shore; his rivals at the
head of the Plain were Miltiades, the chief of the
ancient house of the Philaidæ, who claimed descent
from Ajax, and Lycurgus. At the head of the
Mountain was Pisistratus, of the race of the Nelidæ,
who, like the Alcmæonids, claimed descent from

Nestor of Pylus. As Plutarch has described them to us, the men of the Plain were chiefly the inhabitants of the plain of Cephisus ;—rich land-holders of a strict conservative type, who wished to retain unimpaired all their ancient rights and privileges. The men of the Shore were the inhabitants of the district known as the Paralia, the coast between Athens and Sunium. They included many of the merchant class, who naturally sought to put the claims of wealth above those of birth. The men of the Mountain were the poor goat-herds of the hilly region between the upper valley of the Cephisus and the sea. They were the radical party of the time, whose only hope of improving their condition lay in breaking the power of their opponents, and removing the barriers of birth and privilege. They had found a leader in the ranks of their opponents, a clever and unscrupulous man, who saw clearly that if he triumphed with the aid of peasants and shepherds, there would be no necessity to share his power with his supporters. In 560 B.C., matters came to a crisis, and Pisistratus established himself as Tyrant of Athens. His success was short-lived. Within a very few years his opponents combined and drove him from the city. He retired to his estates in the neighbourhood of Marathon, biding his time. It was not long before the rival parties quarrelled, and Pisistratus at once seized the opportunity to win over Megacles by promising to marry his daughter, (the child of Agariste). By this means he became tyrant of the city a second time. He fulfilled his promise of marrying the daughter of Megacles, but having no

wish that his elder sons should be displaced by any
child of hers, he treated her in a manner which
allowed no hope of offspring.   When Megacles became aware of this, he at once threw up all connection with Pisistratus, and went back to his old friends
of the Plain.   Pisistratus was once more obliged to
retire before the combination, and on this occasion
he was driven from Attica.   He crossed over to
Eretria in the neighbouring island of Eubœa, where
he remained for ten years, strengthening his position
by all possible means.   His rivals at Athens looked
idly on, while he collected mercenaries and amassed
money.   At length, believing himself able to win his
way back by force, he landed at Marathon, and
marched to Athens by the road which, leaving the
famous plain at the southern end, crosses over by
Hymettus to the city.   At Pallene, where the
Athenians came out to meet him, an engagement
took place, in which Pisistratus, by his superior
strategy, outwitted and defeated his enemies.   For
the third time he appeared in Athens.   He was now
careful to establish his power on a firm foundation ;
he surrounded himself with mercenary troops, and
drove his rivals out of the country.   Among many
others Megacles and the Alcmæonidæ found themselves exiles from their home.

For thirty years or more (541–509 B.C.), they ate
the bread of strangers.   In this period Megacles died,
and his place as head of the family was taken by Clisthenes, his son by Agariste.   As a young man, Clisthenes was probably more active than his father in
his efforts to regain his position at Athens, and after

the death of Pisistratus, in 527, the prospect was more encouraging. The sons of Pisistratus, Hippias and Hipparchus, who were associated in the government, were not the equals of their father; they had but succeeded to the throne, which he had won. Their conduct soon aroused such bitter hatred that a conspiracy was formed against them, and though Hippias escaped, Hipparchus was slain. This event, which took place in 514, produced a change for the worse in the character of Hippias; he became morose, suspicious, and oppressive. Uncertain of his position at home, he looked for support abroad, and married his daughter to the son of the Tyrant of Lampsacus, through whose good offices he hoped to find favour with the Persian monarch.

The Alcmæonidæ were doubtless well aware of the state of feeling at Athens; they thought the time had come for driving out the tyrant by force, and with this object they entered Attica and established themselves in a fortified position at Lipsydrium, on the slopes of Mount Parnes. But the attempt proved premature. Hippias was able to expel them from the country.

Thus baffled, the exiles sought assistance in another quarter. In 548 the temple of Delphi had been burned down. The rebuilding was made a national work; money was collected from far and near that a temple might be raised worthy of the most famous oracular shrine in the world. The Alcmæonidæ undertook to carry out the reconstruction, and fulfilled their obligations with the greatest liberality, building the front of the temple with

Parian marble, when nothing more than ordinary stone was required by the terms of the contract. From this time the family was naturally in great favour at Delphi, and they now made use of their position. They induced the priestess—it was said by bribes—to impress upon all the Spartans who came to the oracle the imperative duty of liberating Athens. The Spartans were slow to answer to the call. They had always been on excellent terms with Pisistratus and his sons, under whose government Athens had been a good neighbour. Why should they begin the quarrel? But the priestess was importunate, and at length Anchimolius, a distinguished Spartan, was sent with an army to expel the tyrants from Attica. The task was not accomplished without difficulty. Anchimolius was defeated, and slain, and even when Cleomenes, the King of Sparta, appeared in person at Athens, it was a mere accident which threw the victory into his hands. The tyrants and their partisans were preparing to sustain a siege in the Acropolis, when news was brought that the children of the family, who were being sent away for safety, had fallen into the hands of the enemy. This at once changed the situation; Hippias agreed to leave the country in five days, and retired to Sigeum, in the Troad.

The departure of their rivals was of course the signal for all the exiled families to return to Athens, and at their head was Clisthenes. What were his views when he found himself once more in the city, it is difficult to say. Perhaps he had dreams of securing for himself the tyranny of which Hippias had

been deprived. He might at least look forward to
an established position as the foremost man in the
city. In either case he was disappointed. No sooner
had he returned than he found himself engaged in
party quarrels. The oligarchical party, (the remnant
we may suppose of the old party of the Plain), of whom
Isagoras was now the leader, had no mind to be the
subjects of the ambitious Alcmæonidæ, and offered
violent opposition to his projects. Finding himself
unable to maintain his position without fresh support,
Clisthenes determined, as Pisistratus had done before
him, to seek the aid of the people; but he sought it
in a different manner. He set about rearranging the
whole constitution of Athens. Increasing the tribes
from four to ten, and the Council from four hundred
to five hundred, he gave the people as much authority in elections as he could, and sought in every
way to emancipate them from the influence of the
great families. Isagoras and his party were taken by
surprise; they at once summoned Sparta to their
aid, and the appeal was successful. Cleomenes, who
was a personal friend of Isagoras, sent a herald to
Athens calling on Clisthenes and the Alcmæonidæ to
leave the city, as being "under the curse." Clisthenes at once retired; he had no wish to see the
Spartans at Athens, and he expected to secure his
recall without difficulty. But Cleomenes was not
contented; he soon appeared with a small force at
Athens, and in concert with Isagoras he drove no
fewer than seven hundred families out of the town.
Then he attempted to destroy the Council, and put
the government into the hands of three hundred of the

friends of Isagoras. The Council refused to submit, and, far from being able to coerce it, Cleomenes and Isagoras found themselves driven into the citadel. Their forces were few in number ; they had made no provision for the siege, and after two days the Lacedæmonians came to terms. With a brutal selfishness, of which this is not the only instance, they secured a free passage for themselves, while abandoning their Athenian friends to the mercy of the conquerors. Clisthenes and the seven hundred were at once recalled ; their opponents were put to death, and the ground was cleared for the great reformation which Clisthenes now proceeded to carry out. It is true that Cleomenes was not inclined to submit to the humiliating repulse which he had received ; and still less so, when he discovered that the Delphian priestess had been bribed into insisting on the liberation of Athens. But he could not induce the Peloponnesian allies, whose contingents formed a considerable part of any force which Sparta could put into the field, to listen to him. A large expedition, which he led as far as Eleusis, melted away, when it heard the object for which it had been collected ; and when Hippias was brought from Asia to Sparta, and a general assembly of the Confederation was held to discuss his restoration, the Corinthians, as the foremost of the allies, declared that they would have neither part nor lot in setting up that cruel and bloodthirsty monster, a Tyrant. The subject was dropped, and never revived. Hippias returned to Sigeum, and Athens was henceforth a free city.

We have unfortunately no full account of the measures of Clisthenes. A few sentences, some doubtful in their meaning, contain all the information which has been preserved of the work of the great Reformer. Yet the expulsion of Hippias and the reconstruction of the Athenian constitution, which immediately followed it, were to the Athenians what the Reformation, the Rebellion, and the Revolution combined have been to Englishmen.

Every statesman is of course guided largely by the circumstances of his time; he cannot advise or legislate in the air, but must have something definite in view. We shall see that Pericles trained the Athenians to acquire and maintain an imperial position. Clisthenes had no such aim; he merely sought to secure Athens against the undue influence of great families and its attendant evils—the outbreak of local and domestic faction and the rise of a tyrant. And in this object he succeeded.

All the villages of Attica were collected into a hundred "Demes," which he distributed among the ten tribes, ten to each. In each Deme he established a local officer, the Demarch, who was supported by a local council. The Demarch managed the affairs of the Deme, arranged for elections, and kept the register of citizens for purposes of contribution or service. The Demes belonging to the various tribes were not adjacent in every case; but sometimes Demes from widely different parts of the country were united in one tribe, doubtless with a view to prevent undue local influence. The whole of the new arrangements were put under the sanction of new religious rites or forms of worship: each Deme had its sanctuary; each tribe its tutelary hero. The political life of the citizens was thus dissociated from the family and domestic life, through which, no doubt, the old houses had largely exercised their power.

Within a very few years after the establishment of the new government, Athens was called upon to undergo a number of trials, each severer than the other; she passed triumphantly through them all, and emerged the greatest city in Greece. "Not in one instance only," says Herodotus, "but everywhere, it is manifest that freedom of speech is an excellent thing; in the days of their tyrants the Athenians were no better in the field than their neighbours, but no sooner had they got rid of them, than they were first of all. It is therefore quite clear that, when held in subjection, they would not do their best, because they were working for a master, but when they were free, every one did his utmost for himself." The historian's remark is true, though in justice to the Athenian Tyrants we must at least allow that their rule, however oppressive, did not prevent the growth of a vigorous population, able and willing to fight their own battles.

DRINKING VESSELS.

DRAPED STATUE OF A WOMAN FROM THE
ACROPOLIS.

Period Preceding the Persian Invasion.

(*Boetticher.*)

CHAPTER II.

XANTHIPPUS AND THEMISTOCLES.

Xanthippus—Birth of Pericles—Ionian revolt—
Miltiades, the son of Cimon—Battle of Marathon—Condemnation of Miltiades—Themistocles—Aristides and Xanthippus oppose Themistocles—The Æginetan war—Party struggles—Themistocles victorious—Construction
of a fleet—The Persian invasion.

ROM the time that his reforms were
completed, little is known of Clis-
thenes.   He is said to have been ostracised, and the
same fate twice befel his son Megacles, whose
daughter Dinomache became the mother of Alcibiades.   But Hippocrates, the younger brother of
Clisthenes, was the father of a second Agariste,
and from this daughter, who married Xanthippus of
the old Athenian family of the Buzygæ, was born
Pericles.

Though not himself an Alcmæonid, Xanthippus
seems to have acquired a considerable portion of
the influence of the family by marrying into it.   For
sixteen years (from 494 to 478) he was one of the
most prominent men in Athens.   It was he who
brought Miltiades to trial; who, with Aristides,
endeavoured to thwart the plans of Themistocles.

In 479 he commanded the Athenian ships at
Mycale; and, in the ensuing spring, he conquered
Sestos. Then, like so many of the leading Greek
statesmen in the evening of their lives, he disappears from our view and nothing more is recorded
of him.

Pericles was probably born about the year 493 B.C.
Even before his birth, indications of his future greatness were not wanting. Herodotus, at any rate,
believed a story, which was current in his time, that
Agariste, a few days before the birth of her great
son, dreamed that she was delivered of a lion. The
year of his birth was not a happy one in Athenian
annals. In 494 B.C. the great city of Miletus had
fallen before the arms of Persia, and the ill-timed
and disastrous revolt of the cities of Ionia, in which
Athens had played no creditable part, was brought
to an end amid universal desolation and destruction.
The victorious Phœnician fleet pressed onwards to
the north of the Ægean with nothing to check its
course. The Chersonese, which for two generations
had been governed by members of the Athenian
house of the Philaidæ, passed into the possession of
the Persians, and Miltiades, the son of Cimon, the
present ruler, came flying home with all his goods
in five triremes, one of which was captured by the
enemy. The bitter feeling aroused at Athens by
these reverses is shown by the treatment of the poet
Phrynichus, who had chosen the capture of Miletus
for the subject of a tragedy. The artistic success
of the drama was so great that the audience were
moved to tears, but the subject was felt to be too

painful for a play, and the poet was fined one thous-
and drachmæ (about £35) for reminding his countrymen of their misfortunes.

On his return to Athens, Miltiades found that he
was by no means at the end of his troubles. We
have seen that the two great families of the Alcmæonidæ and Philaidæ had stood at the head of rival
parties at Athens in the political factions of the sixth
century; Megacles, the grandfather of Agariste, had
led the Shore; Miltiades, the uncle of the present
ruler of the Chersonese, had led the Plain. Though
the old factions were at an end, the Alcmæonidæ
were by no means pleased to see the chief of their
rivals back in the city. Miltiades had shewn himself
daring and unscrupulous in his management of the
Chersonese; his wealth was great; his family had
been conquerors at Olympia; he was perhaps descended from Cypselus, the Tyrant of Corinth, and
for many years of his life he had occupied the position of an irresponsible despot. Would such a man
consent to be an equal among equals in his old city?
In the interval which had elapsed since Miltiades had
taken the place of his elder brother, Stesagoras, in
the Chersonese, Athens had gone through the crisis
which we have described in the preceding chapter.
When he left the city, the tyrants were still on the
throne; when he returned, the reforms of Clisthenes
had been firmly established for more than ten years.
To a man of such experiences, accustomed to the
unlimited exercise of personal power, "freedom of
speech" was not likely to commend itself. Xanthippus
and his friends determined, if possible, to get rid of

the danger. They brought an action against Miltiades, immediately after his return to Athens, charging
him with tyrannical government in the Chersonese.
The charge was ridiculous. The Athenians had
nothing whatever to do with the government of the
Chersonese. The first Miltiades had gone out at the
invitation of a native tribe to protect them against
the incursions of their neighbours on the north, and
the "tyranny" thus acquired had remained in the
hands of the family ever since. Under such circumstances Miltiades was, of course, acquitted; the plot
of his enemies entirely broke down.

Three years later came the invasion of the Persians
under Datis and Artaphernes, ending in the battle of
Marathon. On this occasion we hear nothing of
Xanthippus, but we can hardly suppose that he took
no part in the defence of his country. It is true that,
fifty years later, in the time of Herodotus, the Alcmæonidæ were suspected of having carried on some
treacherous negotiations with the invaders. It was
even said that they raised aloft the shield which gave
the signal to the Persians to re-embark from Marathon
and hasten to Athens in the hope of surprising the
city. And those who were hostile to the family
might remind the Athenians that they owed their
wealth in a great degree to the tyrants of Sardis and
Sicyon; that Clisthenes himself had sought the aid
of Persia in strengthening his position against Isagoras. But even if the story of the shield is true,
there is no proof that Xanthippus acted with the
Alcmæonidæ in this matter; and in the great invasion
of Xerxes in 480 B.C. he certainly took a prominent
part in the destruction of the Persian fleet.

In the next year (489 B.C.) Xanthippus was the chief actor in a scene which has left a lasting stain on himself and his city. The victory of Marathon was chiefly due to Miltiades; it was he who brought on the engagement, and he was chief in command on the day when the battle was fought. Such a brilliant success greatly improved his position in the city, and excited in his enemies a still deeper hatred. Ever on the watch for an opportunity to pull down their rival, it was not long before they found one. Soon after his victory Miltiades came before the Athenians with a request that a squadron of seventy ships might be placed at his disposal. The purpose for which he required them he would not disclose, though pledging his word that the expedition would add largely to the wealth and prosperity of the city. The request being granted, he sailed with the ships to Paros, an island which at this time was subject to Persia. From the Parians he demanded one hundred talents,* and when they refused to pay he blockaded the city. So vigorous and successful was the resistance offered that, after a long delay, Miltiades, himself dangerously wounded, was compelled to return home. His enemies, with Xanthippus at their head, at once attacked him for misconduct in the enterprise. They declared that he had deceived the Athenians, and, so far from adding to their wealth and prosperity, had wasted the treasure and lives of his fellow-citizens. For such an offence death was the only adequate penalty. Miltiades was unable to reply in person; he was carried into court, while his friends pleaded his cause. The

---

* A talent may be roughly estimated at £200.

sentence was given against him, but the penalty
was reduced from death to a fine of fifty talents.
So large a sum was more than even Miltiades could
pay; he was thrown into prison as a public debtor,
where he soon died from the mortification of his
wound.

In the account which Herodotus gives of this
event we are informed that Miltiades attacked Paros
from motives of private vengeance, and that he received his wound while seeking an interview with
the Parian priestess of Demeter. But as we are not
told what was the object of the interview, and as the
cause assigned for the private quarrel is quite incredible, this account is not of much value. On the other
hand it is obvious that Miltiades, if he wished to detach the wealthy island of Paros from Persia, would
desire his object to be kept as secret as possible. He
well knew that a project openly discussed in the
Athenian Assembly would be known at Paros long
before he could reach the island. The secrecy of the
expedition was therefore justifiable. The object was
not less so. Paros as a subject of Persia was a source
of danger in the Ægean; if the Athenians conquered
the island they would have a base of operations in
the Cyclades, from which they could intercept such
an expedition as that which brought Datis to Marathon. But Miltiades failed, and failure at the moment was intolerable. In the animation of their
recent victory the Athenians forgot how inadequate
were the means at their disposal for the capture of
walled cities; they thought that there could be no
limits to their success; and the enemies of Miltiades

took advantage of this feeling to bring about his ruin. His condemnation was one in a long series of similar punishments. The Athenians never learnt to be just to those who served them, or to distinguish between treachery and errors of judgment.* It was the natural result of such conduct that those who entered their service were compelled to sacrifice their devotion to their country to the precautions necessary for their own safety.

We have very little information about the state of Athens immediately after the battle of Marathon. So far as we can tell, for the chronology is most uncertain, she was now engaged in a war with Ægina, which though at first carried on with vigour, at length lapsed into inactive hostility, neither side being able to inflict any serious mischief on the other. Meanwhile a man was rising to power who may be said to have created the history of Athens for the rest of the century,—Themistocles, the son of Neocles.

What we know of the birth and early life of this eminent man is derived from the biography written by Plutarch, a late author, whose accuracy depends on that of the writers from whom he collected his information—writers often divided by centuries from the facts which they recorded. We are told that he was not born of true Athenian blood, his mother being an alien. The sons of such mixed marriages

---

* " The law of treason neither could nor ought to be enforced against an act which was an error of judgment, not of intention, which was in good faith intended not to impair the well-being of the state, but to promote and augment it."—Bagehot, " English Constitution," p. xxxix.

were not without political rights at Athens, but they
lay under certain social disadvantages. They could
not train or exercise with the young Athenians of
pure descent; a separate gymnasium was assigned
to them—the Cynosarges—on the banks of the
Ilissus, outside the walls of the city. From his
early youth, therefore, Themistocles found himself
separated from those ancient families, who had been
the ruling power in Athens. He could not expect
the support which came to them from their equals.
Yet his spirit would not allow him to be content
with any but the foremost place in the city. While
he was yet a boy his schoolmaster had predicted his
future greatness; whether he would be famous for
his virtues or his vices he could not say, but famous
he would certainly be. His father, observing his
inordinate ambition, sought to win him from a public
career by pointing to the hulls of some disused
triremes. These had once been employed in the
service of the city—gallant ships, the pride of those
who manned them; and what were they now? But
Themistocles was not to be shaken in his purpose.
As a young man he had fought at Marathon; and
the trophy of Miltiades would not let him rest. Was
it possible for him, without friends, without wealth,
to win success even more brilliant than that of
the great chief of the Philaidæ? Was it possible to
raise Athens, which had just achieved so remarkable
a victory, to a position of irresistible power, and
wrest from Sparta the leadership of Greece?

On the very day of Marathon, Themistocles had
probably made up his mind that the Persians would

visit Greece again.   What was to keep them away,
so long as they were masters of the Ægean?   He
was also aware that Athens, above all cities, was the
object of the wrath of Darius.   How could she be
saved?   Recent experience was entirely in favour of
the army.   At Marathon the Athenian hoplites had
put to flight a host ten times their own in number;
but the fleet had been unable to reduce the single
city of Paros.   For the last twenty years Athens
had been uniformly successful on land, while nothing
decisive had been done in the maritime war with
Ægina.   With such evidence before them, few men
would have ventured to strike into the line which
Themistocles took—a line which implied an entirely
new departure in the military history of Athens.
With an insight almost incredible he perceived that
the Athenians could become a maritime nation, that
Athens possessed harbours large enough to receive
an enormous fleet, and capable of being strongly
fortified; that in possession of a fleet she could not
only secure her own safety, but stand forth as a rival
power to Sparta.

But how could Themistocles induce the Athenians
to abandon the line in which they had been so
successful for a mode of warfare in which even
Miltiades had failed?   After the fall of the great
general, the conduct of affairs was in the hands
of Xanthippus, whom we know, and Aristides.
Both these men after the battle of Salamis took
a prominent part as leaders of the Athenian fleet,
but ten years earlier they were by no means prepared for the change which Themistocles was medi-

tating. This is more especially true of Aristides.
He had been a friend of Clisthenes; he was known
as an admirer of Spartan customs; and doubtless
looked on a trained army as the great bulwark
of a state. He had been second in command at
Marathon, and was now the most eminent general
at Athens. From him Themistocles could only
expect the most resolute opposition.

Xanthippus and Aristides could reckon on the
support of old traditions and great connections.
Themistocles had no support of the kind. He had
to make his party. He began by collecting round
him a few energetic men, who were perhaps convinced by his arguments, or at any rate jealous of the
power of the great families. These he formed into
an association for the spread of his views,—the first
instance, so far as we know, of a political "club" at
Athens. At a later time such clubs were common
enough; in fact they were the principal means by
which the aristocratical or oligarchical party at
Athens preserved what influence it had. They
were always regarded with some suspicion, and the
more severely they were treated the more dangerous
they became. In this early instance the significance
of the movement was probably disregarded. Conscious of their own position, Aristides and Xanthippus looked with contempt upon the knot of men
who began to gather round their unmannerly and
uncultivated leader.

And they might perhaps have maintained their
position if it had not been for the Æginetan war.
That unlucky struggle had begun, soon after the

reforms of Clisthenes, with an unprovoked attack of the Æginetans on the coast of Attica (506 B.C.). It was renewed when the Æginetans gave earth and water to the heralds of Darius in 491, and though suspended at the time of the Persian invasion, it broke out again with renewed ferocity soon afterwards. The Æginetans succeeded in carrying off a mission-ship, which was conveying some of the leading Athenian citizens to the festival of Poseidon on the headland of Sunium. The Athenians, in revenge, attempted a *coup d'état* in concert with Nicodromus, a dissatisfied Æginetan oligarch, who promised to raise the people at the same moment that an Athenian fleet attacked the city. But the Athenians had not sufficient ships for the purpose—for Ægina could put seventy vessels on the water,—and while they were obtaining others from Corinth, time passed on, and they arrived at Ægina a day too late. The Æginetan oligarchs got rid of their domestic enemies by a horrible massacre, and after some contests fought with varying fortune, they finally succeeded in defeating the Athenian fleet. From this time onwards hostilities ceased on a large scale; each city ravaged the coasts of the other as opportunity offered.

Such experiences naturally caused a change in the minds of the Athenians. Had they driven the Persians into the sea only to be defeated, harried, and defied by a neighbouring island? If they could have the Æginetans on land they would soon give an account of them; but now the warfare lay on a different element. It was clear that the old arrangements for the navy were quite inadequate to the

task which was now required of them. Yet the
leaders of the state made no proposals. They
seemed content with a navy of fifty or seventy ships,
regardless of past defeats and present devastations.
Miltiades had been condemned for his failure at
Paros, but failure at Ægina was treated in quite a
different manner. These may have been the mur-
murs which Themistocles and his associates sought
to diffuse through the city. In the confidence that
they were gaining ground, he came forward publicly
with proposals of naval reform, and, as he expected,
he drew upon himself the strenuous opposition of
Aristides.

We need not assume that Aristides had contracted
that dislike of a seafaring population which was so
marked a feature among the philosophers of the next
century; but he could not avoid seeing that a fleet
was useless without rowers, and that the rowers
would be drawn from the lowest class of citizens.
The defence of the city would no longer be in the
hands of that middle class, who were at least able to
supply themselves with a suit of armour, but in the
hands of men who must be paid for their labour.
Aristides was slow to perceive that this class might
be as patriotic and trustworthy as the citizens of
higher position. At a later time he redeemed his
error, but for the present he employed all his influence in thwarting the plans of Themistocles. So
severe was the contest that the public peace was in
danger. Aristides was heard to confess that the
Athenians would be wise if they threw both himself
and his opponent into the pit into which great
criminals were cast.

Affairs were at a dead lock. It was clear that nothing decisive could be done in the Æginetan war unless the proposals of Themistocles were carried ; it was equally clear that they never would be carried while Aristides and Xanthippus were at hand to oppose them. Under these circumstances recourse was had to the safety-valve of the constitution. Ostracism was proposed and accepted ; and in this manner, by 483 B.C., Themistocles had got rid of both of his rivals in the city.

He was now master of the situation. The only obstacle to the realization of his plans was the expense involved in building ships. And this he was able to meet by a happy accident, which brought into the treasury at this time a large surplus from the silver mines from Laurium. Various accounts are given of the precise method in which the fleet was built, and none is perhaps more worthy of credit than another. But, by the summer of 480, the Athenians, who previously had borrowed twenty ships of the Corinthians in order to bring up their navy to a total of seventy, were able to launch a hundred and eighty vessels, besides providing twenty for the use of the Chalcidians of Eubœa. These, or the greater part of them, as we know, on the testimony of Herodotus, were primarily built with a view to the war with Ægina, but, when the news of the second Persian invasion arrived, that quarrel was made up, and the Athenians were at liberty to devote their whole strength to the salvation of Greece.

At the same time, Themistocles set about the fortification of the Peiræus. Down to this time the harbour of Athens had been the open roadstead

of Phalerum, which, though spacious and convenient
was exposed to the wind, and without any protec
tion from attack. A large fleet could not be allowed
to remain there; harbours and convenient docks
were an indispensable part of the policy which
endeavoured to turn Athens into a maritime power.
A little to the west of Phalerum a rocky promontory
runs out from the shore of Attica into the Gulf of
Salamis. Connected with the land by a somewhat
narrow isthmus, the headland becomes broader as
it enters into the sea. It is pierced by three deep
basins, each with a narrow entrance, but varying in
size. Themistocles at once perceived that these
basins were the harbours which he required. In
the largest, which was called Peiræus, all the ships
of Athens could, if necessary, be collected. The
other two, if smaller, were even more defensible.
He resolved to make this promontory the port of
Athens, and to fortify the harbours for the protection of the ships. Could he have carried the
Athenians with him, he would have made the
Peiræus the capital of the country, in order that
the ships and the city might be in close connection.
But for this the people were not prepared. They
clung to the ancient rock, round which were gathered the most sacred legends of the past—the seat
of temples hallowed by immemorial antiquity.

This ambitious scheme was suspended by the
disasters of the years 480–479, in which Xerxes
attempted to avenge the defeat of his father Darius,
and bring Greece into subjection to Persia. As
everyone knows, the attempt ended in utter failure.

The Persian fleet was broken at Salamis, and finally destroyed at Mycale; the greater part of the army hastened back with Xerxes, and those who remained behind with Mardonius were cut down with pro-digious slaughter on the battle-field of Platæa. The historian can hardly have a more delightful task than to trace, even in such outlines as our knowledge permits, the steps by which a mere handful of brave and patriotic men delivered their country from the Persian despot. Of nine tenths of the wars which have destroyed empires and laid waste whole terri-tories, we may say that the world has gained nothing by them; but there can be no doubt that the loss of Greek civilization would have been irreparable. And there can also be no doubt that the glorious victory which saved so priceless a possession was chiefly due to the Athenians, and among the Athenians to the incomparable genius and courage of Themistocles. But we cannot here enter on this subject; we are only concerned with the effect which the Persian war had on the position of Athens among Greek cities, and the stimulus which it imparted to the Greek mind.

We must also remember that among those who saw the desolation of the city, and were carried away to escape the ravages of the Barbarians was Pericles, now a boy of thirteen years of age. Of this flight Plutarch has recorded an incident which is worth repeating. When Xanthippus embarked on board ship to cross the gulf from Attica to Salamis, his favourite dog was forgotten, or reached the shore too late to be taken on board. Unable to

bear separation from his master, the dog sprang into
the sea and swam the whole breadth of the gulf, behind the ship. But the effort was too great for
his strength; on reaching the island he fell down
exhausted and died.

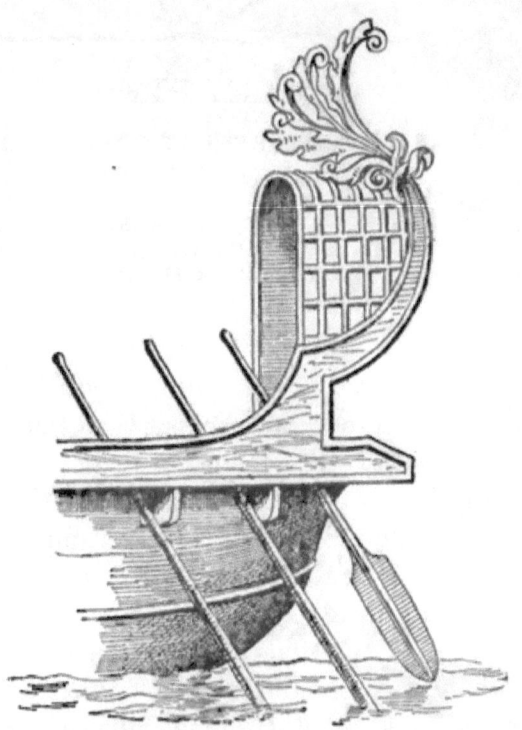

STERN OF AN ANCIENT GALLEY.
According to Bafins.

CHAPTER III.

THE CONGRESS AT CORINTH, AND THE DELIAN LEAGUE.

The congress at Corinth in 481 B.C.—Rise of Athens —Pausanias at the head of the fleet—His treachery —Formation of the Delian league—Aristides and Cimon.

HEN it was known in Greece that Xerxes was on his march into Europe, it became necessary to take measures for the defence of the country. At the instigation of the Athenians, the Spartans, as the acknowledged leaders of Hellas and head of the Peloponnesian confederacy, called on those cities which had resolved to uphold the independence of their country, to send plenipotentiaries to a congress at the Isthmus of Corinth. When the envoys assembled, a kind of Hellenic alliance was formed under the presidency of Sparta, and its unity was confirmed by an oath, binding the members to visit with severe penalties those Greeks who, without compulsion, had given earth and water to the envoys

3

of Xerxes. This alliance was the nearest approach to
a Hellenic union ever seen in Greece; but though
it comprised most of the inhabitants of the Peloponnesus, except Argos and Achæa, the Megarians,
Athenians, and two cities of Bœotia, Thespiæ and
Platæa, were the only patriots north of the Isthmus.
Others, who would willingly have been on that side,
such as the common people of Thessaly, the Phocians
and Locrians, were compelled by the force of circumstances to " medize."

From the time at which it met in the autumn
or summer of 481 to the autumn of 480 B.C., the
congress at the Isthmus directed the military affairs
of Greece. It fixed the plan of operations. Spies
were sent to Sardis to ascertain the extent of the
forces of Xerxes; envoys visited Argos, Crete,
Corcyra, and Syracuse, in the hope, which proved
vain, of obtaining assistance in the impending struggle. As soon as Xerxes was known to be in Europe,
an army of ten thousand men was sent to hold
the pass of Tempe, but afterwards, on the advice of
Alexander of Macedon, this barrier was abandoned ;
and it was finally resolved to await the approaching
forces at Thermopylæ and Artemisium. The supreme authority, both by land and sea, was in
the hands of the Spartans ; they were the natural
leaders of any army which the Greeks could put into
the field, and the allies refused to follow unless the
ships also were under their charge.

For this reason Eurybiadas the Spartan, though
he had only ten vessels under his command, was
chosen general-in-chief of the whole fleet. Of the

HEAD OF A WOMAN FROM A MARBLE BUST FOUND
ON THE ACROPOLIS.

Period before the Persian Invasion.

(Boetticher.)

other cities, each sent one commander, with full powers at the head of her contingent. Themistocles commanded the Athenians, Adimantus the Corinthians. From the time that hostilities actually commenced at Thermopylæ till the return of the fleet after the victory of Salamis to the Isthmus, the direction of affairs was, of course, taken by the general-in-chief. The commanders were allowed to discuss matters in a common assembly, but the final decision rested with Eurybiadas. Of the council or congress at the Isthmus we hear nothing at this time. But when hostilities were suspended, the congress re-appears, and the Greeks once more meet at the Isthmus to apportion the spoil and adjudge the prizes of valour. In the next year we hear of no common plan of operations, the fleet and army seeming to act independently of each other; yet we observe that the chiefs of the medizing Thebans were taken to the Isthmus (Corinth) to be tried, after the battle of Platæa.

It appears then that, under the stress of the great Persian invasion, the Greeks were brought into an alliance or confederation ; and for the two years from midsummer 481 to midsummer 479 a congress continued to meet, with more or less interruption, at the Isthmus, consisting of plenipotentiaries from the various cities. This congress directed the affairs of the nation, so far as they were in any way connected with the Persian invasion. When the Barbarians were finally defeated, and there was no longer any alarm from that source, the congress seems to have discontinued its meetings. But the alliance remained; the cities continued to act in common, at any rate, so far as naval operations were concerned, and Sparta was still the leading power.

On the other hand, the relative position of the states was greatly altered by the events of 480 and 479. In the first place, there were states which had joined the invader, and states which had resisted him. Thessaly and Thebes had done their best to place a foreign ruler over Greece; Argos, in spite of her ancient traditions, had been neutral or worse. The action of these states was not forgotten, if it was not punished. Thebes and Athens had already quarrelled over the allegiance of Platæa; the cities were now more divided than ever; and all hope of the union of Northern Greece, so vital a point in the defence of the country, was at an end. In like manner the long-standing separation of Argos and Sparta was more clearly marked than before. The approach to confederation, which the war seemed to have created, had been accompanied by an increase of the divisions, an aggravation of the hatreds, which rent Hellas asunder.

And this was not all. The part which Athens played at Artemisium and Salamis created a great impression in Greece. Her neighbours and rivals in trade, the Æginetans and Corinthians, saw with surprise and alarm that she had risen at a single leap to a position far above their own. She was now the greatest maritime power of any single state in Greece; and though in the war she had consented to follow the lead of Sparta, it was clear to everyone that Themistocles and not Eurybiadas had been the real power in the fleet. In this case also the war, while seeming to unite Hellas, had created two leading cities, where previously there had only been one. Over against the great Dorian city of the Pelopon- nesus stood the Ionian city of Central Hellas. The trained courage of the Spartan hoplite was matched by the skill of the Athenian sailor.

The events which immediately followed the final defeat of the Persians gave prominence to this new division. Athens made it clear that she intended to pursue an independent line. She did not break loose from the confederation which had been formed in 481 ; she was still the ally of Sparta, and looked to Sparta to lead the allied forces, but in all that con- cerned her own safety she claimed to be free and unfettered. The Athenians had hardly returned from Salamis to Athens—which the Persians had lev- elled to the ground—than they began to build a wall round the city far larger and stronger than any which had previously existed. This was done on the advice of Themistocles, who saw that such a protection was absolutely necessary, if the Athenians were to devote themselves to the sea. Without such a wall the city would be exposed to the attacks of their neighbours —attacks which could only be successfully repelled by a large and well trained army, equal to the best soldiers which the Peloponnese and Bœotia could bring against it, and such an army was impossible at Athens. His advice was the more readily accepted at a time when the citizens, who had been twice driven out of house and home in two successive years, were in a mood to make sacrifices for the protection of the city. The walls began to rise. No sooner did the neighbouring allies see what was going on than they called on the Spartans to put a stop to the ambitious project. The situation was difficult; Sparta as the head of the alliance might make suggestions to the Athenians, but she could hardly venture to interfere in a more decided manner. She sent envoys to Athens pointing out the danger of walls; should another invasion occur, Athens if a walled city might become what Thebes had been in the last: the base of operations for the invaders. Sparta herself had no walls; why should Athens need them? The Athenians were not deceived, but they could not openly resent this interference. Themistocles found it necessary to outwit the Spartans and protract the negotiations till the walls were of a height which made the city defensible. Then he threw off the mask and boldly declared that Athens had a right to take whatever steps she pleased to ensure her own safety. She chose to have walls and she would have them. There the matter ended. It could not indeed be carried further without an appeal to arms, and as yet the memory of the services of Athens was too recent to admit of any but a friendly feeling between her and Sparta.

In the fleet also the Athenians had been able to assert their independence. The Spartan king Leotychidas had succeeded Eurybiadas as high admiral, and under his command the allied squadrons won the victory of Mycale, 479 B.C. The Greeks had been assisted by the Samians and Milesians—who were glad to turn upon their oppressors,—and when

the fleet returned to Samos, after the battle, the
Chians and Lesbians and others asked to be received into the alliance.   The Greeks now found
themselves face to face with a question of no little
importance.   Were they to undertake the defence
of the Greeks on the islands and the mainland
of Asia?   It was obvious that they could only
undertake it, if they were prepared to maintain
a fleet which could keep the Persians out of the
Ægean.   The Peloponnesians, with the Spartans
at their head, were unwilling to charge the confederacy with such a burden.   They proposed that the
Ionians should be removed from their present homes,
and placed in the peninsula, in the ports of the medizing Greeks, whom they would expel for the purpose.
But the Athenians, who were now commanded by
Xanthippus, the father of Pericles, took another
view : the Ionians were their colonists, and they alone
had a right to decide on their future.   They determined that they should remain where they were, and
themselves undertook their protection.   To this view
the Spartans assented, and soon afterwards Leotychidas and the Peloponnesian contingents sailed
home, leaving the Athenians to carry on the war by
themselves.   Nothing daunted, the Athenians attacked Sestos, and continued the siege till they
captured the city, in the spring of 478.

By land and sea Athens had carried her point,
even against the wishes of Sparta.   But the cities
were still on the best of terms ; the old alliance remained, and, as we have said, Sparta was regarded as
the leading city in Greece.   When in the summer of

478 a new expedition was sent out to carry on the
war, it was placed under Pausanias, the general who
had commanded the united forces at Platæa as
regent for his nephew, the infant king of Sparta.
The Ægean had been cleared of Persian ships by
this time, but the ambition of the Greeks grew with
their success. They wished to make another invasion impossible. With this view, Pausanias attacked
Cyprus, the best station from which to keep watch
on the Cilician plain, the rendezvous of the Persian
troops, when required in the west. He succeeded in
conquering the greater part of the island, though we
are not told that he left any garrison to retain what
he had won. From Cyprus he proceeded to Byzantium, the key of the Bosphorus; this city also he
succeeded in taking, and at the capture many Persians of high rank fell into his hands.

Among the spoils left on the field after the battle
of Platæa was found the tent of Mardonius, the
Persian general. This was no other than the tent
of Xerxes, which at his departure the King had left
for the use of his successor in the command. It
was, of course, constructed with royal magnificence,
resplendent with gold, and the richest embroidery;
a sight such as had never before come under the
eyes of the astonished Greeks. When Pausanias
saw it, he bade the attendants prepare a meal as
they were accustomed to prepare it for Mardonius,
and at the same time gave orders to his Helots to
cook a common Spartan supper. Then he summoned the captains of the Greeks to see the difference. "How foolish," he exclaimed, "were the

men who while they enjoyed the one sought to rob
the Greeks of the other!" The sight of this magnificence seems to have sunk deeply into the mind
and memory of Pausanias. Forgetting the infinite
difference between freedom and slavery, he con-
trasted the bare and dreary life of a Spartan with
the softness and splendour of a Persian satrap.
His successes in the last two years had raised him
to the foremost rank in Greece, and he had felt no
scruple in claiming for himself the honours which
had been won by the devotion of others. Was he
to abandon his "great place" and return to Sparta,
to be the subject of an infant king? Was he, whose
name was inscribed on the serpents at Delphi and
the cauldron at the Bosphorus as the captain of the
Greeks, to be recalled to Sparta by the uncontrolled
decision of the ephors? His ambitious hopes led
him to dream of a far different position. Might he
not fill the place which Mardonius had failed to fill,
and govern Greece as the Viceroy of Persia ?

With these schemes in his mind, Pausanias entered
into negotiations with the Great King. He sent the
prisoners taken at the capture of Byzantium back to
Persia, excusing their departure to the Greeks under
the pretence that they had escaped. He also wrote a
letter to Xerxes, in which he proposed to become the
son-in-law of the king (as Mardonius had been of Darius), and requested that a trustworthy person should
be sent down to the coast, with whom he could develop
his plans. Xerxes eagerly entered into the scheme.
Pausanias received ample promises of support, and
a Persian was sent to co-operate with him. Unfor-

tunately for his own purposes, he was unable to conceal his delight. He already regarded himself as a
servant of Persia. In Persian dress, with a body-guard
of Medes and Egyptians about him, he made a tour
through Thrace, where a number of fortified posts
were still held by the King's troops. His conduct towards the allies became more intolerable every day.
He made the lives of the men miserable by harsh punishments, and when their commanders interfered, he
refused to hear them. The irritation, especially of
the Ionians, was increased by the politic courtesy of
the generals of the Athenian contingent, Cimon
and Aristides. At length the smouldering fires
broke into flame. The allies, with the Samians at
their head, transferred their allegiance from the
Spartan commander to the Athenians, and in spite
of all his negotiations with Persia, Pausanias was
not in a position to prevent the change by force.
Meanwhile the Spartans heard of the dispute, and
having before had some suspicion of the motives of
Pausanias, they recalled him from Byzantium. This
step left the course clear for the Athenians. They
assumed the command, and when a successor to
Pausanias was sent out from Sparta, he was not
received by the allied fleet. The Spartans were, in
fact, no longer recognised as the head of the maritime forces of the Hellenic alliance, and as the
rest of the Peloponnesians, who naturally followed
the lead of the Spartans, also ceased from this
time, to send contingents to the Hellenic fleet, the
Athenians and their allies were left in control of
the sea. The Ionians could now claim to be as

supreme on the water as the Dorians were on the land.

Thucydides tells us that the Spartans were not un-willing that the command of the fleet should pass over to the Athenians. They felt that their citizens were becoming corrupted by their residence and service abroad; Spartan simplicity was not proof against the temptations which Persia could offer; the seclusion of the valley of the Eurotas became dreary to those who had mixed with the life and movement of the sea. And at the same time they thought the Athenians loyal friends, who would carry on the maritime war in the cause of Hellas. Of their ability and energy there could, of course, be no doubt.

Thus within three or four years of the battle of Salamis, united Greece had fallen into halves. The great alliance still existed, but Sparta had practically gone back to her old position as leader of the Pelo-ponnesians. Athens had risen to be the first city of Central Greece and head of the maritime forces of the nation. As on the one hand, the Ionian allies of Athens had renounced allegiance to the Spartan commander, so, on the other, the Dorian cities of the Peloponnese had withdrawn their contingents from the allied fleet. Athens and Sparta, Ionians and Dorians, began to be ranged in opposition.

The division was increased by the use which the Athenians made of their position as head of the Hellenic fleet. They had established their power in Central Hellas by surrounding their city with

impregnable walls; they now proceeded to consoli-
date the bond which united them with their allies
into a firm and lasting league. Still remaining
allies of the Spartans, they nevertheless formed a
fresh alliance of their own. This was the famous
Delian confederacy—the foundation, we may say,
upon which the Athens of Pericles and the Peloponnesian war was reared. The avowed object of the
Athenians in forming the league was to compensate
themselves and their allies for their losses by devastating the King's country. They had no sooner
been acknowledged leaders of the fleet in the
Bosphorus than they proceeded to form a synod,
to which all the allied cities, great or small, should
send a deputy, each deputy having an equal vote
on the board. As a second step, it was necessary
to arrange which of the cities should provide ships,
and which should provide money, for the war.
Some cities, such as Chios, Lesbos, Samos, Naxos,
and others, in spite of the requisitions of Xerxes,
seem to have been able to furnish ships at once;
others had either lost their vessels, or for some
other reasons found it difficult to build any. For
their convenience a scale was fixed by Aristides,
according to which their " tribute " to the league
was to be paid, and the Athenians were charged
with the collection of it, a new office being created
at Athens for the purpose—the so-called " Hellenic
Treasurers." What money was collected was placed
in a common chest in the temple of Apollo at Delos,
which was also selected as the common meeting-
place of the synod. The alliance was confirmed by

solemn oaths, which were ratified, as the custom
was, by sinking masses of iron in the sea; when
these should reappear, the oaths would cease to be
binding.   In the enthusiasm of the moment it
seemed that the alliance would last for ever.

The Athenians who took a leading part in the
formation of the league were Aristides and Cimon.
Aristides we know.   After his ostracism in 483 he
had returned to Athens on the eve of the battle of
Salamis, either under a public resolution, or because
he felt that, at such a time, he might disregard the
law in offering his services to his country.   Whatever his old opposition to Themistocles had been, it
was forgotten now, and no one rendered more efficient aid in carrying out the plans of his rival for the
development of Athenian maritime power.   Cimon
was the son of Miltiades, and inherited his father's
military genius; from this date, till his death in 449,
he takes the first place among Athenian generals.
Both Aristides and Cimon were men eminently fitted
to make Athens popular with the allies.   As Aristides
was renowned for his upright character, so was Cimon the delight of the society in which he moved,
the idol of his soldiers.

Splendid as the fortune of Athens was in every
respect at this time, it was in nothing more remarkable than in the number of great men whom she had
at her disposal.   And for a time, at any rate, old
animosities were forgotten; all worked together in
harmony for the good of their city.   Happy would
it have been for the reputation of the republic if this
harmony had continued.

CHAPTER IV.

THE EARLY YEARS OF THE DELIAN LEAGUE—THE FALL OF PAUSANIAS AND THEMISTOCLES.

Changes in the period—Early history of the league —The Athenians become more despotic—Reasons for the change—Internal affairs at Athens, after 478 — Xanthippus — Aristides — The Solonian classes—Law of Aristides—Decline of the popularity of Themistocles—His personal character— Ostracism of Themistocles—End of Pausanias : His second recall, treachery, and death—Themistocles charged with " medism "—He is compelled to take refuge in Persia—His death—Estimate of his guilt.

IN 476 B.C., the Delian league was formed, amid universal enthusiasm, and at the Olympian festival of that year Themistocles was the "observed of all observers," as the man who had saved his country. In 466 Naxos, the most important of the Cyclades, the last of the larger islands to fall under the Persian yoke, and the first to break loose from it, was in revolt against the Athenians, and Themistocles was flying from his country to seek the protection of the Persian king. A change so striking of necessity excites our curiosity; we would fain trace the steps by which it was brought about. Who was to blame for consequences so disastrous? Was it the Athenians, who in the plenitude of their power destroyed the fair promise of united action in Hellas, in order to establish a maritime empire in the place of an equal league of confederate cities? Or did the allies, in the feverish restlessness of Hellenic independence, refuse to submit to the control inseparable from any form of confederation? Was Themistocles a traitor to the country which he had served so well, an associate of Pausanias, and a hireling of the Persian king; or were his exile and flight due to party feuds and political strife?

On the answer to these questions our judgment of the Athenians in this great period of their history must largely depend. And unhappily the answer is vague and uncertain. With the help of Thucydides we can trace a faint outline of the causes which led to the revolt of Naxos; we can see that there was negligence on the one side, and ambition on the other. But at the causes which brought about the fall of Themistocles we can only guess; so far as we know, no truthful record of the events of this period of the domestic history of Athens was ever made, or, if made, it was not preserved. The last days of the greatest of Athenians became a myth; the manner of his death and the place of his burial were unknown.

The first achievement of the new league was the capture of Eion, a town at the mouth of the Strymon in Thrace. This success was gained under the command of Cimon. Not long afterwards, but how

long the meagre record of Thucydides does not allow
us to determine, the island of Scyrus was acquired
by Athens. The inhabitants, who were Dolopians,
were reduced to slavery and their land divided among
Athenian citizens. This fate, we are told, the Dolopians brought upon themselves. Their island was little
better than a nest of pirates, and it was at the request
of the Delphian Amphictyony that the Athenians
entered upon the crusade against them. After this a
war broke out between the league and Carystus, a
town in Euboea. Some time was spent in indecisive
warfare, but at length terms were proposed upon which
both sides could agree. The next event recorded by
Thucydides in the history of the league is the revolt
of the Naxians, who were reduced by a siege. This
was the first allied city which was enslaved contrary
to "Hellenic law," but afterwards the same fate
overtook the rest, "each as its turn came." Various
reasons were given for these acts of aggression on the
part of Athens, but the most common was the failure
to supply the tribute and ships, or the refusal to join
in an expedition. The Athenians were extreme in
their exactions, and caused great irritation by using
compulsion upon men who had never been accustomed to endure any hardship. And by this time
they were not so popular in the command as they
had been. They were not content with their old
position as an equal among equals, and they found it
easy to reduce those who revolted. For this the
allies were themselves to blame. Owing to their
aversion to service, which took them from home, the
greater part preferred paying money to providing

ships, and thus they not only supplied the Athenians with money to increase their fleet, but when they revolted, they were as deficient in skill as in resources. At first, we are told, the Athenians were inclined to insist on receiving the vessels according to the original agreement, but Cimon pointed out that it was far more to the advantage of Athens to allow the allies to have their own way. The revenues of the city were increased at the very time when the power of resistance declined, with the inevitable result that the Athenians became not merely the leaders, but the rulers of the confederacy. In the same careless spirit the allies seem to have neglected the attendance at the synod at Delos, upon which their existence as equals in the league depended. The synod was in fact allowed to fall into decay. Before the death of Cimon it had probably ceased to exist; and even the chest of the allies had been transferred to Athens, where it was, in effect, administered by the Athenian council. It was reserved for Pericles to carry out the change further, and to insist that the Athenian empire had taken the place of the Delian league. The change was perhaps inevitable; or at least, the choice lay between two alternatives. Either the Delian league must be broken up into a number of independent navies, which might or might not act together, or it must be consolidated in the hands of Athens. The first alternative was impossible, so long as Persia was a dangerous power; and when by repeated defeats Athens had crippled her great enemy, she had achieved a position which left the old equality no more than a fiction. Had the Peloponnesians

4

remained in the alliance, the preponderance of
Athens might have been obviated ; there would at
least have been two great states, round which the
allies could have ranged themselves, and the division
of power, though fertile of dissensions, might have
saved the weaker cities.   Unfortunately the treachery of Pausanias rendered such an arrangement impossible ; owing to his conduct the Spartans were
not only hated abroad, but found themselves involved in serious danger at home.   The rest of the
Peloponnesians were unable to take an independent
line.

Of the internal affairs of Athens after the building
of the city walls we know very little.   Four great
names are before us : Xanthippus, Aristides, Themistocles, and Cimon.   Of Xanthippus we hear no
more after the fall of Sestos, in 478 B.C.   That he
died is more than probable, for if he had lived it is
difficult to understand why his name is never mentioned.   His birth, his wealth, his success, and his
ambition would have secured him a leading place in
the politics of the day.   We must, therefore, think
of Pericles as deprived of his father's guidance at
the age of fifteen.   At this critical period of life he
was left to shape his own career, and select the
party to which he would attach himself.   Of the
part which Aristides took in the formation of the
Delian league we have already spoken.   His action
as commander of the Athenian fleet is a proof, as
we have said, that he no longer cherished his old
opposition to the maritime plans of Themistocles.
He had, in fact, so fully identified himself with the

forward policy, which made the lower classes all-important for the service of the city, that he proposed to relieve them from the restrictions hitherto laid upon them. By the arrangements of Solon, the citizens of Athens were divided into four classes, according to their wealth. In the highest class were placed those who derived from landed property an income of five hundred medimni (seven hundred and fifty English bushels) of corn, or equivalent produce; in the second, those whose income from similar sources amounted to three hundred medimni; in the third, those whose income amounted to one hundred and fifty medimni. Into the fourth class, who were known as the Thetes, or " day labourers," fell all the citizens whose income derived from landed property was less than one hundred and fifty medimni, and all whose income, no matter how large, was derived from other sources than land. To each of these classes duties were assigned according to their means, and privileges granted according to their duties. The first class bore the heaviest burdens, and enjoyed the exclusive right to the highest offices. The members of the second class, who were known as the Knights, were liable to the charge of providing a horse in the service of the city ; the members of the third class were called the Hoplites, or Heavy-armed ; every man was expected to take his place in the army, when called upon, and to furnish himself with a suit of body-armour. These two classes shared with the first the privilege of election to the council of Five Hundred, and perhaps some other offices were open to them.

The Thetes were excluded from office of any kind, and the only duty demanded of them was that of attending the hoplites in the field as light-armed soldiers.

The Solonian scheme had undergone considerable modifications at the hands of Clisthenes in regard to the three higher classes, by which many of the old restrictions had been removed, but no change had been made in regard to the fourth class. They were still excluded from every kind of office, though as rowers in the ships they had recently been called upon to take a far larger share in the service of the state than ever fell to their lot as light-armed soldiers. Aristides saw the injustice of the restriction. He had aided Clisthenes in throwing open office to the higher classes; he now went further in the same direction, and proposed that members of the fourth class should be eligible to the archonship.

So far as the poorer citizens were concerned, the proposal was rather a compliment than an advantage. Few of the members of the fourth class, whose position was due to their poverty, would be able to support the expense attending high office, or even to give up the time necessary for the discharge of their duties. But with the men who were placed in the class because their income was derived from trade and not from land, the case was very different. They were by this time a numerous and increasing body, eager, no doubt, to be released from the restriction which lay upon them. The proposal of Aristides placed them on an equality with the rest of the citizens, and opened careers which they felt themselves able to pursue. At the same time it gave to capital employed in trade an importance hitherto reserved to capital invested in land.

But where, we ask, was Themistocles when this proposal was made? Why did he allow a measure, at once so popular and so obviously favourable to his own views of the future of Athens, to be passed by Aristides? Our authorities tell us that Aristides was opposed to the extreme democratic views of Themistocles. Yet Aristides passes a measure more democratic by far than any which we know to have been passed by Themistocles! Are we to suppose that these two great men were once more opponents, as of old, but on a different ground? Does Aristides attempt to outbid Themistocles in winning the popular vote? Or was the measure of Aristides, however democratic in appearance, a modified form of some still more extreme measure contemplated by Themistocles?

What is certain is that, after the building of the city walls and the fortification of the Peiræus, which he persuaded the Athenians to complete —for a beginning had been made a few years previously—when the walls were finished, the popularity of Themistocles began to decline. We never hear of him in any public capacity; he carried no important measures. Full of schemes, as he must have been for the aggrandisement of Athens, and the extension of her power, he found himself not only unable to carry them out, but even to maintain the position to which his great achievements had raised him. This change in his po-

sition can hardly be explained by the extreme
nature of his views on the democracy, for the
most democratic measure of the time was carried by Aristides. It was due partly to the character of Themistocles himself, and partly to the
state of parties at Athens at the time. Themistocles was not a man likely to attract the love
or respect of those with whom he lived and worked,
let his services be never so great. He was too
purely intellectual, too intent on doing what was
best to do, without regard to the means by which
he did it. His conduct towards the Spartans shows
him in a disagreeable light, and many of those who
approved of the result of his policy would not hesitate to condemn the manner in which the result had
been attained. We have no reason to suppose that
he ever entertained any other than patriotic motives
in his dealings with Persia, but the secret and
tortuous arts by which he brought about the
battle of Salamis would not be forgotten by those
who wished to ruin his character. This dislike
and distrust were perhaps increased by defects of
manner. Themistocles is described to us as insolent
and overbearing ; he did not disguise his contempt
for those around him ; he was never weary of dwelling on his own merits, a weakness not uncommon
among Athenians. And this may have been the
reason that the "club," on which he relied ten
years before, was no longer willing to support him.
His old friends grew weary or afraid of one who
posed as a "necessary" man ; for, on the one hand,
the step was short from the necessary man to the

tyrant; and, on the other, though it was true that in great emergencies Themistocles, more than any other Athenian, was competent to guide the state, the case was altered when the danger had passed away. Cimon and Aristides were far better fitted to carry on the work of the Delian league. It is indeed probable, though there is no authority for saying so, that it was in the management of the confederacy that Themistocles and Aristides once more came into opposition. For if Themistocles could have carried out his own views, Athens would not have entered the confederacy as an equal among equals; she would at once have occupied the imperial position, which she gained some twenty years later, and the Ægean would have become an Athenian lake. The opposition of Cimon to Themistocles can be also explained by the different views which they took of the proper policy for Athens to adopt towards Sparta.

However this may be, the party leaders at Athens were able to keep Themistocles out of power. Cimon was the head of the Philaidæ; Aristides carried on the policy of the Alcmæonidæ. Both were sincere patriots—Cimon the more aristocratic, Aristides, though also of an ancient family, the more democratic, in his views. Each could count on a great following: the landed gentry, as we should call them, had for a century looked on the Philaidæ as their leaders; the merchants and traders —the Parali of the preceding century—had been raised to power in the state by the recent measures of Aristides, and at the same time the whole of the poorer classes, whether living by agriculture or trade, had been freed from an invidious restriction. But Themistocles was without a following; the peasants and poorer farmers, who had once supported Pisistratus, no longer formed a third party, and if they had, Themistocles, whose desire was to make Athens a maritime power, was not likely to be their leader. Under such circumstances it was not difficult for Cimon and Aristides, by combining their influence, to destroy the position of Themistocles. In 471 B.C., the opposition reached a climax; ostracism was demanded, and Themistocles was expelled the country.

On his banishment he retired to Argos. Whether he was prompted by his old hatred of Sparta, or whether he suspected that Spartan influence had been active in procuring his exile, we do not know; but we can hardly doubt that he chose Argos as a place of retirement because it offered a convenient base of operations against Sparta. And though the feeling between Argos and Athens, owing to the conduct of the Argives in the Persian war, was far from friendly, the Argives may have been pleased to have among them an Athenian who was better able than any other Greek to aid them in their designs on their detested neighbours.

To Argos Themistocles went. At this point his life becomes linked with the fate of Pausanias, who, when we last heard of him, had been recalled by Sparta from the command of the fleet at Byzantium.

After his recall Pausanias remained at Sparta but a short time. He was too deeply interested in his negotiations with the Persian king to abandon his aims at the first check. In a single vessel he sailed from the coast of Argolis to the Hellespont, on the pretext that he wished to join in the war as a private person. By some means, perhaps on the score of the great services which he had rendered to Greece at Platæa, he obtained an entrance into Byzantium, and established himself there in some degree of power. But his position was not such as to enable him to take any active steps in concert with Persia; year after year passed on, and nothing whatever was accomplished of the promises which he had held out to the King. His treachery meanwhile grew more and more apparent, until at last the Athenians found it necessary to expel him from Byzantium. He retired to Colonæ, a city in the Troad, where he was at least within easy reach of the satrap of Phrygia. But the suspicions of the Spartans had been aroused; ere long a Spartan herald appeared at Colonæ, bidding him return home on pain of incurring the displeasure of the Spartans. Pausanias did not venture to disobey; a breach with the authorities of his government, apart from the personal danger to himself, would have been fatal to his plans, which embraced an entire change of the situation in Peloponnesus as well as in the Ægean. On his previous recall he had been punished for some injuries which he had done to private persons, but on the graver charge of treachery he had been acquitted. He was now thrown into prison by the ephors, whose power was such that they could imprison even the kings of Sparta on bare suspicion. It was not long before he found his way out, when he at

once challenged his enemies to produce their charges.
For a time no one came forward. Many suspicious
actions of Pausanias were remembered ; his conduct
at Byzantium ; his affectation of the Persian dress
and manners ; his ambitious inscription on the tripod
at Delphi, in which he claimed the honours won by
Greece for himself; but certain proof was not to be
had. What touched the Spartan authorities even
more nearly was the report that he was intriguing
with the Helots, of whose rebellious spirit they were
in constant alarm. And it was true that Pausanias
had been in treaty with them, promising them freedom and civic rights if they would revolt. Still,
there was no incontestable evidence to hand, which
would justify the ephors in going to extremities
against a citizen of the royal blood, and the most
successful of Spartan generals.

At length a favourite servant turned informer.
Observing that of the messengers whom Pausanias
sent to Asia none ever returned, he opened the
despatches placed in his hands, in alarm for his own
safety. He found, as he expected, that directions were
given for his death. He at once showed the letter
to the ephors. Their suspicions were of course confirmed, but they still wished to hear something from
the lips of Pausanias himself; a despatch might be
forged, and there was the greater fear of this, because in order to hide his opening of the letter the
servant had in fact forged the seal of Pausanias. A
plan was arranged by which the truth was brought
to light. The servant, as if in fear for his life, took
sanctuary at the temple of Poseidon, on the pro-

montory of Tænarus, in the south of Laconia. Here he built a hut, divided by a wall into two compartments, in one of which he concealed the ephors, while he was visited by Pausanias in the other. The conversation which passed between him and his master was so arranged as to leave no doubt whatever of the guilt of Pausanias.

The ephors returned to Sparta, intending to arrest him. But even now they were not really in earnest in their work. They did not send to his house, or attempt to take him by surprise, and when they met him in the street, one of the body gave him a sign of warning, which enabled him to escape for the moment. He turned and fled. Before the pursuers could come up, he had taken refuge in a chamber adjacent to the temple of Athena of the Brazen House, and within the sacred precincts. Here he was at least safe from violence. But Spartan cruelty was a match for Spartan superstition. Unwilling to remove the suppliant, the ephors found means to defeat his object. They unroofed the chamber in which he lay, and finding that he was certainly there, with no means of egress but the door, they built up the doorway, and left him to starve. It is said by later writers that his own mother laid the first stone in this iniquitous work. When he was at length on the point of death they drew him out of the sacred place; if it was sacrilege to remove a suppliant, it was pollution for anyone to die in a temple. He was no sooner removed than he expired. Not long afterwards the Spartans appear to have felt some scruples about the manner in which they had dealt with him. They consulted Apollo of Delphi, who, besides other instructions, informed them that they had brought a curse upon themselves, and must offer two bodies in place of one. This was the curse of Athena of the Brazen House. The Spartans endeavoured to expiate their offence by erecting two bronze statues of Pausanias.

The chronology of this period is too uncertain to allow us to speak with confidence, but it is probable that Themistocles was at Argos when the treachery of Pausanias came to light. For the Spartans it was highly inconvenient that one who had shewn so strong a determination to dislodge them from their position as leaders of Greece should become influential in a city more famous in legend than their own, and a bitter enemy from the earliest times. As they could not call on the Argives to expel him, they devised a more secret and a more certain method of attaining their object. In the papers of Pausanias they professed to find evidence which involved Themistocles in his guilt. And though they could not appeal to any overt act in support of such a charge, they could remind the Athenians that Themistocles was known to have entered into secret communications with the Great King at the battle of Salamis. Themistocles had enemies enough at Athens, who were willing to take up the charge. An Alcmæonid, by name Leobotes, impeached him before the assembly, and the Athenian people were persuaded to send envoys to join the Spartans in arresting him as a traitor to Greece.

Themistocles received timely warning of their approach, and retired from Argos to Corcyra, a city which, in spite of her conduct during the Persian war, he had in some way befriended. Even here the Spartans followed him; and the Corcyræans finding themselves unequal to his protection, conveyed him to the opposite shore. Here also his enemies pursued him. He was compelled to seek shelter with Admetus, the king of the Molossians, who, though Themistocles had opposed him in some negotiations with the Athenian people, refused to surrender the suppliant, and sent him safely to Pydna in Macedonia. From Pydna he took ship to Ionia. But misfortune pursued him still. The ship in which he was carried was driven by a storm to Naxos at the very time when the city was being blockaded by the Athenians. Themistocles saw his danger, and sending for the captain, told him who he was, and offered a large sum of money on condition that he would neither land at Naxos nor allow anyone to leave the ship. If he refused, he would denounce him as an accomplice in his flight. The captain accepted the money and Themistocles was safely landed at Ephesus.

From Ephesus he entered into communication with the Persians. In a letter to Artaxerxes, who had just succeeded his father Xerxes, he offered his services to Persia. It was true that he had done the Great King more harm than anyone else, but he had also done him greater service, for it was owing to his advice that the bridge over the Hellespont had not been broken down, and Xerxes had been

enabled to retire in safety. He was now driven
from his country as a friend of the King. In a
year's time, if permission were given, he would
himself explain to Artaxerxes why he had come to
Asia. Artaxerxes was delighted at the thought
that his great enemy had come over to him. When
the year was ended, Themistocles appeared at Susa,
and at once became the most influential of all the
Greeks who had ever visited Persia. He was made
governor of Magnesia in Ionia, a convenient station
from which to keep watch over the seaboard. With
oriental magnificence certain cities were set apart
for his maintenance. Magnesia itself, a city with a
revenue of fifty talents, supplied him with bread;
Lampsacus with wine; Myus with meat. For the
time, he was a Persian satrap, enjoying the special
favour of the King.

But no result followed. The victory of Cimon at the
Eurymedon in 466 had crushed any immediate hope
of invading Greece. Themistocles had to confess in
secret that the power which he had created was too
great for him to destroy. According to one account, he put an end to his own life because he
could not fulfil his promise to Artaxerxes; but
Thucydides, who was at pains to make careful inqui-
ries about his great countryman, assures us that he
died a natural death. A monument was erected to
his memory in the market-place of Magnesia, and
Plutarch's personal friend, Themistocles of Athens,
enjoyed the honours which were bestowed on his
posterity, even in the second century A.D., in that
city. But his bones, so at least his family asserted,

were secretly brought home and placed in Attic
earth.

Of the genius of Themistocles it is needless to
speak.   It is attested by the victory which he won,
and the career of the great city, to which he gave,
as it were, a second foundation.   In defence of his
honesty, we may say that there is no reason to suppose that he cherished treasonable designs against
his country before the moment when it was no
longer possible for him to remain safely in it ; and
when the combination of his enemies in Sparta and
Athens drove him out of Hellas, there was no place
but Persia to which he could retire.   It is extremely
doubtful whether there was any real ground for the
charge of medism upon which he was hunted out of
Greece.   The evidence comes to us from a very suspicious source—from the Spartans, who knew that
Themistocles was their enemy, and who had at the
time very urgent reasons for securing his expulsion
from the Peloponnesus.   Unhappily, the enemies of
Themistocles at Athens were only too ready to join
in the work.   They had succeeded in banishing him
from the city, but they knew that while he was in
Greece he might return and find some means of re-
venging himself upon them.   It did not occur to
their minds that the honour of their city was bound
up with that of her greatest citizen.   In the malice
of party spirit they forgot what they owed to the
world and posterity.

The leader of the attack is said to have been an
Alcmæonid, but whether Pericles took any part in
it is unknown. Assuming that Themistocles was

condemned in 467 or 466, Pericles would be twenty-six or twenty-seven at the time. His mind was already occupied with politics, and, as we shall see, he came forward in a very few years as the leader of the popular party; but his sympathy with the views of Themistocles must have been too great to allow him to share in the feud which drove him to the court of Persia. Nevertheless, the flight of Themistocles and the death of Aristides, which seems to have occurred about the same time, left the way clear for the new leader of the democracy.

COIN OF ELIS, REPRESENTING THE
OLYMPIAN ZEUS.

CHAPTER V.

DECADENCE OF SPARTA—REVOLT OF THE HELOTS— BREACH BETWEEN SPARTA AND ATHENS.

Decadence of Sparta—Invasion of Thessaly—Attempt on the Delphian Amphictyony—Troubles in the Peloponnesus—Earthquake at Sparta and revolt of the Helots—Athens under Cimon—Battles of the Eurymedon—Revolt of Thasos—Assistance sent to Sparta.

FROM the time that she withdrew her contingent from the Grecian fleet Sparta began to decline rapidly in prestige and power. Her want of firmness in investigating and punishing the conduct of Pausanias allowed events to take a turn which was disastrous to her reputation and even to her power; while the growth of democratic feeling, fostered no doubt by the example of Athens, was raising an amount of hostility, or at any rate of disaffection, in the Peloponnesus, to which she had hitherto been a stranger.

As a means of increasing her influence on land in compensation for the loss of her influence in the fleet, Sparta took up the line of punishing those states which had supported Xerxes in his invasion

of Greece. The patriotic states were indeed pledged
to this step, but the Athenians were far too busy
with their new confederacy to give much attention to
the claims of the old alliance, and the moment was
favourable for independent action on the part of
Sparta. Among the most flagrant offenders were the
Aleuadæ, the princely house which practically governed Thessaly. They had not only received the Persians into their country, and conducted them to the
south of Greece, but they had even sent envoys to
Persia with the object of bringing about the invasion. To punish such conduct Leotychidas, the
king of Sparta, was despatched at the head of an
army into Thessaly. Unhappily for Sparta, Leotychidas was more corrupt, or at least less able to
conceal his corruption, than Pausanias himself. He
received bribes from the Aleuadæ with so little
secrecy that he was found with the money in his
tent. The army was at once recalled ; Leotychidas
was put on his trial and condemned. He fled for
refuge to Tegea in Arcadia, and so unfriendly were
the terms which now prevailed between Sparta and
her ally, that the Tegeatæ refused to give him up.
He was succeeded on the throne by his son Archidamus.

The first attempt to pursue a patriotic policy had
ended in failure and disgrace. The second also
proved abortive. From very ancient times a league
of twelve tribes had met at Thermopylæ and Delphi, which was known as the Delphian Amphictyony.
It was perhaps in the first instance founded for common worship and defence, but at the time of which

we are speaking its functions were almost exclusively
religious; very rarely did it take a part in the political
affairs of the country.   At the Persian invasion a
large proportion of the cities and tribes forming the
league had gone over, either voluntarily or on the
compulsion of powerful neighbours, to the side of the
Persians.   The Spartans now proposed to purge the
Amphictyony by the expulsion of the medizing members.   The proposal was strictly in accordance with
the resolution which had been taken in 481 B.C. to
punish those Greeks who failed in their duty to their
country, but nevertheless the aims of Sparta were
suspected.   It was thought that she wished to gain
for herself a preponderance in the council of the
league, and by this means to lay the foundation of a
confederacy in Northern Greece, which would be as
fully under her control as the confederacy in the
Peloponnesus.   On these grounds Themistocles at
once came forward to oppose the proposal of the
Spartans.   His arguments, whether well founded or
not, proved convincing ; in spite of its delinquencies
the Amphictyony remained without change.

The attention of Sparta was soon recalled
from these more distant projects by troubles nearer
home.   We have seen that the Tegeatæ refused to
give up Leotychidas at the request of the Spartans.   A war appears to have broken out between
the cities, in which the Argives came to the help of
the Tegeatæ.   The Spartans were victorious, but
the victory cannot have been very decisive, for Leotychidas remained safe at Tegea till his death, and no
steps were taken against Argos.   Not long after-

wards the whole of Arcadia, with the exception of the Mantineans, took the field against Sparta. The armies met at Dipæa, where a great battle was fought, in which the Spartans were again victorious. But though she proved her power in the field, it was obvious that a spirit of independence was gaining ground among her neighbours and allies which threatened her ascendancy at the very time when there was no one at Sparta of sufficient ability and character to counteract it. For in this crisis of her history Sparta was as deficient in great men as Athens was prolific of them.

The same tendency appeared in a great revolution which about this time took place in Elis. Hitherto that state had been oligarchical, and a warm friend of Sparta, but after the Persian war a reaction set in, which now showed itself in a very definite step. The constitution was changed in the direction of democracy, and the change was marked and confirmed by the formation of a large central city, called Elis after the country. Up to this time the great families which had governed Elis had lived in small towns; and indeed a country life was at all times characteristic of the Eleans. The change which now took place transferred the ruling authority to the citizens who were gathered into the new city.

More important were the changes which went on in Argos. Ever since the great defeat by Cleomenes of Sparta, in which six thousand Argives perished, the city had devoted her attention to recovering and consolidating her power. A hard task lay before her. So low had she been brought by her disaster, that the slaves or serfs had usurped the dominion of the country after the slaughter of their masters, and not till these were deposed was Argos her true self. This exhaustion was put forward as a plea by the Argives for their omission to send help against Persia in 481 B.C. Slowly the city recovered her strength, and when she found Sparta occupied with her Arcadian neighbours, she seized the opportunity to break up all the independent towns in the vale of Argos, and concentrate their inhabitants in the city. The ancient towns of Mycenæ and Tiryns, in spite of their legendary glory, and the patriotic part they had played in the Persian invasion, ceased to exist. Those of their inhabitants who were not embodied in the Argive community were driven out to find shelter wherever they could. By this means Argos rose once more to the condition of a flourishing state. At the same time, the concentration of somewhat hetero-geneous elements in the city may have strengthened the democratic tendencies of the constitution, so as to draw her nearer to Athens. At any rate we hear of a king of Argos in the Persian war, and we never hear of one after.

Thus was the influence of Sparta limited on every side at the moment when the conduct of her leaders excited hatred and suspicion throughout Greece. But these were not the whole, nor by any means the greatest, of the troubles by which she was now beset. As we have seen, Pausanias was suspected of inciting the Helots to revolt. The Helots were principally the ancient population of Messenia, whom the Spar-

tans had reduced to serfdom, a brave and hardy
race, who tilled the soil in remote farms and hamlets,
on a sort of metayer system, under which a certain
amount of the produce was paid to the Spartan
owner. They never forgot their lost independence,
or regarded the Spartans as any thing but conquerors, whom they would strike down in a moment, if
the opportunity occurred. This feeling was well
known to their masters, who dreaded nothing so
much as a revolt of the Helots, and took the most
atrocious measures to prevent it. They had recently
torn some Helots from the sanctuary at Tænarus,
and put them to death in spite of the divine protection to which they were entitled, an act which had
brought on them the curse of Tænarus. The present
time was naturally a period of excitement among the
Helots; they saw with delight the repeated attacks
upon Sparta, and felt that a support was at hand
which had hitherto been denied to them. They
were also moved by the promises of Pausanias, who
no doubt held out a hope of Persian help.

With the death of Pausanias and the destruction
of the Persian army at the Eurymedon the worst
danger might seem to have passed away (466 B.C.).
But in the autumn of the year 464 a sudden disaster
overtook Sparta which brought her to the very brink
of destruction. A terrific earthquake laid the city
in ruins. Only five houses were left standing ; more
than twenty thousand persons are said to have perished. In this fearful moment Archidamus the king
saved his country. While others were dazed with
terror at the falling ruins, or lamenting the loss of

their property, he gave the signal for war, and by this means drew the Spartans out of the city. It was the salvation of the Spartan name. For the Helots no sooner heard of the earthquake than they flocked together to complete the ruin of their hated masters. Messenia broke into revolt, and though the rebels could not penetrate to Sparta, they entrenched themselves firmly on Mount Ithome, the ancient stronghold of their race. From this centre they carried on a predatory warfare, often inflicting severe loss on the enemy. In vain did the Spartans endeavour to dislodge them from their fortress; in vain did they call on their allies for help. The Messenians held out, and every attempt to capture Ithome only ended in new disaster.

In this critical state of their affairs the Spartans determined to apply for help to the Athenians, who had a great reputation for their skill in capturing fortified places. The feeling between the cities was not very good; when the earthquake occurred, the Spartans were about to invade Attica in spite of the peace which nominally prevailed. But there had been no open breach, and in the hope that their secret intentions were unknown the Spartans in the year 463 B.C. despatched Periclidas to Athens.

That city had been rising to power and reputation under the command of Cimon, who, for a few years, was without a rival. The Delian confederacy was becoming more and more an Athenian empire, and after the reduction of Naxos it was clear that Athens was resolved to keep the league together by force. The policy was justified, at any rate, for the moment,

by the events which followed the fall of Naxos. The
battles of the Eurymedon, which took place in 466
B.C., were perhaps the most overwhelming defeats
ever suffered by Persia, but unfortunately no contemporary description exists of them. Thucydides
briefly records the fact that the Athenians and their
allies, under the command of Cimon, conquered the
Persians on land and sea at the river Eurymedon, in
Pamphylia, and destroyed two hundred Phœnician
vessels. Later writers have a good deal more to tell,
but it is extremely doubtful whether they had any
real knowledge of what they pretend to describe.
The accounts are neither very credible nor very consistent. Perhaps we may venture to record the few
details which Plutarch, who is far more cautious than
Diodorus, has given in his " Life of Cimon." He
tells us that after altering the shape of the Athenian
vessels so that more hoplites or heavy-armed soldiers could be placed on board, Cimon set sail from
Cnidus with two hundred triremes to Lycia, where,
with the help of the Chian contingent in his fleet, he
won over the important town of Phaselis for the confederacy. Off the coast of Lycia he was informed
that the Persian fleet lay at the mouth of the Eurymedon, while a further contingent was expected
from Cyprus. Without a moment's hesitation he
attacked the fleet in the Eurymedon, defeated it,
and captured not less than two hundred vessels.
Pursuing his success he landed his troops and defeated the Persians a second time on shore, gaining
possession of the camp and an immense booty. After
this victory he went in search of the eighty ships at

MT. ITHOME.

In the Foreground is a Portion of the Wall of Messene, and Gate-way.

(From a Photograph by Mr. Clark.)

Cyprus. These also he destroyed, thus annihilating the whole of the Persian fleet, and defeating any hopes, if any had been cherished, of an invasion of Greece.

The victory of the Eurymedon brought the cities of Caria within the Delian confederacy. It is, however, remarkable that no attempt was made to appropriate Cyprus. That island, so important as a military post, was allowed to remain in the hands of Phœnician princes, though Athens could now sweep the shores on every side.

Such successes confirmed the Athenians in their imperial policy. Soon after their return from the Eurymedon they quarrelled with the Thasians about their mines on the opposite coast, and demanded a share in their trade with the Thracians (465 B.C.). They were eager to establish themselves on the Strymon, and were jealous of the prosperity of the island, which seemed to stand in the way of their own ambitions. The Thasians answered by revolting from the league. Cimon was at once sent to blockade the city, and about the same time no fewer than ten thousand colonists, partly Athenian and partly allies, were sent to occupy the important station of the Nine Ways on the Strymon. Could a vigorous colony be planted there in Athenian interests, it would greatly curtail the trade of the Thasians, and appropriate a large part of the profits of that district. So far as the colony was concerned, however, the project came to a most disastrous end ; the warlike natives of the district were jealous of the interference of strangers, and combined their forces for attack. A fierce en-

gagement took place at Drabescus, in which the whole
of the immigrants were cut down.

Nor could Thasos itself be taken without a pro-
tracted siege. The Thasians were rich; their walls
were strong; their town well prepared for resistance.
They even induced the Spartans to take up their
cause and invade Attica in order to divert the attention of the Athenians, a scheme which only failed
owing to the earthquake and the revolt of the
Helots. But Cimon was not to be shaken off. After
a siege of two years Thasos succumbed. Henceforth she became a tributary ally of the Delian
confederacy, or, more precisely, a subject city of the
Athenian empire (463 B.C.).

On his return to Athens Cimon was by no means
received with universal congratulation. In his absence the popular party had gained ground, and
among their leaders was Pericles, who now appears
for the first time in the history of Athens. At his
instigation or, at any rate, with his consent, a charge
was brought forward that Cimon had failed in his
duty: he might have acquired a portion of Macedonia for Athens, had he not been bribed by King
Alexander to let the opportunity slip. The charge
was, no doubt, without foundation, and disgraceful
to those who made it, but it is an indication of the
state of party spirit at Athens. The reign of Cimon
was at an end; the harmony in which parties had
worked together since the expulsion of Themistocles
was at an end also. A new democracy was rising under the auspices of Pericles, which would be satisfied
with nothing less than absolute and direct supremacy.

At this juncture came the application of the Spartans for aid in capturing Ithome. Cimon was in favour of sending help; Ephialtes—at this time the foremost man in the new democracy—was against it. Cimon declared that he could not stand by and see Athens deprived of her yoke-fellow; Ephialtes would not raise a finger to prevent the ruin of a city which never looked with favour on democratic principles. Cimon gained the day. He was despatched with a force to the Peloponnesus. But Ithome was strong enough to resist even Athenian skill. The siege lingered on, and at length the Spartans became suspicious of the Athenians. They were conscious that they at any rate had been secret and treacherous in concerting operations with the Thasians against the Athenians; they were also probably aware of the opposition which had been made to their request at Athens, and though they might have confidence in Cimon, they distrusted his soldiers. Suavity was not a Spartan virtue; no sooner had these suspicions arisen, than the Athenians, alone of the allies who had come to the assistance of Sparta, were sent home in a, most ungracious manner. Cimon saw himself compelled to lead back in disgrace the army which he had with so much difficulty persuaded the Athenians to send out. The rebuff was fatal to him and to the Athenian friends of Sparta, and his opponents were not slow to avail themselves of the opportunity which the failure of his policy afforded.

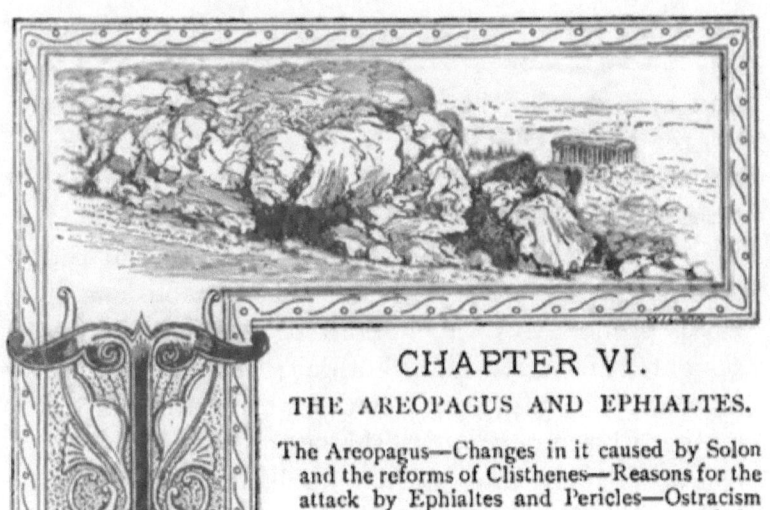

CHAPTER VI.

THE AREOPAGUS AND EPHIALTES.

The Areopagus—Changes in it caused by Solon
and the reforms of Clisthenes—Reasons for the
attack by Ephialtes and Pericles—Ostracism
of Cimon—Curtailment of the powers of the
council—Assassination of Ephialtes.

HE next appearance of Pericles in public life, after the attack on Cimon, is closely connected by ancient authors with the fall of the council of the Areopagus. In concert with Ephialtes, he succeeded in reducing that ancient council from a position of supreme authority in the state to that of a court for the trial of murder and arson—solemn functions, which it had long discharged, but which obviously carried with them no political importance. The change was one of great significance in the constitutional history of Athens, and it is said to have removed the last serious check on the development of democracy. Pericles appears to have been the prime mover in the work, though the measures were actually brought forward by Ephialtes.

Of the origin and history of the council we have very uncertain information. It was a debated question even in the time of Aristotle, whether it had existed before the days of Solon or not. The more probable account seems to be, that from immemorial time cases of murder had been tried on the sacred Hill of Ares, which lay to the north-west of the Acropolis. Here on a bare and rugged table-land of naked stone, Ares had himself been tried for the slaughter of his son Halirrhothius; Cephalus for the murder of Procris; and Orestes for the murder of his mother Clytemnestra. At this last great trial Apollo had pleaded the cause of his suppliant, and Athena had presided in the court. Legendary as these stories are, they mark out the Hill of Ares as an ancient place of judgment, and in this respect they are confirmed by the little historical evidence which we possess. In the eighth century, B.C., the Messenians were willing to refer their quarrel with Sparta to the decision of the Areopagus, and in Solon's " Law of Amnesty," those men were exempted from its provisions who had incurred the sentence of that court. The council of the Areopagus then was an ancient place of judgment for the most serious offences which can arise in a community. It was characteristic of Greek religious feeling to regard such a tribunal as under the special protection of the deities, whose care it was to see that bloodshed did not go unpunished. The Furies, the dread spirits who moved in the darkness of Erebus, ever ready to hear the cry of those who called upon them, were thought to have taken up their abode in a cavern at the foot of the hill. It was not less characteristic that the ritual observed at the trials in this hallowed place should

be of a primitive kind. The court was held in
the open air, that no one might be polluted by
coming into the same chamber with the man guilty of
blood. Two rude stones, the Stone of Outrage and
the Stone of Shamelessness, were assigned to the
accuser and the accused ; the judges sat on the bare
rock. No mitigating circumstances could be taken
into consideration ; no penalty was inflicted less than
death, though the accused might avoid execution by
going into exile.

Solon seems to have availed himself of the sanctity which surrounded this ancient judgment-seat to
create a council whose powers extended far beyond
the punishment of bloodshed. He ordained that
the nine archons, who in his day were the chief executive officers of the city, should enter after their
year of office into the council of the Areopagus, and
that the court thus enlarged should be the supreme
guardian of the welfare of the city. It watched over
the laws, to the end that they might be duly carried
out ; it even went beyond the law in enquiring into
the moral conduct of the citizens. It punished the
idle and extravagant ; it weeded out from the city
every noxious growth ; it was a wakeful guardian
over those that slept, the like of which could not be
found in the broad island of Pelops (the Peloponnesus)
or in far-off Scythia, a land of mythical righteousness
and mysterious power.

Such was Solon's council, as Plutarch and Æschylus
describe it to us. Of the real working of the institution we know little or nothing. In the long period
which elapsed between Solon and Pericles (one hun-

dred and thirty years), we only hear of the Areopagus twice ; a citizen is said to have cited Pisistratus the tyrant before the court, but when Pisistratus appeared, in answer to the summons, the accuser thought it prudent not to come forward.   This incident, which is recorded by Aristotle, is a proof that under the tyranny of Pisistratus the Areopagus, like all the other institutions of Athens, was allowed to continue in existence, and also that its powers, like those of all other public bodies, were at this time little more than nominal.   We also learn, on the same authority, that the Areopagus came forward with some vigorous measures at the time of the Persian war, and "braced the constitution."   What the measures were is uncertain, unless Aristotle refers to an incident mentioned by Plutarch, who informs us that the council provided the poorer citizens with means to pass over from Athens to Salamis, and thus enabled the whole city to act together in offering defiance to the invader.

The political changes of Clisthenes in 509 B.C., were not without effect on the Areopagus. He did not interfere directly with the council, nor with the archons who composed it.   But the creation of the board of the ten generals greatly diminished the power of the archons as executive officers.   For thirty or forty years after this time we find great names in the list of Athenian archons, but it is not as archons that they exercised great power.   The generals were of far more importance, especially from the time of the second Persian invasion in 480 B.C. As it became less influential, the archonship

became less attractive;—and the change naturally
caused some alteration in the class of men who
sought the office. This was still more the case
when, on the proposal of Aristides, the archonship
was thrown open to the lowest class of citizens. In
fact the archons soon became little more than a
mayor and aldermen, with special functions in the
administration of law. And as ex-archons formed
nearly the whole of the council of the Areopagus,
any change in the archons of necessity produced
a change in the council.

We naturally ask: If such were the case, why
should the council have been worth attacking; and
why should the curtailment of its powers be regarded as the turning-point in the development of
democracy? The first of these questions is more
easily answered than the second. The Areopagus
was worth attacking by a democratical reformer,
because the existence of it involved two principles
which democracy could not tolerate. The members
held office for life; and they were not responsible to
any higher authority for the proper discharge of
their duties. As a rule, every public officer at Athens
—and members of the council were regarded as officers,—from the highest to the lowest, held office for
a year only; and at the end of the year he was not
released from responsibility till he had rendered a
satisfactory account of his office. The exception
implied that there was a power in Athens which the
people could not touch;—a superior court, in which
only a part of the citizens shared. This was not the
worst: in the life tenure, and in the freedom of the

THE AREOPAGUS AND THESEUM.
From the South-East.
(Curtius and Kaupert.)

members from responsibility, the council of the
Areopagus presented a striking resemblance to the
Gerousia at Sparta. To some Athenians this might
be a recommendation; to Pericles and his party,
who were convinced that Sparta was the great
obstacle to the final realisation of their views, it was
an additional cause for dislike. These then were the
reasons why the democracy wished to remove the
council. It was the last vestige of a form of constitution which they had renounced; it was an anomaly
which stood in glaring contrast to the legislation of
the last thirty years.

It is another matter, when we ask what was
gained by its removal. How could the council be
said to limit the freedom of the citizens, and impose a check on the growing spirit of democracy?
Why did aristocrats like Cimon contend for its
preservation? Its authority, so far as we know, had
greatly declined; and it was not easy to make it an
instrument of aristocratical power when the archons
were chosen by lot, and the members of the fourth
Solonian class could enter their names for the office.
We can only reply that our information is so defec-
tive that, for aught we know to the contrary, the
council may have exercised a great influence on
social life in Athens, even after Clisthenes. A council which had the right to make annoying enquiries
would perhaps seem more powerful than it really
was, and its power must have been most odious
to those who were rising into public life. The more
a man attracted notice, the more was the Areopagus
likely to have an eye upon him. Or it may have

6

had a large control over the administration of the
law. The paid juries of Athens were the creation
of Pericles; the elaborate system of legislation by
means of the Nomothetæ, was certainly not earlier
than Pericles (if, indeed, it was so early). Before
these came into existence, the Areopagus may have
exercised considerable power, judicial and legal.
Moreover, the mere fact that the Areopagus was
attacked by Pericles, and that its fall was succeeded
by the development of the jury-courts, with which
the democracy was so closely linked, would create in
later ages the impression that its removal was the
last step in the development of democracy, or, from
another point of view, that its power had been in
some way a check on the democratical spirit. In
any case, the later writers who speak of the power
of the Areopagus cannot have known very much
about it. It was to them an ideal; they saw in
it the check which the Athenians of their own day
greatly needed; but whether the reality corresponded
to their conception of it, is more than we can say.

That the aristocratical or Spartan party at Athens
should support the Areopagus was inevitable. The
council was in some respects a distinctly oligarchical
institution. Even if largely filled from the lowest class,
which is very unlikely, it was capable of being influenced by corporate party feeling; it naturally was
jealous of its power, as all corporations are; it had
great traditions. However dissatisfied aristocrats
like Cimon might be with the alterations in the
Areopagus caused by the law of Aristides, they supported it as the remnant of a constitution to which

they looked back with reverence and pride. Cimon had acquiesced in the maritime development of Athens ; he had taken a leading part in establishing the Delian confederacy; he had not attempted to oppose the admission of all classes to office. But in the Areopagus he probably saw, like Solon himself, an anchor of the state, and he supported it with all his influence.

The attack was begun during the absence of Cimon from Athens, and probably when he was absent assisting the Spartans at Ithome in 463. This expedition, as we have seen, had been taken against the advice of Ephialtes, who may very well have compensated himself for his defeat, by bringing forward measures which, as he well knew, Cimon would oppose. And when Cimon did return, he returned in such disgrace that the balance of power was thrown into the opposite scale.

Of Ephialtes who led the attack we only know that he was the " Incorruptible " of this period of Athenian history. Poor, active, and fearless, he busied himself with bringing accusations against the rich who enjoyed office. By this means he became a power in the state ; he was the People's Friend of the new régime. As he had opposed the proposal to send assistance to Sparta, the discourteous conduct of the Spartans in sending the Athenians home brought him a new accession of strength. Had he not shewn himself a better judge of the situation than the great general? The Spartans were utterly untrustworthy, as he had said, and it was impossible to be on terms with them. In these views he had

Pericles with him. The aims of Pericles went far beyond anything of which Ephialtes was capable ; but Ephialtes had made a hit, and Pericles found in him a very useful ally.

Though Ephialtes could take advantage of the absence of Cimon on military expeditions to bring forward his sweeping measures, nothing could really be done so long as Cimon led the opposition. Soon after his return from Sparta a proposal was made that there should be ostracism in the city. No doubt the ground had been prepared ; Ephialtes and Pericles had made such progress in popular favour that they could look forward to the popular vote with confidence. Even if the measures by which Pericles gained his ascendancy—the payment of the juries, the distribution of public money at festivals, and the sending out of colonies—came later, his friends had no doubt been assiduous in spreading abroad the belief that popular measures and reform could not be carried out so long as Cimon was in Athens.

Ostracism was a device for putting an end to faction and strife in the city. It is said to have been invented by Clisthenes, but we find it in other cities than Athens, and we do not know where it was first established. The people were asked in the sixth prytany* of the year, whether it was their wish that ostracism should take place. If they agreed, an assembly was held in the market-place in the eighth prytany, which would fall in the spring, in which they gave their votes against any citizen they pleased by writing his name on what the Greeks called

---

*A prytany is a tenth part of the Attic year.

ostraka, *i. e.* on small pieces of earthenware. No name was proposed to them ; no charge was brought against anyone ; each citizen wrote on his tablet the name of the man who in his judgment was most pernicious to the peace of the community. If six thousand votes were recorded against any one citizen, he was expected to leave the city in ten days, and to remain beyond the borders of Attica for five or perhaps ten years. His property was not touched ; his civic rights remained unimpaired. A decree of the people could at any moment reinstate him in his full privileges as an Athenian citizen. In the days of Clisthenes, when a political opponent was ready to call in the power of Sparta, ostracism might be of some value ; a man against whom six thousand votes were recorded would be proved to have little support to offer to his foreign accomplices. But on the whole the institution contributed little to the security or peace of Athens. As a political engine, it was nearly always worked for party ends, and the instance of Cimon was no exception to the rule. No one could seriously maintain that his presence endangered the public peace, or that Athens was better without him than with him.

Ostracised he was, and with him went the great defender of ancient institutions. Ephialtes was now quite free to carry out his reforms, for Cimon stood so high as the leader of his party that there was no second to take his place. The Areopagus was at once stripped of a large portion of its functions, and ceased to be a political power in the city. What were the precise functions taken from it, and what was done to compensate the city for the loss, are doubtful. One authority tells us that a number of legal cases were removed from its jurisdiction, and in a quotation from Aristotle's "Constitution of Athens" we find that even Themistocles endeavoured to restrict the judicial powers of the council. If this be true, the fall of the Areopagus was, no doubt, closely connected with the development of the popular jury-courts. An obscure notice informs us that the function of watching over the laws, which was now removed from the Areopagus, was transferred to seven Nomophylakes or Guardians of the Laws, who had a seat in the council of Five Hundred and could at once interfere if any proposal were made which seemed to contradict the laws. But these Nomophylakes are never mentioned by any ancient author, and there may be a confusion between them and officers of the same name who existed at Athens at the end of the fourth century.

In this uncertainty we must suppose that the curtailment of the Areopagus, which is so universally ascribed to Ephialtes and Pericles, consisted in removing from it the supervision over the laws which it had previously exercised, and in cancelling its censorial powers. Henceforth the Areopagus was no more than a court for the trial of murder; it could not interfere in the private life of the citizen; it had no power to prevent the alteration of the laws. It is quite possible, as we have said, that under the disguise of censorial supervision, the Areopagus had acquired a good deal of judicial power in excess of what really belonged to it. If this were the case, this power was now transferred to the law courts.

The ostracism of Cimon and the fall of the Areopagus were great victories for the democratic party. Ephialtes was now the first minister of Athens; and the way was clear for any reform which he and Pericles might propose. They had the people with them, and the opposition was helpless. The aristocratical party could only look forward to the complete overthrow of their influence and their principles. They became desperate, and endeavoured to avert by illegitimate means, what they could no longer resist in the assembly. Within a few years after the overthrow of the Areopagus, Ephialtes fell by the knife of an assassin. The name of the murderer was at a later time asserted to be Aristodicus, a native of Tanagra in Bœotia; whoever he was, he was only a tool in the hands of a party. Those who could never speak evil enough of Pericles asserted that he had removed from his path an associate who had acquired an inconvenient degree of power, but this is the mere malignity of personal hatred. It was no doubt the oligarchical party, whom he had pestered by his prosecutions, and whose prospects he had ruined, that secured his removal. It is a coincidence worth mentioning that about the time of the death of Ephialtes some members of the oligarchical party were in treasonable correspondence with the Spartans. As Ephialtes had always been a strong opponent of the Spartan party at Athens, those who wished to restore Spartan influence might feel that their aims could not be realised so long as he was in power. As a first step to efficient co-operation he must be removed. But whoever were the immediate

authors of the deed, it is satisfactory to know that
Cimon was away from Athens at the time when this
murder, the first political assassination at Athens,
was committed.

Ephialtes was a " Radical," as Themistocles had
been before him. Like Themistocles, he was desir-
ous that Athens should be a naval power ; and, like
him, he was extremely opposed to any union with
Sparta. But unlike Themistocles, he was free from
the suspicion of bribery. And though he fell a victim
to the ferocity of party strife, he was more fortunate
than Themistocles in retaining the favour of his own
adherents to the last. What his ulterior views may
have been, we cannot say. Were his democratical
measures shaped like those of Themistocles with a
view to an Athenian empire, or did he also wish,
like Pericles, to secure the conditions of a noble life
for every citizen of Athens? or, like later dema-
gogues, to provide an easy subsistence for the mob
of the city? These are questions which we cannot
answer. With the assassination of Ephialtes, Pericles became the acknowledged leader of the Athenian democracy, and he kept the position till his death.
All the measures passed in that period are his work ;
whether he carried out the ideas of Ephialtes, or
Ephialtes had been put forward to prepare the way
for the ideas of Pericles, it is impossible to decide.

CHAPTER VII.

THE FIRST WAR BETWEEN ATHENS AND SPARTA.

Renewal of the war in the East—Outbreak of war in Hellas—Battle of Tanagra—Battle of Œnophyta—Cimon recalled—Disastrous failure of the Egyptian expedition.

HE churlish and suspicious rudeness with which the Athenian troops had been dismissed from Ithome by the Spartans created a reaction in the feelings of the Athenians towards that city. Hitherto, in spite of the efforts of Themistocles and others, and though various causes of complaint had arisen, the two cities had preserved the appearance of friendship. Even those Athenians who would have claimed the supremacy at sea for themselves were willing to allow that the Spartans were the rightful leaders of the Greeks on land. Harmonious action between the great cities was the best warranty of the safety of Greece. But now the irritation was uncontrolla-

ble, and it was decided not only to break off the
alliance which had existed since 481 B.C., but to take
up a line which made it clear that Athens was as
willing to support the enemies of Sparta as she
had been to support Sparta herself.

Argos was of course at all times hostile to Sparta.
As we have seen, the city had recently recovered a
considerable degree of power, and at the same time
changes had taken place which made the democratic
feeling there stronger than ever.

Thus there were now two bonds to draw Athens
and Argos together—hatred of Sparta, and democratic sympathies. At the moment both these feelings were almost at fever heat at Athens, owing to
the influence of Ephialtes. Under such circumstances the events of 480 B.C. were forgotten; Athens and Argos became allies.

The step is significant of the change which had
taken place in Greece since the Persian war. *Then*
oaths had been sworn binding the patriotic Greeks
to take vengeance on those who had so foully be-
trayed their country; Argos and Thessaly were out-
casts from the circle of Greek cities, and Sparta had
herself undertaken an expedition to punish the Thessalians for their conduct. *Now* the Athenians, to
whom all the rest of the Greeks owed their freedom,
who had twice abandoned their homes, and undergone the greatest privations in the cause of Hellas,
were content to enter into an alliance with a city
which, to say the best of her, had pursued a weak and
temporising policy. But the Athenians did not stop
here. With Argos to aid them they renewed the

old alliance with Thessaly, which had existed in the time of the tyrants. They knew by experience that Thessalian cavalry were valuable in the field, and they could reckon on the hatred of the Thessalians for the Spartans. In this second alliance they not only disregarded the part which the great princes of Thessaly had played in bringing Xerxes into Greece ; they forgot the character of the Thessalian people, who were not less treacherous than brave. In the hour of peril, as we shall see, they had bitter reason to repent their mistake.

These proceedings did not amount to open war with Sparta, but they were nothing less than open preparation for war. And they were succeeded by a number of events which made war inevitable. The years 460 and 459 B.C., during which the two cities were nominally at peace, were years of great military activity on the part of the Athenians. Never before did they exhibit so plainly the strength of the city ; never before was their strength displayed in a manner so likely to rouse the suspicions of their neighbours.

The Spartans had by this time succeeded in crushing the rebellion of the Helots. For about three years after the dismissal of the Athenians in 463 B.C. the fortress of Ithome held out, then it capitulated, and the defenders were allowed to depart on condition that they would never set foot in the Peloponnesus again. The Athenians, who had recently taken Naupactus, a town near the mouth of the Corinthian gulf, from the Ozolian Locrians, allowed the exiles to settle there. The permission

was equivalent to establishing the deadliest enemies
of Sparta in a position where they could at any
moment land on the shores which they were forbidden to tread.

The next step aroused the wrath of a city which
had formerly been on the most friendly terms with
Athens, but from henceforth became her most active
enemy; a city to whose unsleeping hatred a large
part of her misfortunes were due. For some time
past the Megarians and Corinthians had quarrelled
as neighbouring states in Greece were only too apt
to do. Some question of boundaries had arisen,
such as centuries before, in the time of Orsippus,
had led to war between the cities. Megara was,
of course, no match for her formidable rival; her
only hope of justice lay in an appeal to Sparta, as
the head of the confederacy to which Corinth and
Megara belonged. But Sparta would not interfere;
she was probably unwilling to incur the enmity of
Corinth, and unable to perceive what would be the
inevitable result of her inaction. She was also still
affected by the panic caused by the recent outbreak
of the Helots, " a turn for the worse " in a long disease which might recur at any time. The Megarians
then applied to Athens, where they found a ready
reception. Nothing indeed could be more opportune. It was the weakness of Athens that her territory could be invaded without much difficulty from
Megara; and through the territory of Megara, along
the eastern extremity of the Corinthian gulf, lay the
route which connected Peloponnesus and Bœotia.
Athenian troops were at once sent to the aid of the

Megarians and, with their consent, garrisons were placed in the two ports of their city : in Pegæ on the Corinthian gulf, and in Nisæa on the Saronic gulf. Nisæa was also connected with Megara by long walls, which were protected by Athenian soldiers. By this measure Megara was not only brought into close relations with the Peiræus, but Athens practically secured a frontier in the Megarid extending from sea to sea, and a station for her ships on the Corinthian gulf. For a time she had effectually blocked the way to Attica from that direction.

At the very time that she was thus irritating her most powerful neighbours, Athens did not hesitate to enter once more upon the conflict with Persia. Egypt had been made a Persian province in 525 B.C.; in the last year of Darius it had revolted, but it was quickly subdued by Xerxes, to whom it had subsequently furnished a very large contingent of ships for the invasion of Greece. In 465 B.C. Xerxes was murdered, and the first years of his successor were occupied with suppressing conspiracies. A rebellion in Bactria then carried him to the eastern edge of his empire. To the oppressed Egyptians an opportunity seemed to have arrived when there was a reasonable hope of shaking off the hated yoke. Inaros, the son of Psammetichus, the king of Libya, which formed a part of the Egyptian satrapy, seized Mareia, a Persian outpost on the south-western shore of the Mareotic lake. He was at once joined by the greater part of Egypt; the Persian governor was expelled; and Inaros elected king of the country. For a short time he remained undisturbed, but in 459 B.C. he became

aware that a vigorous attempt was about to be made
to recover Egypt. His own forces were inadequate
to resist the army which was being brought against
him, and he sent to Athens for assistance.

For some years after the decisive victories of Eurymedon the Athenians had sent out no expeditions
to the East, but at this time they had just despatched
two hundred ships to Cyprus. That island, in spite
of the victories of Pausanias and Cimon, had never
been acquired by the Greeks. It formed no part of
the Delian league ; there was neither ally nor colony
among its numerous cities. It was a wealthy island,
well situated for trade with the East, and exceedingly valuable as a military station. It lay opposite
that Cilician plain which formed the rendezvous of
the Persian Empire ; it commanded the cities of Asia
Minor and the mouth of the Nile. With Egypt in
revolt and the Egyptian fleet detached from the
service of the king, there was a reasonable hope of
annexing the island to the league.

But on receiving the application of Inaros the
project of acquiring Cyprus was abandoned for the
time, and the fleet was ordered to proceed to Egypt
to co-operate with the rebels. Egypt was not only
the more valuable prize of the two, a country which
could at once supply vast stores of grain, and furnish
a number of brave and experienced seamen, but the
conquest of Egypt carried with it the conquest of
Cyprus. The temptation was irresistible ; the gathering clouds at home were disregarded, and at the
moment when the war with the Peloponnesians was
inevitable, Athens sent more than half her fleet to

the Nile. She may have felt that even without these ships, her position at the head of the Delian confederacy rendered her far more than a match for any combination which would be brought against her; she probably overestimated the effect of the revolt of the Helots on the Spartan state. Whatever her views, we may observe that she would never have permitted such a division of her forces had she intended to make any serious attack upon Sparta. As yet, it would seem, Pericles was unable either to restrain the Athenians from the Persian war or to concentrate their energies on the conflict with their rival.

The situation did not escape the watchful eye of the Corinthians. They were encouraged to resist the next movement of the Athenians by open force. On the coast of Argolis lay the small town of Halieis. Unimportant in itself, the place possessed a convenient harbour, and formed an admirable station for any power which desired to control the navigation of the Saronic gulf. In the hands of the Athenians Halieis would be a rival to Epidaurus and Hermione; and now that the Argives and Athenians were allies, it might afford Argos some compensation for the loss of her old trading-stations at Epidaurus and Ægina. There were other reasons also which made the acquisition of Halieis desirable to the Athenians. The town was inhabited by the Tirynthians whom the Argives had expelled from their ancient home; and there is reason to suppose that it was in some connexion with Sparta. To the Corinthians and Epidaurians nothing could be more disastrous than an Athenian settlement in this region. Already ships were at Pegæ watching the entrance to the great western port of Corinth; from Peiræus and Nisæa they commanded the northern half of the Isthmus; if they were settled at Halieis, the Saronic gulf would be entirely in their hands. The Epidaurians were even more closely touched, as their territory lay nearer Halieis. When, therefore, the Athenians landed on the Argolic coast they were met by a combined force of Corinthians and Epidaurians. It is certain that the Athenians were defeated, though they afterward succeeded in gaining a footing in the town of Trœzen, a still better station than Halieis. The defeat was overweighed by a victory over the fleet of the enemy at Cecryphaleia, a small island off the coast. Insignificant in themselves, these skirmishes were not insignificant in the history of Greece. They were the first steps in the disruption of the Hellenic league which had been formed at the Isthmus in the autumn of 481 B.C. for the defence of Greece. For years it had been obvious that Greece was parting into two camps, but now for the first time had hostilities broken out.

The next movement was of far greater importance, opening a new scene in a drama, in which, more vividly perhaps than elsewhere, we perceive the dire effects of neighbourly hatred and commercial rivalry among the Greeks. Since the general pacification of 481 B.C. Athens and Ægina had been on friendly terms, but now, owing, perhaps, to some hints from the Corinthians, the suspicions of the Æginetans were aroused. Were they not being surrounded by the

ACHO-CORINTHUS AND TEMPLE.

From the North-East.

(*From a Photograph by Mr. Clark.*)

Athenian power? Was not their union with Athens *
treachery to the older allegiance, which they owed
to the Peloponnesian confederacy? At the present
moment, with two hundred ships in Egypt, Athens
could not be a match for the combined Corinthian
and Æginetan fleets. Whatever the impulse under
which she acted, Ægina now went to war with
Athens, and all the bitter feelings of the ancient feud
were once more aroused. An obstinate battle was
fought off Ægina between the fleets of the two cities.
The Athenians were victorious, capturing no fewer
than seventy of the ships of the enemy. They then
landed on the island and proceeded to besiege the
city. The Peloponnesians sent over a small force
to aid the Æginetans, but it was of no avail. Meanwhile, the Corinthians, believing that the whole force
of the Athenians was now employed, resolved to
create a diversion by seizing the passes of Mount
Geraneia, which divided Megara and Corinth, and
invading the Megarian territory. But the Athenians
were equal to the occasion; they met the Corinthians with a force composed of their oldest and youngest men, under the command of Myronides, a general
who had served in the Persian war. The first engagement ended with doubtful success; a second
was decisively in favour of the Athenians.

While such were the achievements of the Athenians abroad, their proceedings at home made it
clear that they intended to secure the position they

---

* The Æginetans were not members of the Delian confederacy at
this time, but they were allies of Athens under the general pacification
of 481 B.C.

7

had gained. They had already built long walls to connect the town of Megara with the port of Nisæa; they now united Athens and Peiræus in the same permanent manner. Of the two walls which were built, one extended from the north-west edge of Peiræus across the marshy ground to the western wall of Athens, a distance of very nearly five miles. The second ran in a direction almost due south from Athens to the eastern edge of the harbour of Phalerum, a distance of four miles. Such an immense work could not be carried out in one year, and there is some reason to suppose that the walls were begun by Cimon and brought to completion by Pericles. The object of the walls was clear. When thus united with the sea, Athens would be impervious to attacks by land. Even if the Peloponnesians succeeded in passing the Megarian frontier and invading Attica, they could inflict no damage on the city. They could lay waste the cornfields of Thria, or the olive-gardens of the Cephisus; they could consume the harvest and carry off the cattle, but they could never separate Athens from the sea. With the building of the walls the policy of Athens under Pericles became possible.

It was time for Sparta to stir, if she wished to keep her allies round her. Her reputation was declining; and the recent movements of Athens seemed to shut her out from any participation in the affairs of Northern Greece. So at least the Phocians thought, and they took advantage of the situation to attack the communities of the Dorians who inhabited the northern declivities of Mount

Parnassus, one of whose towns they captured.   The
Lacedæmonians could not allow a state which they
acknowledged as their "mother city" to be laid
waste.   Nicomedes, who was regent at the time in
behalf of Plistoanax, the young son of Pausanias,
was at once despatched to Phocis with a large force
of Spartans and allies.   He crossed the Corinthian
gulf and marched through Bœotia into Phocis, which
he quickly compelled to make such terms as he
pleased, and restore the captured town.   But now a
difficulty arose.   How were the Peloponnesians to
return?   They had crossed the gulf on their way
out without attracting the notice of the Athenian
ships at Pegæ, but they could not expect to do this
a second time.   To cross Geraneia was still more
impossible, for the passes were held by Athenian
troops.   For the present it seemed best to remain
in Bœotia.   The delay was not without advantage.
If Bœotia could be raised from the degradation into
which it had sunk after the battle of Platæa, and
made a solid power, it would form an excellent
counterpoise to Athens.   The natural centre of the
country was, of course, Thebes.   In 480 B.C. that city
had been governed by one or two powerful families,
who had been instrumental in bringing the Persians
into Bœotia.   After the battle of Platæa the leaders
of these families had been executed or expelled,
but, so far as we can make out, an oligarchy still
continued at the head of affairs.   This oligarchy the
Lacedæmonians now attempted to make the ruling
power in Bœotia, by bringing the smaller allies into
a sort of dependent alliance with Thebes.   And this

was not the only result of their stay in Bœotia.
The present policy of Athens, external and domestic, was not approved by all the citizens. The
limitation of the powers of the Areopagus, the
constant prosecutions of Ephialtes, had roused the
fiercest passions of the oligarchs. They would
gladly have seen some check placed upon the development of the demos, which now, as in the days
of Clisthenes, seemed to be carried to victory on a
wave of enthusiasm. More especially they were
opposed to the building of the long walls, which
implied a complete change from Athens as the head
of Attica to Athens as a trading city, relying wholly
on her fleet. They foresaw that a union of the port
and town would give a new accession of strength to
the rabble of artisans and sailors. Their influence
was no doubt far less in the Peiræus than in the
city, as it was far less in the city than in the
country. With these views they entered into negotiations with the Spartans in order to secure their
assistance. The negotiations could be carried on
the more readily as the Spartans were now at Tanagra, a town in the extreme south of Bœotia, and on
the borders of Attica.

Pericles and his friends became alarmed. They
were aware of the treachery in the city and resolved
to attack the enemy before it went further. They
called upon the Argives for one thousand heavy-
armed soldiers, and on the Thessalians for a troop of
horse. Help came from other cities also, and the
whole available force of the city was put in the field.
The battle was hotly contested, but ended in favour

of the Spartans. The result was largely due to the treachery of the Thessalians, who went over to the enemy in the midst of the engagement, thus depriving Athens of the assistance which was specially needed against the excellent cavalry of the Bœotians. The Lacedæmonians were now at liberty to return home by land. They marched through Megara and the Isthmus, laying waste the country as they went, and on their return they suspended a golden shield in front of the temple at Olympia as a thank-offering for their victory (457 B.C.).

At last the fatal event had happened: Sparta and Athens had come to blows. The result was partly due to the action of the oligarchs at Athens, who wished to call in the aid of Sparta to their own support; partly to the desire to cut off the Spartan army before it could return home. The battle of Tanagra was the first occasion on which the Spartans and Athenians had been in conflict since the time when Cleomenes led his forces—sixty years before— to Athens to expel Clisthenes; it was a step in that fatal progress which soon divided Greece into oligarchical and democratical parties, each eager to pull down the other, let the result be what it might.

The victory cannot have been very decisive, or the Spartans would have been able to support their party at Athens and hinder the building of the walls. At any rate, they made no other use of it than to convey their troops safely home. Whether Bœotia was secure from any further attack on the part of Athens, they did not enquire. Yet it was pretty clear that a territory lying between Phocis and Attica, both of

which countries were at the time bitterly hostile to
Sparta, was in some danger. The result of their
carelessness was soon apparent. Sixty-two days
after the battle of Tanagra the Athenian forces were
again in Bœotia under the command of Myronides.
The battle took place at Œnophyta, not far from
Tanagra, and ended in a most decisive victory for the
Athenians. All Bœotia was now at their feet. They
demolished the walls of Tanagra and reduced the
country to the condition of a subject ally. At the
same time Phocis passed out of the Athenian alliance,
while the Locrians of Opus, who may have fought in
the allied army against Athens, were kept in submission by the surrender of one hundred of their richest
citizens (456 B.C.).

Not long afterwards the Æginetans, who had been
closely besieged since their great defeat nearly two
years before, came to terms. They surrendered their
ships, dismantled their walls, and agreed to pay tribute to Athens as members of the Delian league.
This was a serious loss to the Peloponnesian confederacy. If the Æginetan fleet was not so large as the
Corinthian, and this is doubtful, the Æginetans were
the better and braver sailors. The prize of valour
had been awarded to them at Salamis; their ships
were known from Palestine to Campania; their trade
penetrated the remotest valleys of Arcadia. The
helpless condition of the Peloponnesians in the
face of vigorous action was never more plainly
demonstrated than by the loss of Bœotia and Ægina; never was the selfish policy of Sparta placed in
a clearer light. Bitter, indeed, must have been the

vexation of Corinth when she saw the Athenians not only established on the coast of Argolis and in possession of the ports of Megara, but also masters of new resources by land and sea.

It was a proud moment for Athens. On land she controlled continental Hellas from the Pass of Thermopylæ to the Isthmus. Phocis and Megara were willing allies; Bœotia and Locris were subject to her power. At home the long walls secured her from attack. In the Peloponnesus, Argos was her ally; she had planted a foot in the north-east coast of Argolis, and was on friendly terms with Achæa. Near the mouth of the Corinthian gulf she held Naupactus. On sea she was without a rival. The Delian confederacy, which was rapidly becoming the Athenian empire, extended from Byzantium to Phaselis, from Miletus to Eubœa. Ægina, her old rival, was humbled, and Athenian fleets swept the shores of the Peloponnesus at pleasure. The Spartans, the only power now capable of vigorous opposition, were little better than caged wolves.

On the internal politics of Athens the battle of Tanagra had a very important effect. When the Athenian army was in Bœotia, Cimon appeared before the generals and begged permission to take his place among the soldiers of his tribe. He was known to be a firm friend of the Lacedæmonians, and he wished to prove that his friendship did not extend to enemies in the field. But the generals refused; there was no place for an ostracised citizen in the Athenian army any more than on Athenian soil. Thus repulsed, Cimon adjured those of his followers

who were most suspected of sympathy with Lacedæmonians to clear his name from every stain of
treachery. They responded to the appeal, and, faithful even unto death, fell on the battle-field to the
number of a hundred. Such a proof of patriotism
could not be denied or ignored. Pericles, who was
himself present at the battle, brought forward a proposal for cancelling the decree of ostracism which
had been pronounced four years previously, and
Cimon was allowed to return to Athens.

Meanwhile, a cloud was gathering in the East.
The great expedition which had been sent out to the
assistance of Inaros had at first met with considerable success. Even before it arrived, Inaros had
defeated the large army which Artaxerxes had sent
against him, under the command of Achæmenes, and
had slain Achæmenes with his own hand. The battle-field of Papremis on the Sebennytic arm of the
Nile was one of the most famous scenes of Persian
disaster. When the Athenian fleet of two hundred
triremes sailed up from Cyprus it had no difficulty
in defeating the Persian fleet of eighty ships which
defended the mouths of the Nile. It ascended the
river as far as Memphis and captured two-thirds of
that city. But here their success came to an end.
The " White Fortress," which formed the stronghold
of the town, was able to resist their utmost efforts,
and the revolution received a serious check.

Artaxerxes was quickly informed of the defeat
and death of Achæmenes. New preparations were
arranged, for at any risk it was necessary to recover
Egypt. Not less than two years (459–457 B.C.)

seemed to have been consumed in getting together a force which should make successful resistance impossible. In the interim Megabazus, a distinguished Persian, was sent to Sparta with a sum of money in the hope that some diversion could be created which would draw the Athenian forces from Egypt. The Spartans were willing enough to take the money, but no active measures followed, and Megabazus soon returned with the remainder of his treasure to Persia.

In the year 457 B.C. Megabyzus, the son of that Zopyrus, whose devotion had recovered Babylon for Darius, marched from Susa to Cilicia, where the forces which he was to command were assembled. He spent no less than a year in practising and drilling his troops, and it was not till the beginning of 455 B.C. that he marched upon Memphis.

The appearance of such a vast armament—the fleet amounted to three hundred triremes—was calculated to fill the Eastern Mediterranean with terror. In spite of the crushing defeats of the Eurymedon ten years before, and the overthrow of Achæmenes at Papremis, Persia could put forth a power which it seemed impossible to resist. The day of vengeance was come at last, and the cities of the coasts and islands would be exposed to the fury of the Phœnician fleet. We may imagine how great was the alarm, when the news came that Megabyzus had utterly defeated Inaros and the Athenians, and had shut them up in Prosopitis, an island formed by two converging arms of the Nile, and a canal which connected them. It was about this time that the chest

of the Delian league was transferred from Delos to
Athens; a change proposed by the Samians. The
only reason given for this change by any ancient
author is that found in Justin, who tells us that the
Athenians removed the money from Delos lest it
should become a prey to the Lacedæmonians, who
were abandoning the alliance. It is possible to connect this statement with the mission of Megabyzus
to Lacedæmon. But the Samians would certainly
be aware of the danger in the East, and it is not
improbable that this was the immediate cause of
their proposal.

The investment of Prosopitis by Persian troops
continued for a year and six months. Weary of
the delay, Megabyzus then drained the canal, at
the base of the island, upon which the Athenians
burnt their ships, in order to prevent them from
falling into the hands of the Persians. The Persian
army could now march dry-shod into the "island;"
and after a severe resistance it was conquered.
Inaros and a number of Athenians escaped to
Byblus, but Megabyzus induced them to capitulate by guaranteeing to Inaros his life, and to the
Greeks an unmolested return. The Greeks marched
through Libya to Cyrene, whence they returned
home, "few out of many." Inaros was conveyed
to Susa, and in spite of the pledges of Megabyzus
was crucified at the instance of Amestris, the cruel
widow of Xerxes, whose daughter Achæmenes had
married.

The disasters of the Athenians were not yet
ended. After the capture of Prosopitis, and in
ignorance of the event, a squadron of fifty triremes

sailed into the Mendesian arm of the Nile. Here they were immediately attacked by land and sea, and the larger part was destroyed.

So after six years ended the great expedition of the Athenians to Egypt. It was the most severe disaster which had overtaken Athens; the first failure in a long series of successes against Persia. To most men the catastrophe would appear an unmixed evil, but Pericles might reflect that such a severe lesson would teach the Athenians not to waste their strength on distant expeditions; and that the transference of the chest from Delos to Athens would in the end prove an ample compensation for the terrible reverse which had fallen on his city.

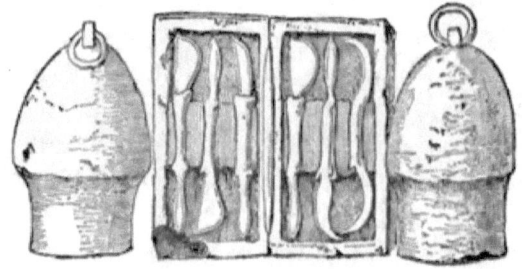

SURGEON'S CASE.
From an Athenian bas-relief.

CHAPTER VIII.

THE LAST YEARS OF CIMON.

War with Sparta—Athenian expeditions round the Peloponnesus—Disasters in Egypt—Cleruchs—Truce with Sparta for five years—Expedition to Cyprus—Death of Cimon—Battles of Salamis—Character of Cimon.

LUTARCH found among his authorities a story that Pericles had made it a condition of Cimon's return to Athens, that he should himself be left undisturbed in the control of the domestic policy of the city, while Cimon led out the fleet against Persia. Whether this story is true or not, it is a fact that Cimon took little or no part in the "Hellenic war" after his return.

In the years which immediately follow the conquest of Bœotia, we hear of two expeditions against the Peloponnesus. In 456 B.C. a fleet was sent round the peninsula under the command of Tolmides, a general who, like Myronides, had distinguished himself in the Persian war. He burned the dockyards of the Lacedæmonians at Gytheum, attacked and captured Chalcis, a Corinthian colony near the mouth of the Evenus, outside the entrance to the Gulf of Corinth, and carried the Athenian arms with

success into the territory of Sicyon. A short time
afterwards (453 B.C. ?) Pericles was again in the territory of Sicyon, and again the inhabitants were defeated, but no lasting settlement was effected.   In
the same expedition Pericles attempted to gain possession of Œniadæ, a city in Acarnania, lying in the
lakes near the mouth of the Achelous, but without
success. We hear nothing of the details of these
campaigns, though they were famous in their day,
and created a great impression in Greece, but we
see that Athens is now endeavouring to obtain the
complete control of the Corinthian gulf, as she had
obtained the control of the Saronic gulf. The
attacks on Sicyon were no doubt made with the
intention of rendering it impossible for a Peloponnesian army to cross from Sicyon to the opposite
shore, as the Spartans had done in their invasion of
Phocis in 457 B.C. It was useless to guard the
passes of Geraneia if Spartan troops could be conveyed from Sicyon to Creusis.

These attempts were not rewarded with encouraging success, and in the north of Greece Athens met
with a definite repulse. At Tanagra, as we have
seen, the Thessalian cavalry went over to the enemy.
The truth was that the common people of Thessaly
were always on the side of the Athenians, whom
they regarded as the champions of liberty, and the
great family of the Aleuadæ also thought it worth
while to cultivate their alliance. But the nobles
and knights of Thessaly—the class between the
dominant family and the subjects—were more inclined to Sparta than to Athens. This middle class

was in the ascendant, as we may see from an incident which occurred at this time. Orestes, the son of Echecratidas, the king of Thessaly, was expelled from Pharsalus. He appealed to Athens for help. The application came when the Egyptian expedition was either destroyed or in a hopeless condition ; yet the Athenians sent a force of Bœotians and Phocians under Myronides, the hero of Œnophyta, to restore Orestes. Nothing was effected. The forces reached Pharsalus, but they failed to take the city, and so annoying were the attacks of the Thessalian horse, that they could not venture far from their camp. In a short time they returned home bringing Orestes with them. All hope of acquiring influence in Thessaly was at an end.

Meanwhile matters were going from bad to worse in Egypt. When the crash came, the Athenians must have felt that the situation was grave (453 B.C. ?). What use would Persia make of her great success? Would she assume the offensive and endeavour to recover what she had lost at the Eurymedon, or perhaps to avenge the defeat of Salamis? What would the feeling of the allies be? Would they regard the defeat of the Athenians in Egypt as an indication of declining power? The expenses of the war with Egypt had compelled Athens to impose heavier contributions on the subject cities, and symptoms of the discontent, which was soon to break out on the Asiatic coast, may have shewn themselves. If she was to retain her hold on the Delian confederacy, it was necessary for her to appear once more in the East with an imposing force.

There must also have been considerable distress at home. The constant service harassed the hoplite class and the loss of men was very great. It may have been with the combined intention of stilling discontent, and securing the power of Athens, that Pericles began, about this time, to send out a number of colonies. In 453 B.C. Pericles himself took one thousand colonists to the Chersonesus, which he secured once more from the attacks of the barbarians on the north. In the same year Tolmides conducted another thousand to Eubœa, where already no fewer than four thousand Athenians possessed plots of land. And not long afterwards a large number were settled in Naxos. These colonists were of the class known as "cleruchs" or lot-holders. They did not cease to be citizens of Athens, many of them perhaps never left the city, but they were provided with plots of land at the expense of the subject or conquered countries. If the colonists left Athens their presence ensured the obedience and loyalty of the regions in which they were planted ; and those who chose to remain at home, living on the produce of their lots, were perhaps by this means qualified to bear the expenses which fell on the heavy-armed soldier.

Under such circumstances, peace with Sparta was almost a necessity for Athens. What forces she had must be devoted to the recovery of prestige in the East, on which the very life of the Delian league was largely dependent. The great commander, whose name would inspire confidence among the allies, was still in the city, and, in spite of the repulse of 463 B.C.,

Cimon was on friendly terms with Sparta ; a *grata persona*, through whom negotiations could be opened. By his intervention a truce was concluded between the two cities for five years. The shortness of the time proves that neither side looked on the present situation as tenable. But the Spartans were irritated and discouraged by the naval expeditions which harassed their coasts, and owing to the loss of Ægina and the humiliation of Corinth, the fleet of the confederacy was seriously damaged. To us it seems almost ludicrous that two belligerent cities should make a peace which was obviously nothing more than a breathing space in which to prepare for the renewal of hostilities on more favourable terms. But in Grecian politics such arrangements were common. It is even stated, though perhaps without sufficient authority, that after the battle of Tanagra Athens succeeded in obtaining a truce for four months from Sparta, in order that she might recover from the blow which had fallen upon her,—and reassert her superiority over Bœotia!

When it was known at Argos that Athens had entered, or was about to enter, into a truce with Sparta, it became necessary to reconsider the situation. If Argos remained unprotected, and Sparta was freed from the fear of attack from Athens, she might have reason to expect the worst. The work of the last ten or fifteen years, during which she had slowly consolidated her power, might be undone in a single battle. Moreover, she had gained nothing by her alliance with Athens. That city, it was clear, sought her own advantage, and not the advantage of Argos. Under such circumstances it seemed prudent to enter into negotiations with Sparta. In 481 B.C. Argos had proposed a peace for thirty years; she now renewed the offer. Sparta accepted it. Knowing that the truce with Athens was nothing more than a cessation of hostilities, it would be an advantage to be secure on the side of Argos, when the war broke out again. A peace was concluded between the two cities; and in spite of the subsequent commotions which shook Hellas, it ran out to the full term, coming to a close in 421 B.C.

When affairs had been settled at home, the Athenians prepared a new expedition to the East. Cyprus was once more the object of attack, and Cimon was the commander. It was now more necessary than ever to hold a station which should command Cilicia and Egypt. In the spring of 449 B.C. a fleet of two hundred ships, supplied by Athens and her allies, was sent out. Sixty ships were detached for the assistance of Amyrtæus, who, even after the annihilation of the forces of Inaros, could bid defiance to Persia in the impenetrable swamps of the Delta. With the remaining one hundred and forty Cimon sailed to Mareion, on the west coast of Cyprus, whence he passed along the south shore and laid siege to Citium, which was at this time governed by a Phœnician prince. The city was defended with the stubborn spirit which has made the sieges of Phœnician cities so famous in military annals. Ere long the Athenian fleet began to suffer from famine, and, to increase the misfortune, their great commander fell sick and died. On his death-bed he is said to

8

have given orders for the besieging forces to retire
and conceal the news of his death. But retirement
was impossible ; a Phœnician fleet had already appeared on the north coast of Cyprus ; to refuse an
engagement would imply the cession of the Eastern
Mediterranean. In spite of the weakness created by
famine and the loss of their leader, the Athenians put
to sea and sailed upon the enemy. The battle took
place off Salamis, and ended in a complete victory for
Athens. The defeated Phœnician vessels fled to the
shore, where the army was drawn up to protect
them, but the Athenians followed close, disembarked
and defeated the army no less than the fleet. Thus
the achievement of the Eurymedon was repeated,
and Athens once more proved her immense superiority over the Persian power. On its return home
the fleet was rejoined by the ships from Egypt,
which do not appear to have rendered any efficient
service to Amyrtæus. Cimon's corpse was brought
to Athens and buried in the sepulchre of the
Philaidæ, outside the Melitian gate of Athens.

The balance was once more in favour of Hellas in
the East, but the success was far from complete, and
it had been purchased at severe cost. The Phœnician fleet had been defeated, but Cyprus was as far
as ever from being annexed to the Delian league.
The island remained a dependency of Persia ; Persian
troops could land on it ; Phœnician princes ruled in
most of the cities. Hellenes and Hellenism had but
a precarious footing. The coveted post, from which
Greece could have thwarted the embarkation of
troops from the Cilician plain and held the Phœni-

cian and Egyptian fleets in check, passed from henceforth out of the grasp of Athenian generals.

And Cimon was dead. The great commander, who for nearly thirty years had led the allies to victory, would lead them no more. We first hear of him in 480 B.C. as an Athenian knight, cheerfully hanging up his bridle in the temple of Athena, in recognition of the change which made it imperative for every Athenian to fight on board ship, as Themistocles demanded. From 478 B.C., when Xanthippus the hero of Mycale disappears from sight, Cimon is associated with Aristides in the command of the fleet. With him he founded the Delian confederacy. From this time forward he was the life and soul of every military undertaking; it was he who secured the Thracian coast for Athens; it was he who quelled the revolt of Thasos; it was he who inflicted the terrific defeat of Eurymedon on the Persian army and fleet. Even after his death his name seems to have inspired victory. He was the greatest seaman Athens ever knew—the Nelson of his time.

His manners and character were those of a soldier. Tall in stature, with hair curling close to his head, and winning eyes, he was a well-known sight in Athens. His accomplishments made him a welcome guest at every social gathering; a song from Cimon was remembered by those who heard it, while others listened attentively to the stories which he could tell in abundance of his military life and experiences. His wealth was great and his liberality unbounded. At times indeed his profusion was such that his enemies accused him of seeking to win the people by unworthy means. He would command his well-clad servants to exchange garments with aged beggars, or he would remove the fences which protected his gardens and orchards, bidding all who passed take what they chose. Or he would squander small coin among those who were willing to pick it up. But he also applied his wealth to nobler uses. He adorned the city with the spoils taken from the enemy; the market-place was planted with trees, to afford the shade so grateful in the fierce heat of summer; the Academy was irrigated and laid out with clear racing courses and pleasant walks; the foundations for the walls which connected Athens and the harbour were begun. The Acropolis was prepared for a new temple; and Pheidias was employed to erect the great bronze statue of Athena, whose bright spear could be seen even by the mariners off Sunium.

Two charges have been brought against Cimon. It is said that he hunted Themistocles out of Athens, thus depriving the city of her greatest man, and that he prevented the destruction of Sparta at the moment when destruction was possible. The charges are not without foundation, though there is much to say on the other side. Cimon and Themistocles were opponents; and Cimon was the winner. But we may observe that Themistocles was never employed as a general in the field after 480 B.C., and though he served Athens in other ways, he did so at the cost of provoking the animosity of Sparta. Whether Themistocles would have succeeded as well as Cimon and Aristides in organising the Delian league, is open to question. It was doubtless a grievous misfortune for Athens that she could not retain Themistocles, but the blame of the expulsion may have been due to his own conduct not less than the jealousy of his enemies. That Cimon persuaded the Athenians to send help to the Spartans at a moment when it would perhaps have been possible to destroy their power by supporting the Helots is undeniable. He was always the firm friend of Sparta; he never accepted the doctrine that Athens and Sparta could not work together; and under his management they probably would have worked together. Co-operation on the lines of Pericles and Themistocles was impossible; to both of these statesmen Athens was an imperial city, and Sparta a rival who must be crushed. To speak of them as Pan-Hellenes is a mistake; they were Pan-Athenians. But Cimon was sincerely Pan-Hellenic, so far as any Greek could be so. He knew that the loss of Sparta would be an irreparable loss to the Hellenic name. He wished to see the two great cities of Greece drawing together in harmony, at peace at home, and united in making war on Persia. With his death all hope of continuing that war, and all hope of lasting peace between Athens and Sparta came to an end.

COIN OF ATHENS, WITH OWL, CRESCENT MOON, AND OLIVE SPRAY. B.C. 450.

CHAPTER IX.

PEACE AND THE SECOND WAR
WITH SPARTA.

HE death of Cimon marks an epoch
in the history of Athens. He
was the last of the great generals who thought
it the mission of Hellas to be at war with Persia.
With him closed the generation of the "Heroes
of Marathon." For the next fifty years Greece is
occupied with the duel between Athens and
Sparta; and it is only when this disastrous episode
comes to an end with the fall of Athens that
the traditional policy is resumed by Agesilaus,
the king of Sparta. Cimon was also the last
leader of his party, who led it as a soldier rather
than as a statesman. Those who came after him
had other views, and other means of carrying them
out. The soldier and the politician began to di-
verge. In this respect the aristocratical party suffered even more than their opponents. Pericles, if
not a great, was a respectable general, as generals

went in Greece; Cleon rendered his country one important service; Alcibiades, if we may count him among the democrats, was probably the greatest military genius of his time. But, with the exception of Nicias, the aristocrats hardly possessed a man after Cimon, who by his success in the field could add to the power of his party at home.

Pericles was now the foremost man in Athens, but he was not yet without opponents. A few years had still to elapse before he could win that undisputed mastership of the city, which he held when at the height of his influence; and they were years full of events. The truce with Sparta had hardly been concluded when troubles broke out at Miletus. That city was famous of old for its factions, though for the last century, partly owing to a better government, and partly to the disastrous Persian conquests which merged party quarrels in submission to a master, we hear little of them. On the reception of Miletus into the Delian league, the oligarchical section were in power, and the Athenians made no attempt to introduce a change. The reception probably took place very soon after the battle of Mycale (479 B.C.), when the democratic spirit was by no means strong enough at Athens to require a similarity of political views in allied states. The victories of the Persians in Egypt may have altered the sentiments of the Milesian oligarchs, and inclined them to closer union with Persia. Or the growing democratical spirit at Athens may have induced the " demos " at Miletus to put forward new claims.

Whatever the cause, about 450 B.C. the oligarchs attacked the people, and renounced their connection with the Delian league. The people, of course, appealed to Athens; the oligarchs sought aid from Persia. It became necessary for the Athenians to interfere. The government of Miletus was reconstructed in the interests of the people, and an Athenian garrison was placed in the city for their protection. Five Athenians were chosen to administer the affairs of the city, and all suits at law for the value of more than one hundred minæ (about £335) were to be brought to Athens for decision. We may observe that this last provision is an indication of that development of the law courts which became so marked a feature of Athenian democracy.

Similar disturbances took place at Erythræ and at Colophon, and similar measures were taken to restore order. The decree by which the constitution of Erythræ was reorganised has come down to us, and parts of it may still be read. The document is interesting, for it was doubtless framed either by Pericles or under his influence. It expresses the Periclean views of the best and safest form of government for an independent state in the interest of Athens. Erythræ was to be ruled by a senate consisting of one hundred and twenty members, chosen yearly by lot. No citizen could offer himself for election if less than thirty years of age. From the senators when elected an oath was required under the most solemn sanctions: "To the best of my power I will advise what is lawful and good for the people of

Erythræ, the Athenians, and the allies. I will not
revolt from the people of Athens and their allies, or
help others to do so ; I will not go over to the
enemy, or help others to do so ; I will not receive
an exile or help others to do so, nor any of those
who have taken refuge with the Medes, without the
sanction of the Athenians and the state. I will not
put any Erythræan to death without the sanction of
the Athenians and the state. If any citizen slay another, he shall be put to death ; and if any citizen
sin against the gods, he shall be put to death ; if
anyone offend against the alliance he shall be banished, and his property shall be given to the
Erythræans. If anyone is convicted of betraying
the city of Erythræ to tyrants, he shall be put
to death, and his children also." The Erythræans
were to send victims of not less value than three
minæ (£10, or a little more) to the Panathenæa,
and, in return, each Erythræan was allowed to
have a portion of the sacrificial food, not exceeding a drachma in value (9*d.*). A further oath bound
the citizens of Erythræ to be faithful to the Athenians and the allies. There were also regulations
about the government of Erythræ, and the duties of
the officers or " overseers " whom Athens sent to the
city, but owing to the imperfect state of the inscription we cannot read what these were.

In these regulations we see that Athens identified
herself with the confederacy : treachery to the alliance was treachery to her. And she did not hesitate
to plant garrisons of Athenian soldiers in the citadels
of allied cities, if the step seemed necessary to secure

their allegiance, or to reduce them to the condition
of subject cities by claiming the sovereignty in their
administration of law.   Naxos and Thasos, Miletus
and Erythræ, were no longer confederates on equal
terms, but on compulsion ; their contributions went
to swell a fund which made resistance on their part
more and more impossible.   Even more significant
were the results of the transference of the chest from
Delos to Athens.   The old Ionian place of gathering
was no longer the centre of the confederacy; to
Athena and not to Apollo were dues paid and victims
brought.   The whole administration of the league
and its funds was conducted at Athens, and perhaps
by this time by Athenians.   At Athens, too, the
more important law-suits of the confederates were
decided.

By common consent all operations against Persia
were discontinued after the death of Cimon.   Neither
Pericles nor his opponents cared to renew the war.
But the Athenian sailors and soldiers remembered
how Cimon had led them to victory, and the sailors
and soldiers were an important element in the state.
Pericles could not fail to perceive the importance of
securing their good-will.   Hitherto they had probably been inclined to take sides with the party to
which Cimon belonged, in spite of the democratic
measures of Pericles.   But now that their great
commander was dead, they were no longer carried
away by the enthusiasm of the soldier for his general,
an enthusiasm against which a merely political
leader is powerless.   A slight impetus might bring
them round to the side which had made them a

power in the state.   Pericles saw his opportunity,
and used it.   He had already sent colonies to
Euboea, Naxos, and the Chersonese, which had been
of service in improving the condition of the citizens
and securing the empire.   He now turned his thoughts
to regions lying outside the range of the confederacy,
if indeed we are right in placing at this date the
establishment of a colony at Brea in Thrace and the
voyage of Pericles into the Pontus.

Our knowledge of the colony at Brea is due to the
fortunate accident which has preserved the decree
under which the colony was sent out.   But for this
we should know nothing beyond the mere fact that
the Athenians had sent out a colony to Brea—
a sufficient proof, if the proof were needed, that
our knowledge of this period is scanty and uncertain to the last degree.   From the decree we
learn that ten commissioners (Geonomi, "dividers
of land") were to divide the land among the colonists.   Democlides, the author of the decree, was
chosen to be the founder of the colony, with full
powers.   All the temples and sacred precincts already
existing on the site were to be carefully preserved,
but no new ones were to be provided.   The colonists
were to send a bull and two sheep to the Panathenæa,
and an emblem to the festival of Dionysus.

The merchants of Athens had long carried on a
trade in corn with the ports of the Black Sea, where
the innumerable colonies which Miletus had planted
were so many stations for shipping the products of
the interior to Greece.   And if it be true that Aristides died in the Pontus, the expedition of Pericles

was not the first which the Athenians had undertaken in that direction. But it was probably the first time that an Athenian general had appeared beyond the Bosphorus with an imposing force. The immediate cause of the expedition seems to have been an application from the inhabitants of Sinope for aid against their "tyrant," Timesilaus. This "tyrant" was, no doubt, an officer representing the Persian power in the city, and any attempt to expel him was equivalent to an attack on the Persian king. This did not prevent Pericles from taking the allied fleet into the Black Sea, or from leaving Lamachus behind with thirteen ships to aid the citizens of Sinope, who, with this reinforcement, succeeded in driving out Timesilaus. Six hundred Athenians were afterwards sent to the city to occupy the lands and houses of the tyrant and his party. This is the only specific act which is recorded of the expedition, though Plutarch tells us, in a vague manner, that Pericles settled all the petitions which the Greek cities brought to him, and exhibited to the barbarian princes and potentates around the greatness of his power and the confidence with which his fleet sailed wherever they chose, and subjugated every sea to themselves. The barbarian princes and potentates would be Teres, the king of the Odrysians, whose dominion extended from the Hebrus to the Danube, and his son-in-law and neighbour beyond the Danube, Ariapeithes, king of Scythia, both princes of great vigour and capacity. The Greek cities on the western shore of the Pontus paid tribute to Teres, and those on the northern were of course the neighbours of the Scythians. It was of great importance that these princes should be on

good terms with the Greeks, and a timely display of
force was likely enough to impress them with a sense
of the power which, if need were, could come to the
aid of the Greek colonies. But even in the Greek
cities there were potentates. In Panticapæum, the
most important trading station in the Pontus, a
family was ruling which claimed descent from
Archæanax, the ancient king of Lesbos. It is quite
possible that Pericles entered into friendly relations
with a city from which more corn was exported than
from any other, for at a time when the granaries of
Egypt were passing into the hands of the Persians,
such a step would be especially opportune. Whether
the connexion was due to Pericles or not, we find,
in the fourth century, the princes of the Cimmerian
Bosphorus making presents of corn to Athens, and
treating the city with the greatest respect and consideration.

This was perhaps the most lasting gain of the great
expedition. Sinope, if relieved for the time, fell back
under the dominion of Persia. And we have no certain evidence that the Athenians established themselves at any other point. It is true that we afterwards find them in possession of Nymphæum, a port
a little to the south of Panticapæum, and that twenty
years later than this expedition, they hold a post at
Chrysopolis, at which they taxed the corn ships on
their way from the Pontus. There is, however, no
proof that we ought to connect these establishments
with the voyage of Pericles.

Meanwhile, in spite of the peace, events were taking place which showed that Sparta and Athens were
still rivals for the supremacy in Greece. In 448 B.C.

the Phocians made an attempt to secure possession
of the temple at Delphi. The shrine lay in their territory, and they had long regarded it as wrongfully
taken from them. Relying, perhaps, on the power
of Athens in Northern Greece, they now seized it
for themselves. The Delphians appealed to Sparta,
who at once responded. Troops were once more
sent across the bay of Corinth, and Delphi was restored to the Delphians. In return for the timely
assistance the Lacedæmonians received the right
of consulting the oracle first, and their name was
inscribed on the front of the great bronze wolf,
which stood near the principal altar at Delphi. No
sooner had the Lacedæmonians departed than Pericles marched to Delphi at the head of a force of
Athenians and gave the temple once more to the
Phocians. The honour of first consultation was now
given to the Athenians, and their name appeared on
the right side of the bronze wolf. Thus were Athens
and Sparta written up as competitors at the most
central shrine of Hellas. These events were known
as the "Sacred War." For the moment no result
followed; but it was now plain to Northern Greece
that in any revolt against Athens they could reckon
on the support of Sparta.

It was not long ere the revolt came. While we
hear of distant expeditions and colonies on the part
of Athens, nothing is recorded of any measures by
which her authority was secured in Bœotia. That
authority rested on the presence of a democracy in
the various states, a democracy which was resolved
that Bœotia shoul᷄ not be subject to Thebes, even

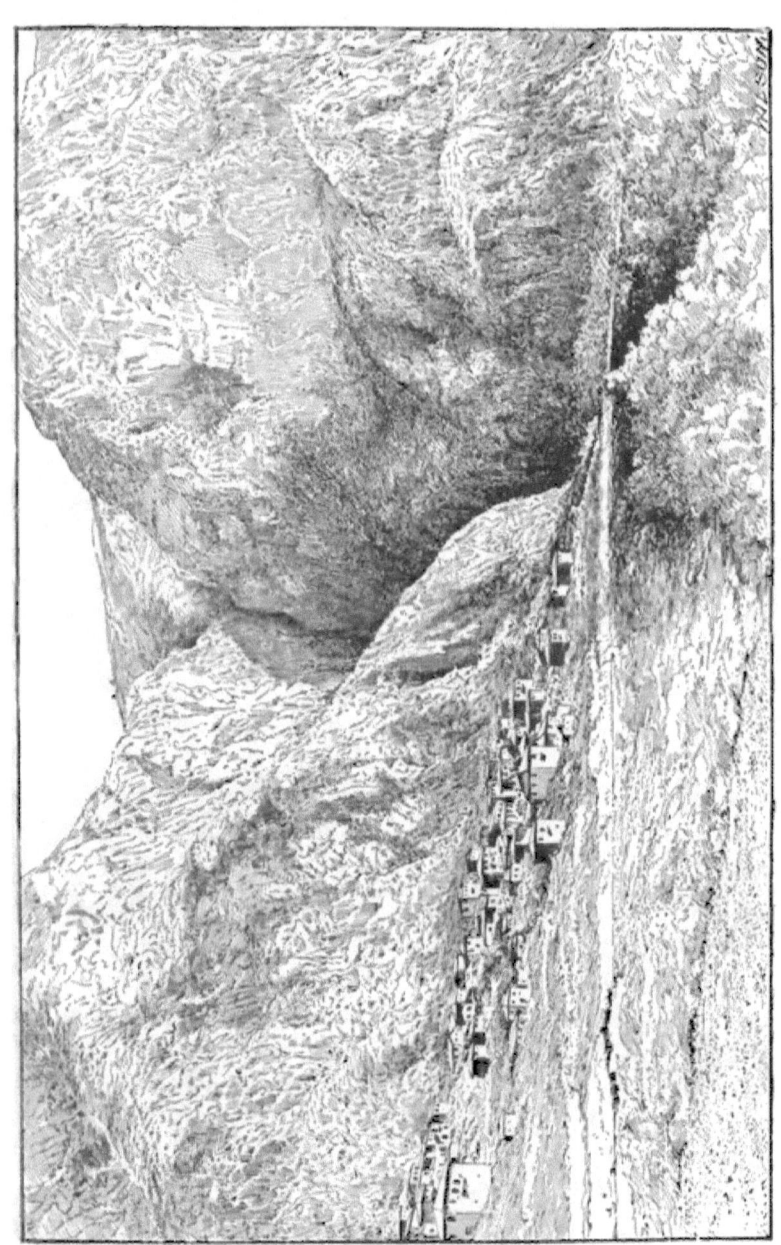

DELPHI—GENERAL VIEW.

Showing the Phaedriddes Rocks and the Ravine of Castalia.

(Redrawn from Photograph by Dr. Lrdf.)

though it must be subject to Athens. The people had been raised to power by the expulsion of the opposite party, but Athens had taken no steps to render the exiled oligarchs powerless for mischief. They gradually returned home, and formed a party, especially in the north of Bœotia, where Chæronea and Orchomenus had resisted the Athenian supremacy. It was an anxious and difficult moment for Athens. To send a small force might entail defeat; to send a large one would require time. Tolmides, who ranked second to none as a general at this time, was in favour of immediate action. Pericles thought the numbers of the army insufficient, and foresaw the disastrous consequences of a defeat. His fears were disregarded. Tolmides carried the day. With an army of auxiliaries and one thousand Athenian troops, for the most part volunteers from the higher families, he set out for Chæronea. By rapid and energetic action he was enabled to capture the town, but here his success ended. He found his forces too small for the numbers which gathered round him. Retreat was inevitable, and retreat was the signal for the enemy to attack. As he passed the town of Coronea, the rebel forces fell upon him and inflicted a severe defeat. His army was destroyed; many were slain, among them Tolmides himself; many were taken prisoners, and remained as hostages in the hands of the enemy. The Bœotians were absolute masters of the situation; a single battle had utterly overthrown the Athenian supremacy in their country. They refused to give up the captives unless the Athenians agreed to evacuate Bœotia, and these terms the Athenians accepted. The oligarchs—the bitter enemies of Athens—returned to their cities, burning with the proverbial hatred of exiles. From this time forward union or common action between Athens and Bœotia was impossible. The Phocians also and the Locrians, finding themselves cut off from Athens, declared their independence. Thus without being able even to put her whole force in the field, Athens saw herself deprived of all her continental power. A single day had removed her frontier from Thermopylæ to Cithæron.

The battle of Coronea was probably fought in the spring of 446 B.C. The summer had even worse news to bring. The island of Eubœa had formed a part of the Delian confederacy from the first; for more than thirty years it had been the faithful ally of Athens, and for two generations Athenian citizens had been settled as colonists in it. But the oligarchs of Bœotia appear to have been able to inspire the oligarchs of Eubœa—the remnant of the old proprietors who had suffered heavily at the hands of Athens—with their own courage and hope. What if Eubœa also could shake off the yoke of the conqueror? The moment seemed favourable now that all Northern Greece was independent. Sparta would doubtless support the attempt; perhaps she had already pledged herself to do so. For the five years' truce was on the point of expiration; and even if it had not expired, the Spartans were not over-scrupulous about agreements, when it was possible to make an effective attack on the enemy. So

Eubœa revolted. Her action was part of a wider
plan. No sooner had Pericles crossed over to the
island than Megara threw off her allegiance ; the
Athenian garrison was partly cut down, and partly
compelled to take refuge in Nisæa. And when the
way over the Isthmus was thus opened the Spartans
hastened to take advantage of it. Plistoanax, the
youthful king of Lacedæmon, invaded Attica with a
Peloponnesian force. Thus was Athens surrounded
on every side; and a combined attack on the city
seemed inevitable.

Athens had no army to put in the field which
could for a moment stand against the enemy, if they
had time to unite. Pericles saw where the danger
lay, and also how it was to be met. He returned in
haste from Eubœa, which, owing to his command of
ships, he had pretty much at his mercy, to Attica.
The Peloponnesian army was already on the Thriasian plain near Eleusis, and had begun to devastate
the country, when suddenly, without any apparent
reason, before even meeting with the Athenian
troops, it returned home. In the minds of the
Spartans there could be but one solution of the
strange event : their king and his adviser, Cleandridas, must have been bribed to leave Attica. The
suspicion was probably correct; Pericles himself
refused to account publicly for all the money which
passed through his hands as general ; he merely announced that he had spent a large sum on " a necessary purpose." This necessary purpose was supposed
to be the retreat of the Peloponnesian army from
Attica. The Spartans fined their king on his return,

9

and as he was unable to pay the sum, he fled in fear
for his life to the temple of Zeus Lycæus in Arcadia,
where for the next nineteen years he remained in a
dwelling so constructed that he could at any moment retire into the temple of the god. The throne
passed to his son Pausanias, who was still a child.
Cleandridas did not even venture to return to Sparta;
in his absence he was condemned and his property
confiscated; we hear of him subsequently at Thurii,
and his famous son, Gylippus, was the saviour of
Syracuse.

Pericles was now able to return to Eubœa. He
took over a force of fifty triremes and five thousand
hoplites, with which in a very short time he reduced
the island to submission. From the Bœotians no
assistance whatever was sent, and without it the
Eubœans were quite unable to meet such a force as
that of Athens. Only in Histiæa, a district in the
extreme north, do we hear of vigorous resistance,
and even there the rebels were soon overcome.
Their punishment was severe; the Histiæans were
expelled, and their territory was divided among
two thousand Athenian colonists. In the south of
the island the constitution of the city of Chalcis was
re-arranged, and here, as in the case of Erythræ, the
inscription containing the details of the arrangement
has been preserved. We can still read the very
words in which Pericles, or his agent, determined the
relation of the subjects to the sovereign city. The
Chalcidians were compelled to swear that neither in
word nor deed would they revolt from Athens, and
should anyone revolt, they were pledged to give in-

formation at once.   Chalcis was to pay the tribute
imposed on her by Athens after due inquiry, and to
supply forces to Athens according to her ability, and
in every way to be a faithful and efficient ally.   On
their part the Athenians guaranteed to the Chalcidians the possession of their city.   Without a
formal trial no Chalcidian was to be punished with
loss of civil rights, banished, imprisoned, put to death
or punished in his property.   In every action the
accused was to be legally cited, and without such
citation no sentence could be pronounced.   Any
embassy from Chalcis which visited Athens was to
be brought before the assembly by the Prytanes
within ten days of its arrival.

Similar arrangements were made with the rest of
the cities of Eubœa.   Documents exist regulating
the trade of the new colony in Histiæa with Athens,
and arranging for the settlement of small actions at
law by the appointment of local judges.   In all these
decrees we observe that Athens does not deal with
Eubœa as a member of the confederacy ; she is a
conquered territory, a subject of Athens, and bound
to serve her interests without reference to any others.
More plainly here than elsewhere do we see the head
of the alliance formed after the battle of Mycale
emerging into the tyrant city which entered into the
Peloponnesian war.

The prompt and complete reduction of Eubœa
was an immense service to Athens.   But even with
this success her condition was sufficiently deplorable.
Four years had elapsed since Cimon's death, and
already she had sunk far below the military eminence

which she then occupied. Operations against Persia were not so much as thought of. The land empire was irretrievably lost; the way from Peloponnesus was again open. The allies in Argos and Thessaly were estranged; Euboea, the greatest and nearest of her allies, had been in open revolt. And this was not all. From the lists of the tribute paid by members of the league which have been preserved in inscriptions, we find that in the assessment of the year 446 B.C. the amount of tribute is very considerably reduced; a large number of cities either withdrew from the alliance or did not pay tribute. In the period 450–447 the number of contributing cities may be put at 190 to 200; in 446–440 the average is 170, and the total amount of contributions only reached 434 talents, of which not more than 400 talents were really paid. In Caria and Lycia more especially there were many defections; the retirement of the Greeks after the battle of Cyprus left them at the mercy of the Persian satraps.

Such a sudden fall from the height of her prosperity naturally produced a feeling of despondency at Athens. It was clear that she could not now keep her allies in hand and sustain the burden of a war in Hellas. At all costs she must come to terms with Sparta and her allies. In the winter of 446–445 B.C. ten plenipotentiaries were sent to Sparta, through whom the Thirty Years' Peace was concluded between the cities. The Athenians renounced all their acquisitions in Peloponnesus: Nisæa, Pegæ, Trœzen, and Achæa. For the rest, each state was to retain its possessions; the Athenians were not to admit Lace-

dæmonian cities, and the Lacedæmonians were not
to admit Athenian cities into their league without
the permission of the other side, but any city which
was independent of either alliance might join which-
ever of the two it pleased.   The Æginetans were
apparently to remain independent, but to pay a
certain contribution to the Athenian alliance ; that is,
they were not to be reduced to the condition of the
Eubœans.   The Argives had no part in the peace ;
they were already at peace with Lacedæmon, and they
might, if they liked, make a separate peace with
Athens.   Should any differences arise between the
cities they were to be settled by arbitration.   The
terms of peace were engraven on stone and set up at
Athens, and in the shrine of Apollo at Amyclæ.   A
bronze copy was also to be seen at Olympia.

THEATRE TICKET.
Athens.

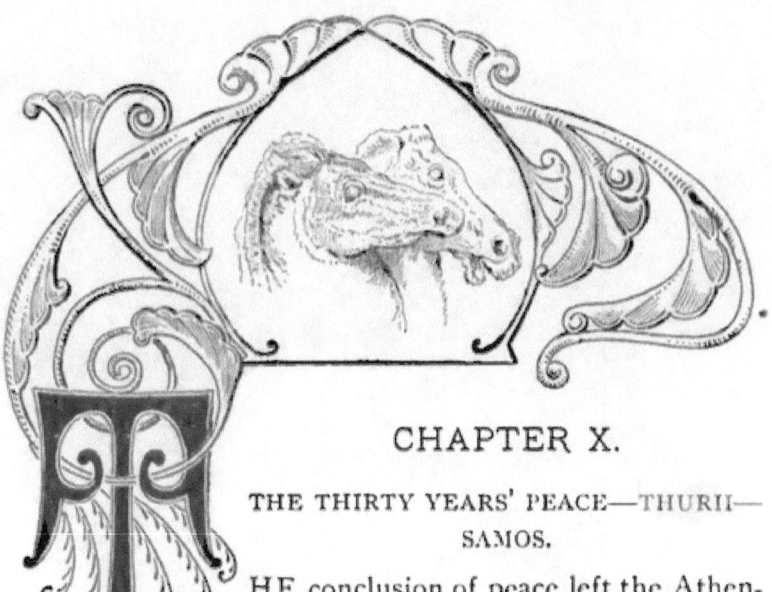

CHAPTER X.

THE THIRTY YEARS' PEACE—THURII—SAMOS.

HE conclusion of peace left the Athenians to their confederacy and their internal politics. There could not now be any difference about war with Persia or peace with Sparta; but it was still possible to contest the development of the democracy, the personal ascendancy of Pericles, and the treatment of the allies.

After the death of Cimon the oligarchical party at Athens had been led by Thucydides, the son of Melesias, a man of high character and a kinsman of Cimon. The better to keep together the party, which had suffered so severely by the death of their great leader, Thucydides organised the oligarchs into a compact body. Hitherto the members had sat here or there in the assembly as they pleased; now they were combined into a single body, and sat in a special place.

FUNERAL MONUMENTS AT ATHENS.

(*Curtius and Kaupert's " Atlas von Athen."*)

Such a consolidation was doubtless needed if the
party was to hold its own against Pericles, who was
rapidly carrying all before him.   For years past he
had provided a subsistence for many of the poorer
citizens by means of his numerous colonies—no fewer
than five thousand Athenians must have been sent
out to the "cleruchies" in the interval between 453
B.C. and 444 B.C.   The new system of juries had also
been established on the fall of the Areopagus, and
the jurymen were paid—a second source of income
to the poor.   Such measures were beyond anything
that the private liberality of Cimon—splendid as it
was—could achieve ; and on Cimon's death no other
aristocrat came forward to aid his party with his
purse.

Pericles did not stop here.   Since the cessation of
the war with Persia there had been fewer drafts on
the public purse, and the contributions of the allies
were accumulating in the public treasury.   A scrupulous man would have regarded the surplus as
money of the allies, which could only be spent on
objects connected with their protection, and with
their approval.   Pericles took another view.   He
plainly told the Athenians that so long as the city
fulfilled the contract made with the allied cities, and
kept Persian vessels from their shores, the surplus
was at the disposal of Athens.   Acting on this principle, he devoted a part of it to the embellishment
of the city.   With the aid of Pheidias, the sculptor,
and Ictinus, the architect, a new temple began to
rise on the Acropolis in honour of Athena—the celebrated Parthenon or " Virgin's Chamber,"—the un-

rivalled triumph of architectural skill, of which we
shall speak in a later chapter. Other public buildings were also begun about this time. Athens was
in fact a vast workshop, in which employment was
found for a great number of citizens. Nor was this all.
Though little inclined to war, Pericles was sufficiently
aware of the value of the Athenian fleet to take steps
for preserving its efficiency. For eight months of
the year sixty ships were kept at sea with crews on
board, in order that there might be an ample supply
of practical seamen. These crews were largely composed of the poorer citizens, who were glad to receive pay for their services. Thus by direct or in-
direct means Pericles made the state the paymaster
of a vast number of citizens, and the state was practically himself, with these paid citizens at his back.
At the same time the public festivals of the city
were enlarged and adorned with new splendour.
There were innumerable processions and spectacles,
contests and dramas to delight the Athenians; and
that all might attend the theatre in which the plays
were acted, Pericles provided that every citizen
should receive from the state a sum sufficient to
pay the charge demanded from the spectators by
the lessee.

We may look on these measures as the arts of a
demagogue who seeks by spending the public money
to secure the public favour. Or we may say that
Pericles was able to gratify his passion for art at the
expense of the Athenians and their allies. Neither
of these views is altogether untenable; and both are
far from including the whole truth. Pericles did un-

THE PARTHENON, IN ITS PRESENT CONDITION.
From the North-West.

(Boetticher.)

doubtedly seek by every means in his power to win
an undisputed position at Athens ; and undoubtedly
he had a passion for art and literature.   He was, if
we please to say it, a demagogue and a connoisseur.
But he was something more.   Looking at the whole
evidence before us with impartial eyes, we cannot
refuse to acknowledge that he cherished aspirations
worthy of a great statesman.   He sincerely desired
that every Athenian should owe to his city the blessing of an education in all that was beautiful, and
the opportunity of a happy and useful life.   If Solon
had laid down rules, not less excellent than precise,
for the education of the Athenian youth, Pericles
would go further, and educate the Athenian man.
The promise of youth is always beautiful ; perhaps
it was nowhere more beautiful than at Athens ; but
it is the performance of manhood which sets the
stamp of value on life.   Pericles wished to influence
that performance, and raise it to a higher level ; he
sought to unite a passionate enthusiasm with clear
and definite aims.   Whether these aspirations could
be realised at all ; whether they ought to be realised
in the manner in which Pericles sought to realise
them, are questions which admit of discussion ; perhaps the experience of the world has driven us to
confess that while leisure is necessary for the development of the highest natures, the mass of men are
only kept from ruin by severe and continuous labour.
But there is no reason to doubt that such aspirations
were cherished by Pericles.

The organisation of the oligarchy by Thucydides
and the development of the democracy by Pericles

naturally caused the opposition between the two to
become more marked than it had hitherto been.
Now, for the first time, as Plutarch informs us, were
the words "oligarch" and "demos" heard in Athens.
They were words of evil omen; though as yet
neither side can have perceived in what the opposition would end. A democracy in a prosperous
country is a very different thing from a democracy
in a poor country; an oligarchy which seeks to
defend its power differs widely from one which
seeks to defend its wealth. But, sooner or later,
the opposition of the Few and the Many passes
over into the opposition of the Rich and the
Poor.

The oligarchs determined to pull down Pericles,
if it were possible. Above all things they endeavoured to cut off the supplies from which he supported his schemes. They pointed out the discontent
which prevailed among the allies, who found their
money used in adorning Athens, not in forwarding
the purposes of the league. They argued that the
money was either required for the purpose for
which it was given, or it was not. If it was not
required, let less tribute be demanded. Was Athens
to be dressed out, like a vain and extravagant
woman, with the spoils of others? Already some
allies had thrown off their allegiance; others were
paying diminished sums. Euboea, a faithful ally for
thirty years, had endeavoured to shake off the yoke,
and others would doubtless do the same; such
flagrant dishonesty in the administration of the
funds would bring the confederacy to ruin.

In answer to such arguments, Pericles held to his opinion; the city, he said, fulfilled its duty to the allies; the contributions were the price of an undisturbed enjoyment of the Ægean, and this Athens had secured. If Athens saved money on her bargain, what was that to the allies? As for the expenditure, it was expedient for the allies, aye, and for all Hellas, that Athens should be beautiful; that her festivals should be splendid; that she should be the home of art and literature; the abode of freedom and culture; the Hellas of Hellas. In such reasoning there was nothing very cogent, at any rate to the minds of the contributing cities, and those who took their part. Athens, they might reply, was not the sole judge of the cost necessary for the maintenance of a free Ægean, but the board of the Delian league, and that board had been set aside. The arguments of Pericles veiled the absurd claim that of two contracting parties one only has a right to decide whether the bargain shall continue. And where was the evidence that the board and Athens had ever entered into such a contract as that behind which Pericles sheltered himself? The Delian league was an alliance between equal states in which Athens ranked with the rest; her present position was an outrage—a tyrannous outrage — on the rights of free Hellenic cities.

The oligarchs probably believed that a large party in the city held these views, and their new organisation gave them confidence. Moreover, the last year had been disastrous; had Cimon been alive, the war

with Sparta might have been averted, or peace
obtained on different conditions. Was it not possible to throw the blame of this on the all-powerful
Pericles? On these grounds they proposed, in the
winter of 445 B.C., that there should be an ostracism
in the city. The people agreed, and the usual arrangements were made. But when the day came for
decision, in the spring of 444 B.C., the sentence fell,
not on Pericles, but on Thucydides.

The sentence left no doubt about the feeling
of the Athenian people, and it was accepted as final.
Thucydides disappeared from Athens, and for the
next fifteen years Pericles was master of the city.
In fact, the oligarchs had chosen a most unpro-
pitious moment. The disasters which marked the
year 446–445 B.C. had without exception been the
work of the oligarchical enemies of Athens; she was
now surrounded by hostile states, all of which were
oligarchical. No wise citizen, even if he disap-
proved of the democracy, could at such a time have
ventured to put the control of his city in the hands
of the oligarchical party. Besides, the measures
which had saved Athens—the reduction of Eubœa
and the removal of Plistoanax from Attica—were
due to the strategy and political skill of Pericles.
The oligarchs had done nothing in this crisis of
their country. Indeed it was their rashness in supporting the ill-advised expedition of Tolmides to
Coronea which had brought the crisis on; had they
listened to the advice of Pericles, that disastrous
blow might have been averted. The plea in
behalf of the allies was not likely to stir the people

at the moment when they had just triumphed over Eubœa, and reduced her from an ally to a subject state. The Athenians had gone too far to return upon their steps. The leader of the allies was in effect what Pericles meant her to be, a tyrant city, and her measures must be taken on that line.

Pericles was now in a strong position, and the next incident which meets us in the history of Athens shows us that he was conscious of his strength. In the year 445–444 B.C., a large present of corn was sent from Egypt to Athens to be distributed among the citizens. The motive of the gift was no doubt a desire to secure the assistance of the Athenians. For though the revolt of Inaros had been crushed, Amyrtæus still remained in the marshes of the Delta, and recent events had prevented the Persian monarch from making any serious attempt to crush him. Megabyzus, enraged at the insult which Artaxerxes had put upon him by refusing to save Inaros from the vengeance of Amestris, had openly revolted from the king, and defeated his armies in two great battles in Syria. Such a division between the king and his greatest general revived the hopes of the discontented princes of Egypt and Libya. It was worth while to attempt to bring a Grecian fleet once more into the Eastern Mediterranean.

Pericles was not to be drawn from his purpose, and the less so as the quarrel between Megabyzus and the king was quickly made up. He accepted the present of Psammetichus, which was apparently

offered without any conditions, but no help was sent
to Egypt. The corn was divided among the Athenians; and in connexion with this distribution
a story is told that Pericles revived, or passed, a law
striking off the list of citizens every one who was
not born of an Athenian father and an Athenian
mother. No fewer than 4,760 persons, it is said,
were struck off the list on the occasion, the total
of the citizens being reduced˙ to 14,240. There
are strong reasons for believing that this story
cannot be an accurate account of what took place.
That Pericles, himself the descendant of an alien
woman, should have been the author of such a
law is unlikely, especially as he had by this time
entered into relations with the Milesian Aspasia.
Such a law was not likely to commend itself to the
statesman who had sent out thousands of Athenians
to dwell among aliens. Should any of these men,
as would be almost inevitable, marry a Naxian or
Eubœan woman, his children would be illegitimate
and incapable of exercising the rights of Athenian
citizens. Nor can he have revived any old law of
the kind. From the seventh century onwards we
can point to instances of Athenians marrying aliens
without damage to the position of their children.
Megacles, the Alcmæonid, married the daughter of
Clisthenes of Sicyon, and his son was Clisthenes, the
Athenian reformer. Cimon and Themistocles were
the sons of alien mothers; yet both were Athenian
generals. Besides, it is impossible that the number
of citizens should have been 14,000 in 445, if in 432
B.C. there were 26,000 Athenians capable of bearing

arms, exclusive of the lowest class, as Thucydides tells us that there were.* But though we cannot suppose that Pericles made any attempt to alter the status of the Athenian citizen, it is quite probable that he was very strict in the distribution of the corn. Five thousand men who attempted to gain a share may have been prevented from doing so ; and the number who received shares may not have been more than 14,000. We may even suggest that as Pericles was opposed to sending help to Egypt, he may have made the distribution of the present as unpopular as he could. He did not indeed dare to propose that the corn should be sent back, but the reception of it might be made a source of heart-burning and jealousy among the citizens, so as to prevent any enthusiasm in the cause of the giver. And we may see in his action on the occasion an indication of the change which came over his policy when he felt his power established. He was no longer, as before, the servant of the people, but their master, and dared to thwart their wishes.

While discouraging all attempts to enter into conflict with the Great King, Pericles was still intent on the extension of Athenian power. We have already seen how anxiously he had striven, in the years of Athens's greatest power, to secure a strong position in the Corinthian gulf. The most important stations in this quarter, Pegæ and Achæa, had been abandoned at the peace. The route to the West now lay over the alien Isthmus, or round the

---

* I deduct 3,000 from the total given in Thuc. ii., 13, for the " metics."

dreaded promontory of Malea. But in those distant regions there were openings which did not escape the eye of Pericles. In Southern Italy there was no Persian monarch, animated by hereditary hatred, and master of innumerable troops; the rivalry of Athenian and Peloponnesian had not yet been carried there. Was it possible to found a city in Italy which should exhibit the spectacle of Greeks from all quarters living harmoniously together, undivided by the jealousies of race or city?

The passion for Italy had long haunted the Athenians. When Themistocles was brought to bay by the Peloponnesian commanders before the battle of Salamis, he declared that Siris had been assigned by an oracle to Athens, and if the Peloponnesian generals abandoned Salamis, he would carry away his two hundred ships and found a new city there. So strong was the attraction which the West exercised on him that he named his two daughters Italia and Sybaris. The feeling is by no means unintelligible. The West was pre-eminently the goal of the adventurer. The Greek cities of Sicily and Italy were prosperous beyond the dreams of hope. The Sicilian princes were the most prominent men in the Grecian world; the luxury of Sybaris had not been surpassed in the East. The stories which came to the ears of the Greeks about Tartessus and Sardinia were greatly exaggerated, but there was daily evidence that valuable products and manufactures, carpets from Carthage and metal-work from Etruria, could be imported from the West. It is remarkable that Athens should never have attempted to secure for herself a footing in this coveted region. Perhaps her trade was not important—or her ships were few—till the Persian war; and for a generation after that event her attention was occupied with the Delian confederacy and the East. But though she had no depôts in the West, we know that the pottery of Athens was exported into Etruria and Campania, into Sicily and Lombardy, early in the fifth century B.C. There is also reason to believe that the Athenians and the Segestæans were brought into some kind of communication about the middle of the century.

To an excited nation nothing could be more welcome than the invitation which now came from the Sybarites, asking for assistance in refounding their ancient city. After the destruction of Sybaris by the Crotoniates in 510 B.C., the remnant of the Sybarites had found a home in Scidros and Laos, where they maintained their own against the attacks of their enemies. About the year 452 B.C., in conjunction with some Thessalians they founded a community which they called New Sybaris, after the old town. This was more than Croton could bear. A resolute attack was made on the city, and five years after its foundation the Sybarites were again driven out. They now resolved to ask the assistance of Greece in founding a state. Ambassadors were sent to Lacedæmon and to Athens, offering in return for assistance a share in the new colony. At Lacedæmon nothing was done, but at Athens the scheme was readily taken up. Not only were Athenians enrolled, but envoys were sent into the

10

Peloponnesus to enlist all who were willing to join. The colony was not to be the colony of any single state, but a colony founded by all Hellas, and a proof of Hellenic unity. In 445 B.C., ten ships left Athens to carry the colonists to their homes; at their head was Lampon, who, though not the founder of the colony, in the Greek sense, was of great authority as a seer, by whose power of divination the scheme had been greatly aided, and might be aided still more. In their choice of a site the colonists were guided by the Delphian oracle, which bade them seek a place "where water was measured and bread was not." They found, near the ancient site of Sybaris, a spring which poured its water through an iron pipe, to which the inhabitants gave the name of "the bushel." This seemed to indicate the measurement of water, and the richness of the soil promised unmeasured abundance of corn. Here, then, was the site indicated by the oracle: it was known as Thurii, from the name of the spring (θουρία, "fast-flowing"), and lay in a plain by the Crathis.

On this land the colonists proceeded to build a town. Among the emigrants was Hippodamus, the architect, who had recently laid out the Peiræus in a rectangular block with intersecting streets. The same regularity was observed in the new city. It was built in an oblong; four streets ran through the length, which were known as the streets of Heracles, Aphrodite, Olympia, and Dionysus. Three streets traversed the width—the Street of Heroes, the Thurian Street, and the Thurina. Such regularity

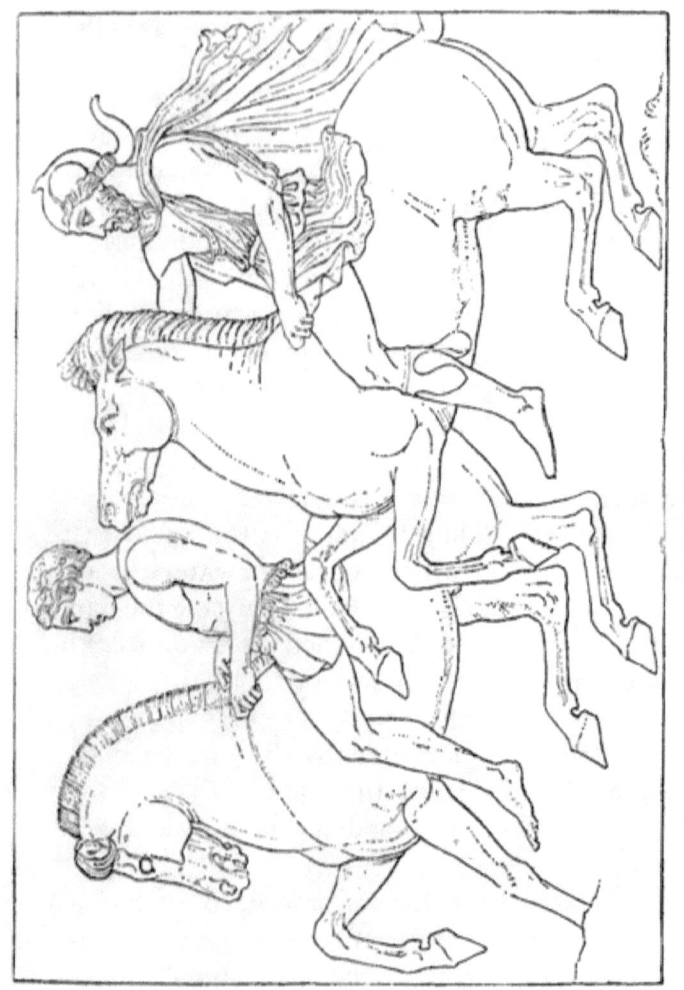

HORSEMEN.

From the frieze of the Parthenon.

(*Boetticher.*)

of structure was new in the Grecian world; in this respect also Thurii was a model city.

The colonists had not long been settled before dissensions broke out amongst them. The Sybarites claimed the first place in the colony; they were not content to hold an equal position with the rest. The highest offices were to be reserved for them; their wives were to have precedence at the sacrifices. They also retained possession of all the land immediately round the city, which was, of course, of the most value. Such claims could not be allowed without conceding that Thurii was not a Hellenic city, but merely the old Sybaris restored and protected by the new settlers. The quarrel led to a battle, in which the unfortunate Sybarites were once more defeated; the greater part were slain, the rest expelled from the country.

This victory left the conquerors in possession of a large quantity of fertile land. They immediately sent to Greece inviting a number of colonists to come and occupy it on terms of equality, an invitation widely accepted. The state now rapidly increased in power; the Crotoniates, after the expulsion of the Sybarites, were, for a time at least, on friendly terms with the settlers, and a popular government was devised, in which all the inhabitants had a share. Ten tribes were established, as at Athens; in three of them were included the colonists of the Peloponnesus; three others comprised the settlers from Bœotia and Central Hellas. In the remaining four were collected the colonists from Athens, Eubœa, and other Ionian

cities, and the islands.   These events took place in
443 B.C.

The colony of Thurii is interesting from many
points of view. It was an attempt to found a colony
which could not be claimed by any Grecian town as
its daughter city. It was intended to prove that
there were circumstances under which the jealousies
of race and city could be forgotten, and Ionian and
Dorian, Athenian and Bœotian, could dwell together
in unity. It was also, from the first, the home of
distinguished men. We have spoken of Lampon
and Hippodamus, both of them men from the Periclean circle, who had aided their leader in his work at
Athens. Herodotus, the historian, was also one of
those who joined the colony. The last fifteen or
twenty years of the life of the great historian were
passed, no doubt with intervals of travel, in his
western home. Thither also went Lysias, the young
son of that aged Cephalus, who is so well known
to all readers of Plato's "Republic." There too
dwelt Tisias, the Sicilian teacher of rhetoric, from
whom Lysias may have learnt his skill as a writer of
speeches. And, as we have said, Thurii has yet
another interest as a town built on the plan of an
architect. It was not a mere collection of houses,
like the Grecian cities, where old and new jostled
each other in gay confusion, but a town constructed
with a view to convenience, health, and protection.
It is from these points of view that Thurii becomes
the ideal colony of the Periclean era; other cities
were of far more use to Athens by supporting her
citizens, or holding places of strategical value; but

none reflects so much of the mind of Pericles as the Hellenic town by the waters of the Crathis—where Herodotus, the most Hellenic of Greek historians, was wont to talk and meditate.

Diodorus, in the account of Thurii from which we derive our knowledge of the city, takes the opportunity to give a sketch of the laws of Charondas. In so doing he makes the incredible blunder of asserting that Charondas, who lived in Sicily some two hundred years before this time, actually composed his code for the benefit of the citizens of Thurii. Such inaccuracy staggers us; we cannot feel that we are justified in supposing that the laws which he quotes were those observed in Thurii; still less that they represent the genuine code of Charondas. But as Diodorus probably copied his account of them from Ephorus, a historian of the fourth century B.C., who was in a position to know what laws passed as those of Charondas at that time, we may assume that the enactments are not pure imagination. They represent rules which were then obeyed in the cities of Magna Græcia. To this extent they are a genuine picture of society and manners among the colonies in Italy. And we may at least say that whatever their value, there is no doubt about their interest.

Under this code, a father who married a second wife to be a step-mother over his children, was not allowed to sit in the public council of his city. For how could one who ordered things so ill for his own family give good advice to the state? Besides, those who had been happy in their marriage ought to be content with their lot ; and those who had not, were foolish to try the experiment a second time. Men who were convicted of dishonest practices at law were compelled to walk the city in garlands of tamarisk ; all the world was to know that they had received the crown of villainy. By this wise law the city was freed from one of the worst pests of Greek society,—the man who made a dishonest use of his legal knowledge. Another law forbade all association with criminals or disreputable persons. Another established compulsory education ; every boy must learn to read and write, and the state paid the teachers. With regard to orphans, Charondas ordained that their property should be managed by the kindred of the father, but the children should be in the possession of the kindred of the mother. The kindred of the mother had no part in the inheritance, and therefore had no motive to make away with the heirs ; the kindred of the father could not come at them. Any citizen who had been guilty of cowardice was not, as in other cities, put to death, but compelled to sit for three days in the market-place in woman's attire. In regard to the letter of the law, Charondas was precise ; bad or good, the law, while it was the law, must be strictly obeyed. If it worked ill it might be corrected, but obeyed it must be.

The method by which Charondas allowed his laws to be corrected is one which is elsewhere mentioned in connection with Zaleucus the law-giver of Locri. It was not likely to make law reform popular. Anyone who chose could plead against a law in the public assembly, but he did so with his neck in a noose.

If he convinced his audience, the law was changed; if he failed, the noose was drawn. Instances are recorded of corrections made even under such severe conditions. It was the law that bodily injuries should be requited by the *lex talionis*: "An eye for an eye, and a tooth for a tooth." This continued in force till a ruffian threatened to knock out the eye of a man who had already lost one; he knew that the law would only deprive him of one of his eyes in return, and yet his opponent would be totally blind. As this was obviously unjust, the one-eyed man obtained a modification of the rule, and henceforth anyone who destroyed the eye of a man who had but one lost the sight of both eyes. Another correction related to divorce. An aged man, who had been abandoned by his young wife, succeeded in persuading the citizens to correct the law which permitted second marriages to divorced persons, to the extent that no woman might marry a man, no man might marry a woman, younger than the husband or wife whom they had abandoned. These stories are ridiculous, but they are probably true. They exhibit the humorous common-sense which meets us in Greek legislation. We know for a fact that Pittacus doubled the penalties for all misdeeds committed in intoxication, and Solon protected heiresses from greed by regulations which appeal to the animal rather than the moral nature of man.

Within a very few years from the foundation of Thurii the attention of Pericles was called away to the extreme east of the Athenian empire, and a struggle began which taxed his resolution and his resources

to the utmost. We have seen that in the year 450
B.C. troubles had broken out in Miletus, in which the
Athenians had found it necessary to interfere; the
constitution had been changed from an oligarchy to
a democracy, and an Athenian garrison had been
placed in the city. Such reforms naturally brought
Miletus into very close connection with Athens.
The democracy there might expect the support of
the democracy of Athens in any contest with oligarchy. It was perhaps in this spirit that they
entered into a contest with Samos for the possession
of Priene, though it is difficult to understand how
two cities belonging to the confederacy of Delos
could contest the possession of a third which was also
an independent member of the same confederacy.
It is possible that the Samians were the aggressors.
They were never very scrupulous in their acquisitions, and they had been at war with Priene in
old days for the possession of certain places on
the mainland. Or it is possible that in Priene
herself there were two factions, one of which
wished to place the town under the protection
of Samos, the other under the protection of Miletus.
Whatever the cause of strife, the cities flew to arms,
and Miletus was defeated. She at once appealed to
Athens, where the appeal was received with favour;
the more so, as it was supported by a party from
Samos who wished to overthrow the government
there. For Samos was in the hands of an oligarchy
composed of the rich landowners of the island, the
very class of men whose power at Athens had been
finally broken by Pericles. Plutarch tells us that the

Athenians called on the Samians to discontinue hostilities and submit the matter to arbitration, but in
Thucydides we hear nothing of this, and the Samians
are treated forthwith as guilty of rebellion. A force
of forty triremes was despatched from Athens in the
spring of 440 B.C. under the command of Pericles. He
met with no resistance, and proceeded to reorganise
affairs in Samos. Fifty men and fifty boys were taken
as hostages from the leading families, and placed with
Athenian colonists in Lemnos. The Samians were
compelled to pay a fine of eighty talents, the oligarchs
were deposed, the constitution was changed into a
democracy, and a garrison was left in the city to
preserve order. These measures were carried out
with the greatest decision and rapidity; in a very
few weeks Samos had been degraded from her
position as one of the most powerful of the allies of
Athens to the rank of a subject, held by a garrison
and punished by a fine. Here, as in Eubœa, the
policy of Pericles had triumphed; the Delian confederacy was a thing of the past.

But Samos was not prepared to submit. The
oligarchs could not forget that Samos had once been
the ruler of the Eastern Ægean; that her fleet was
still a great power. The city was strongly fortified,
and help might be expected from Persia. A number
of the discontented citizens left the island and entered into communication with Pissuthnes, the
satrap of Sardis. With his support they returned
at the head of a body of men by whose aid, in
concert with their friends, they succeeded in capturing or expelling the Athenian garrison and re-

covering possession of the city. The old constitution was at once restored; and before the Athenians had time to stir the hostages were removed from Lemnos. The work of Pericles was undone in less time than he had taken to do it.

Athens found herself face to face with a powerful ally in revolt. The danger was great; greater even than at the revolt of Eubœa. There was imminent risk that the war with Persia might be opened again, and Athens might be alone in the contest. Sparta certainly would not join her, and who could tell whether the allies would remain faithful? Samos was taking every step to strengthen her position, the leaders of the democracy were expelled from the city, the officers and garrison of the Athenians, who had been captured, were placed as hostages with Pissuthnes, the aid of the Spartan confederacy was invoked. In order, if possible, to cut off any assistance from Miletus, the Samians at once sent an expedition against the city. Could they capture it before the arrival of the Athenians, such a signal success might induce all the cities of Asia Minor to join in the revolt. Byzantium had joined already, and the cities of Caria were uncertain.

The whole policy of Pericles was at stake. Instantaneous action was necessary. A defeat at Samos would undo the work of years. Sixty ships were at once ordered to Samos, and apparently all the ten generals, with Pericles at their head, went over in charge of them. Part of the fleet was despatched to watch for the Phœnician ships, which were reported to be coming up from the south, part

was sent to bring reinforcements from Chios and
Lesbos. With the remaining vessels Pericles attempted to cut off the Samian force which was
engaged on the mainland in attacking Miletus. A
severe engagement took place in which both sides
claimed the victory. The Samians were able to force
their way through to Samos; while Pericles was able
to blockade the harbour. Further operations were
deferred till reinforcements came up.

Twenty-five triremes now arrived from Chios and
Lesbos, perhaps under the command of the poet
Sophocles, whom we know to have been a general in
this war, and hear of at Chios; forty, from Athens.
Thus reinforced Pericles was able to land forces at
Samos and draw lines round the city, which he also
blockaded by sea. While he was thus engaged the
news arrived that the Phœnician fleet was at hand.
Pericles at once set out to intercept it with sixty
ships. It was better to call off half his forces
than to engage with the Phœnicians off the shore of
Samos, where the Samians would be at hand to take
part in the battle. The Phœnician fleet did not appear, but meantime the Samians were able to break
through the sixty-five ships which Pericles had left
behind. For fourteen days they were masters of the
sea and could carry into the city whatever provisions
they pleased. Then Pericles returned. The Samians
attempted to cut him off from the island but in vain.
They were defeated, and the city was once more
blockaded by sea and land. It was now midsummer
440 B.C., and the generals for the year came into
office at Athens. Pericles was re-elected and re-

mained with the fleet, but the rest of the commanders at Samos were replaced by new officers,
who brought large reinforcements. First forty and
then twenty ships were brought from Athens; Chios
and Lesbos added thirty to the triremes previously
sent, and the total amount of the fleet was more
than two hundred sail. It was apparently an overwhelming force, yet the Samians defied it. Their
walls were strong; their city well stocked with provisions; they could still hope that assistance would
come from Persia or from Peloponnesus. So they
held out, month after month, waiting for help which
never came. The Persians failed to seize the opportunity; the Peloponnesus decided, on the motion of
the Corinthians, that they would not go to the aid of
a city which had revolted from her leader. To do so
might form a very inconvenient precedent; were the
Megarians to revolt and Athens to aid them, Corinth
would find herself in the same difficulties as before
the peace of 445 B.C. By this time the prospects
of the Samians were gloomy enough. At length
when nine months had passed, and the supplies in Samos were exhausted, the city agreed to a capitulation.
The terms were severe; all the triremes of Samos
were to be given up to Athens; the walls of the city
were to be thrown down; the cost of the war was to
be defrayed by the Samians, and hostages placed
with the Athenians as a surety for good behaviour.
The oligarchs who had brought about the revolt
were of course expelled from the city—we find them
afterwards at Anæa on the mainland opposite,—and
a democratical form of government was established.

Duris of Samos, a late and untrustworthy historian, had horrible stories to tell of the cruelty of Pericles toward the Samian trierarchs and marines. They are doubtless fictions; the Greeks were not merciful to the captives who fell into their power, but they were content with putting them to death. They did not add torture to bloodshed.

The cost of the war had been enormous; if we exclude all the previous operations, the siege of eight months with two hundred triremes would require 1,600 talents, if we allow a drachma a day as the entire cost in food and hire for each man on board a trireme. So far as we can judge from a mutilated inscription, 1,276 talents, in addition to the ordinary income from the league, were paid out of the treasury of Athens in the war, this implies a total expenditure of more than 2,000 talents; if the Samians paid even half this sum, it would be a severe tax on the island for many years.

Once more was Pericles victorious. When he returned to Athens, in the spring of 439 B.C., he might feel that his policy was now fairly established. In her dealings with Samos, Athens had acted from first to last as an imperial city. To her the complaints of the Milesians had been brought ; she had interfered as a sovereign in the domestic politics of Samos. She had employed the fleets of Chios and Lesbos, and the money of other cities, to reduce Samos to subjection. She had compelled the city to accept a form of government in harmony with her own. To those who had eyes to see, such conduct proved only too clearly that Athens claimed sovereign rights over the confederacy, and was resolved to use them for her own advantage.

The measures which Pericles took on the news of the revolt of Samos were not less clear-sighted than rapid. The attempts to cut off the Samians on the mainland from the island, and to meet the Phœnician fleet before it could reach Samos, were excellent pieces of strategy. Yet we notice that here, as elsewhere, the Greeks were helpless in the presence of a walled city. Thasos, Ægina, Samos, had bidden defiance to all the skill of the best Athenian engineers. Famine or treachery alone could bring a strongly fortified place into the possession of the enemy. In the case of Samos, we must allow that Pericles was highly favoured by fortune. Had the Persians taken up the cause of the Samians, as it was their interest to do; had the Chians and Lesbians joined in the revolt, or even refused to send ships to subjugate an ally; had the Corinthians been less short-sighted in their advice, the event of the war would probably have been different. It is interesting to know that the defence of Samos was conducted by a man whose name is remembered in another sphere. Melissus, who defeated Pericles, and defied his forces so long, was a philosopher of the Eleatic school. As Pericles occupied his leisure with the speculations of Anaxagoras on the physical world, so did Melissus ponder the problem of the Many and the One, striving to find beyond and behind the change and decay of all visible things a reality which was always and everywhere the same.

With the fall of Samos, Byzantium also came in

and resumed her place as a subject state of Athens, and though a number of Carian cities broke away from the confederacy at this time, and were never recovered—and troubles were not wanting in the Thracian quarter,—Pericles, on his return to Athens, was at the height of his reputation as a general. Twice in a moment of supreme danger he had saved Athens. The first success had been overshadowed by the peace which it had been necessary to make with Sparta, but the conquest of Samos was clear gain to the city. Yet his victories were won at the cost of those who had once been free and independent Greeks. When the last solemn rites were paid, after the custom of the Athenians, to the dead who had fallen in their country's cause, Pericles was chosen to pronounce the funeral oration over them. He dwelt on the immortality of the glorious dead ; on the fair promise of the lives that were ended ; "the loss of her youth was to the city what the loss of spring would be to the year." But they had fallen in a noble cause, and achieved a famous victory. When he descended from the tribune, widows and orphans crowded round him with flowers and garlands, but Elpinice, the now aged sister of Cimon, turned away, with the bitter words: " Why these flowers and crowns? Not in war against Medes and Phœnicians, as my brother, but in conflict against a friendly and allied state, has Pericles led our citizens to death."

CHAPTER XI.

AMPHIPOLIS—THE COMING WAR.

Founding of Amphipolis—Splendour of Athens—Pan-Hellenic scheme of Pericles—His imperial policy—Growing opposition to Pericles.

HE success of the Athenians at Samos did not enable them entirely to repair the breaches which the revolt had made in the confederacy. When we compare the lists of the tribute paid by the allies in the Delian confederacy in the years just preceding the outbreak of the revolt with that of 436–435 B.C., we find that no fewer than twenty-two of the Carian cities are wanting in the later list, and that these cities no longer form a separate district, but are united with the Ionian. In Thrace also there had been disturbances. The cities on Pallene had fallen into arrears with their tribute or refused to pay it. In this district Athens was able to restore order, and the defaulters were punished by the exaction of higher sums; Scione, for instance, pays fifteen talents in the list of 437 B.C. instead of six talents, and many towns that hitherto had been subordinate to neighbouring cities, were now detached and formed into independent mem-

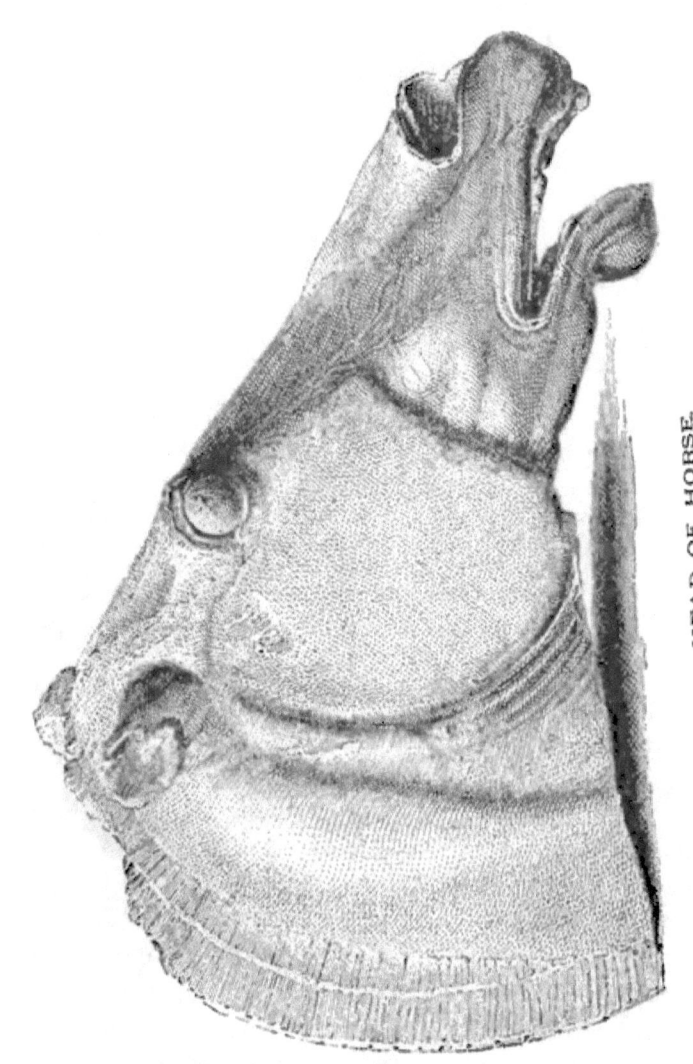

HEAD OF HORSE.

From the eastern gable of the Parthenon.

(Boetticher.)

bers of the league. But the revolt of Byzantium, and the uncertain fidelity of the Chalcidic cities, seem to have convinced Pericles that something had still to be done to secure the interests of Athens in this quarter. How keenly he felt the necessity of providing for a close and unbroken connexion between Athens and the north, he had already shewn by his voyage into the Pontus and the colonies he had sent out. With the exception of Naxos, the cleruchies of Pericles were all planted in a line more or less direct between Athens and Byzantium. Chalcis secured the south of the Euripus, Histiæa the north; Brea was in the territory of the Bisaltians; the Chersonese commanded the Hellespont. At all these points Athenian colonies were established of such a nature that their loyalty to Athens could never for a moment be called in question.

Another site remained, more valuable from every point of view; a site where the Athenians had already attempted to establish themselves, but only to meet with overwhelming disaster. At the point where the Strymon leaves Lake Cercinitis are the " Nine ways," —the centre to which all the roads from east and west, north and south converge in order to strike the bridge over the river. Here in 465 B.C. Leagros had led out an Athenian colony of 10,000 men, all of whom had perished at Drabescus, in conflict with the warlike tribes of the district. It was a severe loss, but a further attempt was worth making; the region was not only rich in all materials required for building ships, but it lay in the immediate neighbourhood of the mines of Pangæum, and above all it com-

11

manded the principal route to the north. In 437 B.C. another band of colonists was led out by Hagnon the son of Nicias, who had been a general with Pericles in the Samian war. He landed at Eion at the mouth of the Strymon, which had long been in the occupation of the Athenians, and from thence forced his way up the river till he obtained possession of the coveted place. Just above the bridge, on an eminence skirted by the river, Hagnon placed his city, which from its site he called Amphipolis. Two sides of the town were swept by the stream and needed no defence; on the third, a wall was built, reaching at each end to the river. The colony was strengthened by settlers from the neighbouring cities of Chalcidice, but so far as we know the native tribes made no attempt to drive out the intruders. Hagnon was regarded as the founder of the city, and public honours were paid to him in this capacity.

Great changes had taken place in this region since Cimon had conquered Eion, and Leagros had perished at Drabescus—changes which perhaps explain the inefficient resistance of the natives to this new attempt of the Athenians. In 464 Alexander was still king of Macedon; the prince who in his youth, by an act of great daring, had cleared his country of the Persians, when sent to demand submission from his father Amyntas. When he came to the throne he had pursued a policy which enabled him to preserve his kingdom from the Persian invaders, without incurring the open hostility of the Greeks. A series of conquests had extended his empire from Mount Bœum to the middle course of the Strymon; and from the mines near·Lake Prasias, which were at his disposal, he received not less than a talent of silver a day. After his death in 454 B.C. his kingdom was divided between his two sons Perdiccas and Philip, the eastern portion, between the Axius and the Strymon, falling to Philip's share. Such a division was in itself a source of weakness, and the weakness was increased by dissensions between the brothers. Perdiccas seems about this time to have entered into an alliance with the Athenians; he was probably not displeased that they should plant themselves in force between Philip and the sea. They would at least be on the spot to render what aid was necessary. To the Athenians also the alliance was for the moment advantageous; it prevented Philip from taking any decisive measures against Amphipolis, but in time they found it more to their interests to support Philip against Perdiccas.

In like manner on the death of Teres, in 440 B.C., the great kingdom of the Odrysians was divided between his sons Sitalces and Sparadocus. They too were soon at variance. The quarrel was a fortunate circumstance for Athens, while it lasted. Some years later, when Sitalces had overpowered and expelled his brother, the Athenians were alarmed at his forces and flattered him by every means in their power. Fortunately the Odrysians never attained consolidation, and the time was not yet come when the powers of the north could make or mar in Greece.

While Athens was thus active, organizing her confederacy and securing her communication with the north, the Peloponnesians had allowed the years to pass in apathy and inattention. At length they awoke to a sense of the situation. It was clear that Athens had abandoned all idea of war with Persia and that the confederacy of Delos was transformed into an Athenian empire, of whose forces the great city was absolutely mistress. And meanwhile in visible greatness Athens had become far the first city in Greece. Her walls were unrivalled, her harbours and docks ample for the largest fleet, and protected by the strongest fortifications. On the height of the Acropolis new temples were rising, surpassing in beauty all that had hitherto been achieved by architect or sculptor, and at the head of all was Pericles, under whose guidance Athens seemed to be forever falling into the greatest dangers only to rise again more splendid than before. An uneasy feeling began to prevail. What would the end be? Who could forecast the action of democracy or penetrate the designs of the silent, self-reliant statesman, who wielded such immense power? Pericles seems to have perceived the discontent. He knew what it foreboded. War with Sparta had perhaps never been wholly absent from his thoughts, even when he concluded the Thirty Years' Peace. In such a struggle it was necessary for Athens to have as large a following as possible. By a wise policy he might at least prevent the growing suspicion that Athens was using her power for her own interest only, and that she was utterly careless of the great charge entrusted to her. He might show the world that if Greece was once more willing to unite against Persia, Athens was

ready to do her part.   If they refused, it was no
longer open to them to charge Athens with any want
of patriotism ; but if by any means Hellas could be
united round Athens, her position would be immense-
ly improved.   Such a union would at once put her
in the first place in Greece, and Sparta in the second.
We are told by Plutarch that at the time when the
Lacedæmonians were beginning to feel great annoy-
ance at the rise of Athens, Pericles encouraged the
people to aim at a still higher position.   With this
object he brought forward a decree that all the
Greeks, whether in Europe or Asia, should be invited
to send envoys to a conference at Athens for the purpose of discussing a number of questions of national
interest.   The temples which the Persians had destroyed were still unrestored ; the offerings vowed at
the time of the great struggle had not been fully
paid ; no definite arrangement had been made for
the control of the sea and the preservation of peace.
These were matters in which every Greek had an interest, and they could only be discussed in a Pan-Hellenic conference.   Twenty Athenians—men of more
than fifty years of age—were chosen, of whom five
visited the Ionians and Dorians in Asia, and the
islands as far as Lesbos and Rhodes ; a second five
were sent to the Greeks in the Hellespont and in
Thrace as far as Byzantium.   Other five went to
Bœotia, Phocis, and the Peloponnesus, from which
they passed through Locri to Acarnania and Ambracia ; the remainder visited the Œtæans, the Malian
Gulf, the Achæans of Phthiotis, and the Thessalians.
But the scheme fell dead to the ground ; nowhere

was there any response to the invitations ; not a single
envoy appeared at Athens. The attempt to make
the city the centre of Hellas completely broke down.

Pericles was not discouraged by the failure of his
plan. He was content that Athens should stand
alone ; that the division which had been slowly widen-
ing since the Peloponnesians withdrew from Byzantium should continue till one or other of the great
cities, which stood at the head of the opposite sections, was brought to submission. And he resolved
that Athens at any rate should not be first in shewing signs of weakness. Let the cost be what it might,
she must still pursue the career of progress on which
she had advanced for the last fifty years. If the rest
of Greece failed to sympathise with a forward movement and preferred to cling to their old leader, so much
the more reason was there for Athens to be resolute
in her purpose and solid in her power. From this
time forward Pericles sought to brace his citizens to
the idea of war with Sparta. He endeavoured to
instil into their minds the greatness of the objects
for which they would fight. He pointed to the glorious city, the like of which could be seen nowhere
else in Greece. He called to their minds all that the
city had been to them ; the happy life they enjoyed
in her, the numerous recreations she provided for
them. He told them of the great empire the city
controlled ; an empire which, he said, would certainly
fall to pieces, if Athens became in any way subject
to Sparta. He enumerated the wealth stored up in
the treasuries of the city, and explained how indispensable money was for the successful prosecution of

THE "FATES."

From the eastern gable of the Parthenon.

war. He frankly avowed that Athens was no match
in the field for the forces which the Spartan confederacy could bring against her; but why need she
meet them? The fair possessions of the wealthy
Athenians in Attica were pleasant and beautiful;
but they were not the city; they were but the orna-
ments of wealth, the "garden of the house." If the
need came they must be abandoned, and he would
cheerfully set the example. The walls and ports,
money and ships:—these were the real safeguards of
Athens. While these remained intact, the enemy
might ride up to the city and she would suffer nothing. Such were the precepts enforced by an eloquence, which left a sting in the ears of those that
listened. They were not enforced in vain. Whatever the wavering and uncertainty of the Athenian
people, the democracy clung with a tenacity rarely
equalled to the war with Sparta.

The policy of Pericles was not without opponents.
There were many in Athens whom his eloquence
failed to convince, and who spoke of him and his
measures with a bitter and even personal hatred.
The oligarchical party, though politically helpless
since the ostracism of Thucydides, was still vigorous.
If it could accomplish nothing in the assembly, much
could be done by the organised co-operation of
clubs, by clever satire, and well-conducted personal
attacks upon Pericles and his friends. The position
of Pericles was not less difficult because it was unique.
Year after year he was elected one of the ten generals, and this permanence gave him a peculiar
authority on the board. Whether he was so formally

or not, he was in reality chairman of the generals, the first executive officer in Athens. It was thought that he superintended everything, and therefore everything could be charged upon him. If any scheme went wrong, it was Pericles who was to blame. More especially did the poets of the old comedy take up this line. Their sympathies were not with the people whom they sought to amuse, but with the people of the age of Cimon, "the men of Marathon;" they praised the good old times and criticised all that was new. Those who listened were willing enough to be discontented. The years of peace left the Athenians with little to occupy their minds. A long peace is always a time of trial for a government, however able and efficient. Men grow captious in their criticisms when they have no severe burdens to bear, no definite aim before them. Besides the comedians, there were men who rightly or wrongly took great offence at the conduct of Pericles. Dracontides scented corruption in the public expenditure; Diopeithes was convinced that the doctrines of Anaxagoras must lead to the overthrow of all sound religion, and bring on the city the dire vengeance of the gods; others saw in Aspasia, the Milesian friend of Pericles, the destruction of Athenian domestic life. These various sections were drawing together, and if they could not reach Pericles himself, they could, when the right moment came, attack him through his friends. For the present they contented themselves with abuse. Aspasia was spoken of as the new Omphale, as the Hera of the Olympian, the child of corruption, an impudent mistress. Pericles was the prince of satyrs, his house was an office for the corruption of female honour. Pheidias was a thief, Anaxagoras an atheist.

While the storm was gathering at home, Pericles was extending the influence of Athens in the West as well as in the north. We have seen how anxious he had been before the peace in 445 B.C. to secure a firm footing at the mouth of the Corinthian Gulf, and the subsequent foundation of the colony at Thurii proves that he had not lost sight of his old policy. A favourable opportunity soon offered for renewing it. On the shore of the bay of Ambracia lay the city of Argos Amphilochicum, so called from the founder, Amphilochus of Argos, who, according to a tradition preserved by Thucydides, founded the city on his return from Troy. It was the greatest city in that region. At a date which we cannot fix, the Amphilochians, being in great distress, invited their neighbours, the Ambraciots, to join in the settlement. The Ambraciots came and after a time, finding themselves the stronger, drove out the Argives and took possession of the city for themselves. The Argives now sought the protection of the Acarnanians and both together appealed to Athens. A fleet of thirty ships was sent under the command of Phormio, who had recently served in the war with Samos. When Phormio arrived, Argos was taken by storm, and the Argives and Acarnanians dwelt together in the place. This was the beginning of the alliance between Athens and Acarnania, which we find subsisting at the time of the Peloponnesian war.

The acquisition of a friendly port on the shore of the Ambracian Gulf was of great advantage to Athens in keeping up a communication with the west. We hear of an alliance between Athens and the Messapians and of the presence of an Athenian admiral, Diotimus, at Naples, and though we have no evidence on which to fix the date of either, it has been conjectured with some reason that they were connected with that advance of the Italian tribes to the west and south which about this time threatened the cities of Magna Græcia. In the Greek cities also of Italy and Sicily affairs had taken a turn which could not fail to attract the attention of Athens. From the first the new colony of Thurii had aroused the jealousy of Tarentum ; war had broken out, and though no decisive result had followed, the Tarentines had acquired an equal share in a new colony on the site of Siris, which the Athenians in the days of Themistocles claimed for themselves. This was a gain for the Dorian element in Italy ; it was hardly less so that the Thurians had been led in their defence by Cleandridas, the Spartan exile, the father of the famous Gylippus. In Sicily also the Dorian cities of Syracuse and Agrigentum had recently made such progress that the Ionians had reason to be apprehensive. It may have occurred to Pericles, that if he could not place Athens at the head of Greece in a combination against Persia, she might at least come forward as the defender and supporter of the Ionians, and he could hardly fail to see that a war of Athens with Sparta meant also a war of Ionians with Dorians, in which the cities of the west

would be called upon to furnish ships to their kinsmen in the east. So much the more important was
it that Athens should be in a position to control the
passage from Syracuse to Corinth.

Thus we see Athens repairing the loss which the
peace inflicted upon her by drawing more tightly
the reins with which she governed the confederacy,
and by strengthening her communications with the
north and the west. It was from these quarters
that the storm finally broke.

THE WRESTLERS.

CHAPTER XII.

CAUSES OF THE PELOPONNESIAN WAR.

The "Corinthian War"—Alliance of Athens and
Corcyra—Battle of Cheimerium—Aspasia.

HUCYDIDES informs us that the
real cause of the Peloponnesian war
was the growing dread and jealousy of the Athenian
power; but the avowed cause was the part which
Athens took in the affairs of Epidamnus and Potidæa.
The contemporary comedians attributed the war to
corrupt personal motives on the part of Pericles—
his wish to shield his own peculations and those of
Pheidias, or to avenge some insult done to Aspasia.
Ephorus, the historian who flourished in the fourth
century B.C., fixes the blame on Pericles, on the ground
that he wished by this means to extricate himself from
the difficulties into which his appropriation of the
public funds had brought him.   In a time of distress
the people would forget to prosecute enquiries, and
the need of their great leader would be felt more

LAPITH AND CENTAUR.
Metope from the south side of the Parthenon.
(*Muller's " Denkmäler der Alten Kunst."*)

severely. But all writers agreed that the immediate cause of the war was the refusal of the Athenians to rescind a decree which excluded the Megarians from trading in the markets of Athens or her allies, and that Pericles, who was the author of this decree, persuaded the Athenians not to rescind it.

That such a trifling matter would never have brought about hostilities between two allied nations without other and more grave causes of ill feeling, is obvious; nor would Pericles have been so peremptory in his refusal to make a slight concession if he had not been persuaded that war was the best policy.

Whatever the immediate cause of the struggle, the question of war or peace was first opened before the Spartan confederacy, and it was opened by Corinth. Ever since the Persian war Corinth had felt that the Athenian fleet was vastly superior to her own, and for years past she had had reasons to fear that Athens would become a dangerous rival in the trade to the west. Before the Thirty Years' Peace, Pericles had endeavoured to acquire the control of the Corinthian Gulf by the settlement of the Messenians at Naupactus, by attacks on Œniadæ and Sicyon, by occupying the Megarian harbour of Pegæ, and by entering into friendly relations with Achæa. When compelled to withdraw from Achæa and Pegæ, he had helped to found the colony of Thurii, and still later he had entered into an alliance with the Messapians of Italy and the Acarnanians of Western Greece. These movements were sufficiently alarming to a city conscious of declining power, as Corinth was, and an incident now occurred which made the intentions of Athens still more clear.

The island of Corcyra had been colonised by the Corinthians in the eighth century B.C. The island —the modern Corfu—enjoyed a most fortunate situation. It was sufficiently distant from Greece to lie outside the currents which disturbed the politics of the peninsula ; and yet it formed a convenient station in the route from Corinth to the west. For almost a generation after the founding of the city, Corcyra and Corinth were on the usual terms of colony and mother-city ; but as the colony grew in power, quarrels arose between them. Before the middle of the seventh century Corcyra had shaken off her allegiance and conquered the Corinthians in a great naval engagement. It was in vain that Cypselus, the first tyrant of Corinth, strove to bring the island into subjection ; the utmost that he could do was to check the extending commerce of the Corcyræans by establishing rival colonies on the shore of Acarnania. His son Periander was more successful ; he brought the rebels back to their allegiance ; but on his death they established their independence once more. These conflicts left bitter memories behind them. In their common festivals the Corcyræans would not allow the Corinthians the customary privileges of founders, and at their sacrifices they denied to a Corinthian the right of receiving first the lock of hair cut from the head of the victim. Such conduct on the part of a daughter city was equivalent to the renunciation of the bond which linked her to the source from which she sprang.

At the time of the Persian invasion the Corcy-ræans were in possession of sixty ships, while the Corinthians had but forty ; in the next fifty years they had increased the sixty to one hundred and twenty, a number far in excess of any navy in Greece but that of Athens. When invited to assist in the deliverance of Greece they had played a double game —promising assistance to the patriotic side, but delay-ing to send it, and waiting for the event. In the subsequent quarrels between Athens and Sparta they had taken no part ; they were allies of neither side. They considered that their position enabled them to stand alone, and it was not their interest to favour one party more than the other.

From Corcyra a colony had been sent out (625 B.C.) to Epidamnus on the Illyrian coast. The leader of the emigrants was Phalius, a Heraclid of Corinth, for it was the custom, when a colony sent out an off-shoot, to renew the connexion with the ancient mother city by bringing thence a founder for the new settlement. The colony was valuable to the Corcyræans, because it secured their trade with the interior of Illyria and Epirus. It rapidly became a wealthy and populous town. The government was a close oligarchy, the supreme council being formed by the heads of the tribes, of whom one was chosen annually to be the President of the city.

This constitution was subsequently modified by the creation of a less exclusive council, and finally, about the year 435 B.C., the people succeeded in driving the oligarchs out of the town and establishing a thoroughly democratic form of government. The exiled oligarchs at once united with the neighbouring barbarians, with whose aid they plundered the property of their opponents. So severe was the damage inflicted, that the Epidamnians were at length compelled to send to Corcyra for assistance. Their request was received with the greatest apathy ; the Corcyræans shewed no inclination to enter into the domestic quarrels of Epidamnus. In their distress, the Epidamnians sought the advice of Delphi. Should they apply to Corinth, the home of their founder, for the help which Corcyra denied ? The oracle approved the suggestion, and to Corinth they went, repeating the command given at Delphi, and offering to place their city in the hands of the Corinthians. Their overtures met with a ready response. The Corinthians were not inclined to forego any claim which they had upon Epidamnus, and their hatred of Corcyra was an additional motive for securing the colony. Without consulting the wishes of Corcyra, they at once invited any Corinthian who pleased to settle at Epidamnus, and a force of troops was sent to protect them in the city.

Upon this the exiled oligarchs went to Corcyra, and entreated the city to restore them. The appeal came at the right moment. When the Corcyræans found that their colony had gone over to Corinth, and had admitted Corinthian troops and settlers, they were highly indignant. Taking the exiles with them they set sail at once for Epidamnus, and demanded that they should be taken back. The demand was, of course, refused, upon which they set about investing the city, with the aid of the exiles and neighbouring Illyrians.

The Corinthians were not less active; they no sooner heard of the investment of Epidamnus, than they proclaimed a new colony to the town. Any Corinthian who chose might go, and he would be an equal among equals in the new city; those who found it inconvenient to leave Corinth at once could secure a place by depositing a sum of money. Appeals were also sent round to friendly cities for ships and money. A large force must be despatched, and a large fleet would be required as a convoy. The Corcyræans now repaired to Corinth, complaining loudly of the injustice done to them. The Corinthians, they said, had no interest in Epidamnus, which was a Corcyræan colony. Let them choose any Peloponnesian state to decide between them; or let the matter be referred to Delphi. Before going further the Corinthians demanded the withdrawal of the Corcyræan troops from Epidamnus. The Corcyræans replied with a similar demand. But all negotiations were useless; the Corinthians were resolved upon war, and sent their fleet to sea. A great battle was fought at the mouth of the Ambracian Gulf, seventy-five Corinthian ships against eighty Corcyræan, in which the Corinthians were entirely defeated, with a loss of fifteen ships. On the same day, Epidamnus was compelled by the besieging force to capitulate. Such disasters were overwhelming, and though hostilities went on for the rest of the year (435 B.C.), the Corinthians did not venture on a second engagement.

The old feud had broken out once more; once more the mother-city had been defeated by her ungrateful daughter. The humiliation was intolerable. The Corinthians were filled with a desire for

revenge. All through the year 434 B.C. and for part of
433, they were busy with building ships and preparing to renew the struggle. The Corcyræans became
alarmed! They were alone, and without allies, while
the Corinthians were members of a great confederacy.
It was necessary to seek assistance from the second
great power in Greece. In 433 B.C. Corcyræan envoys
appeared at Athens asking that the island might be
admitted into the Athenian alliance. Their position
was difficult, for they had to clear themselves of the
two charges to which their conduct was open. Was it
not inconsistent for a state, which had refused to
become the ally of others, to be now seeking an
alliance? Was it not ungrateful for a colony to be
engaged in war with her mother-city? They confessed that they had made a mistake in standing
apart from an alliance with the Grecian cities ; but a
mistake was pardonable when it proceeded from no
bad motive. And it was now impossible to adhere
to a policy which left them alone, while the Corinthians could bring all the Peloponnesus against them.
The war with Corinth had been forced upon them, in
spite of their appeal to arbitration. It was the duty
of a colony to treat her mother-city with all proper
respect and deference, but she could not submit to
injustice. The colonists were the equals of those
whom they had left behind ; and it was the duty of
a mother-city to treat them as such. After this
justification, the Corcyræans attempted to shew that
the Athenians would not be guilty of a breach of the
treaty with Lacedæmon, in accepting them as allies.
Technically this was true ; by the treaty it was open

to either side to receive as allies states who were as
yet the allies of neither. But the slightest reflection
was enough to shew that a mere alliance was not
what the Corcyræans wanted. They wanted help,
and how could the Athenians help them without
coming into collision with the Corinthians? This
difficulty was perhaps forgotten when the Corcyræans pointed out that war between Athens and Sparta
was inevitable and even imminent. Let the Athenians choose whether they would enter into the war
with the navy of Corcyra—the second largest navy in
Greece—as an ally or an enemy. From Corcyra too
more conveniently than from any other state they
could control the route to Sicily, if it should prove
important to send ships thither, or to cut off those
which came from the west.

In reply to these arguments the Corinthians, who
had at once sent an embassy to Athens to oppose
the request of their enemies, had much to say of the
iniquity of the Corcyræans, both in their general
conduct and in their treatment of their mother-city.
They had of course to veil as best they could their
own refusal to submit the points at issue to arbitration ; but on the other hand they had no difficulty
in shewing that an alliance between Corcyra and
Athens must lead to a breach of the peace between
Athens and Corinth. They could not deny the great
advantage which Athens would gain by the addition
of the Corcyræan navy to her own, but the war in
which this navy was to be of such signal service was
still in the future ; there was no reason why it should
come soon ; and it might not come at all. They

reminded the Athenians that they had restrained the Peloponnesians from interfering to help the Samians against Athens; let the same principle be maintained now. Whatever the balance of immediate advantage, in the long run an honest and consistent policy was the best.

The Athenians were at first inclined to listen to the Corinthians, who, whatever their conduct to Corcyra, had justice on their side in opposing the alliance. But on further consideration they resolved to enter into a defensive alliance with Corcyra. They believed that war with Sparta would come, and, with that danger before them, they wished to have Corcyra on their side. They also felt that Corcyra was an important station on the way to Sicily and Italy—a station which they could not allow to fall into the hands of their rivals and enemies. It was at once determined to send ten ships to Corcyra with orders not to attack the Corinthians, but to act with the Corcyræans, if any attempt were made to land on their island, or on any territory belonging to them. For in this case the Corinthians would be the assailants, and the Athenians would be merely defending allies, whom they had a right, under the treaty, to receive. Soon afterwards, feeling that ten ships were an inadequate force, they sent off twenty more. The first squadron was under the command of Lacedæmonius, the son of Cimon, and two others.

From this narrative, which has the authority of Thucydides, we can hardly avoid drawing the conclusion that there was a great diversity of opinion at

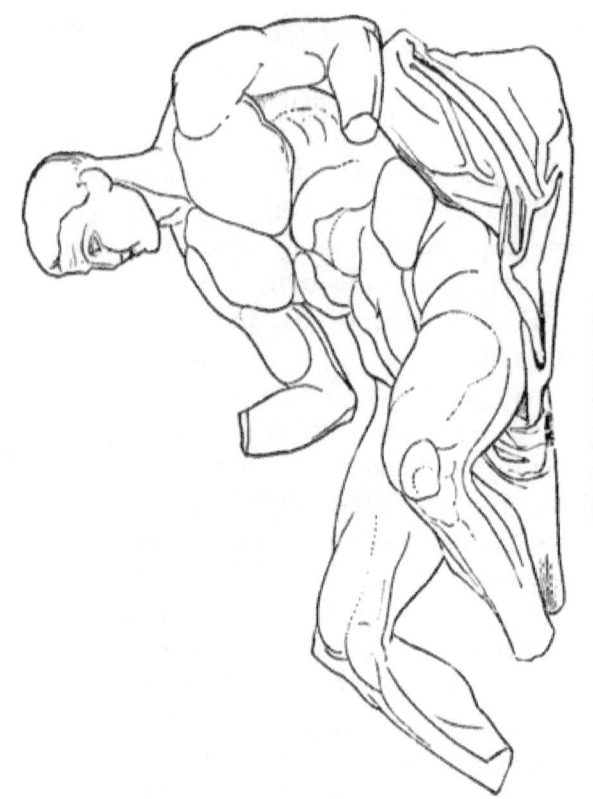

THE "THESEUS."

From the eastern gable of the Parthenon.

Athens about the Corcyræan proposal. Pericles was no doubt strongly in favour of accepting it ; he would employ all his eloquence to put in the most striking light the two reasons which eventually determined the choice of the Athenians. But the opposition was also very strong—that is, there was a large party at Athens, which did not believe that war with Sparta was imminent, or perhaps inevitable, which wished to restrain Athens from any conduct likely to bring on a war, and which still cherished the hope that the international relations of Greece might be guided by principles of equity rather than expedience. How small was the encouragement given to Pericles is shewn by the fact that Lacedæmonius —the son of his old opponent—was put in command of the squadron ; and that the squadron was so insufficient. Lacedæmonius might be trusted to do nothing, if he could help it, which would irritate the Spartans, and with so few ships he could neither alarm the Corinthians into acquiescence nor render any real service to Corcyra. Indeed both parties seem to have felt that the despatch of such a force was ludicrous. It was one of those half-measures which always entail fatal consequences.

The Corcyræans and Corinthians now prepared for battle. The Corinthians equipped ninety ships of their own, and obtained sixty more from their allies. With those they sailed to the mainland opposite Corcyra, where they pitched a camp near the promontory of Cheimerium. The Corcyræans met them with one hundred and ten ships and the ten Athenian vessels. A severe engagement took place

—the most severe which had yet been fought between two Hellenic fleets. The Corcyræans were
successful on their own left wing, and not only drove
the Corinthian allies to shore, but even landed and
destroyed the vacant tents ; but on their right, where
they were engaged with the Corinthians themselves,
they were defeated. Unhappily it was at this point
that the Athenian ships were stationed. For a time
they endeavoured to abstain from any actual collision, " but when the Corcyræans fled outright and
the Corinthians pressed them hard, then every man
fell to work ; all distinctions were forgotten ; the time
had arrived when Corinthian and Athenian were
driven to attack one another." *

The Corinthians pursued their enemy to the shore,
and then began to collect their own wrecks and
dead. These they conveyed to the mainland, where
the barbarian allies were at hand to protect them.
They then formed afresh for a second attack, and
the Corcyræans sailed to meet them. The war-cry
had already been sounded, when the Corinthians
suddenly retired. Twenty vessels were seen sailing
up, which proved to be the second squadron from
Athens. These joined the Corcyræan fleet.

The next day the Corinthians did not venture to
renew the attack. Enough if they could get away
with their prisoners without being captured by the
Athenians, whom they now regarded as declared
enemies. In order to ascertain what opposition
would be offered, they sent a few men in a boat
to the Athenians, upbraiding them with their action,

* Thuc. i., 49 Jowett.

and calling upon them, if they were at war, to take
the crew of the boat and deal with them accordingly.
But the Athenians merely replied that they were defending their allies ; if the Corinthians were going to
sail against Corcyra, resistance would be offered, but
not otherwise.   The Corinthians then set up a trophy
in honour of victory, and sailed home.   Among their
captives were two hundred and fifty of the most influential men at Corcyra.   These they treated with
great consideration, in the hope that by their influence the city might yet be won; the remaining
captives, who were slaves, they sold.

" Thus the war ended to the advantage of Corcyra,
and the Athenian fleet returned home.   This was
the first among the causes of the Peloponnesian war,
the Corinthians alleging that the Athenians had
taken part with the Corcyræans, and had fought
against them, in defiance of the treaty."

What was the result of the Corcyræan victory at
Epidamnus, we are not informed ; nor what became
of the Corinthian captives there.   But the Corinthians must have seen with intense irritation the
fruits of their final victory over the Corcyræans
snatched from their hands by the appearance of the
second Athenian squadron ; and their anger would
not be lessened when they found that Athens followed up the alliance with Corcyra by giving
favourable audience to envoys from Leontini and
Rhegium (Chalcidian towns in Sicily and Italy) and
entering into an alliance with Zacynthus.   The influence of Corinth in the West was in greater danger
than ever.

Another cause of quarrel soon arose, and in this case also it was the Athenians and Corinthians who were brought into collision. Potidæa, a Corinthian colony on the isthmus of Pallene, was a tributary ally of Athens, but governed by magistrates sent annually from Corinth. The Athenians, aware of the hostile spirit which now prevailed at Corinth, were afraid that the Potidæans might be induced to revolt. They had the greater reason for alarm, because Perdiccas, king of Macedonia, their former ally, had now become their enemy, and was doing all that he could to kindle war between Athens and Sparta. The revolt of Potidæa, under such circumstances, would be followed by the revolt of Chalcidice. To prevent this disaster, the Athenians called on the Potidæans to raze their walls, and give hostages for good behaviour; and, in order to secure the execution of this demand, they directed the generals of an expedition, which they were about to send against Perdiccas, to put in at Potidæa. The Potidæans in their distress sent envoys to Athens to obtain if possible some remission of the demand. The Athenians were inexorable, and when the envoys found that negotiations were useless, they passed on to Lacedæmon, where they received a promise that, if the Athenians attacked Potidæa, the Peloponnesians would invade Attica. When the Potidæans heard this, they determined to revolt. They were joined by the Chalcidian Greeks and the neighbouring Bottiæans, and on the advice of Perdiccas, the Chalcidians even abandoned their small settlements on the coast, and gathered at Olynthus, which they

formed into a strong city. Aid was also sent from
Corinth to support the rebellion. The Athenians on
their part reinforced their former expedition, which
had abandoned the hope of reducing Potidæa, and was
occupied with Macedonia. A peace was made with
Perdiccas—who had no sooner got the Athenian army
out of his country than he reverted to his old position,
and sent two hundred horse to aid the rebels—and
the whole force moved upon Potidæa. A successful
engagement enabled them to drive the Potidæans
and Corinthians into the walls of the city, which they
at once cut off from the mainland. With the aid of
subsequent reinforcements they cut off the other
side also, towards the isthmus, and the ships prevented any communication from the sea. Though
Athens and Corinth were nominally at peace, the
Athenians were now blockading a Corinthian garrison in a Corinthian city!

The excitement at Corinth was great; it was unfortunate for the peace of Hellas that, of all the
cities of the confederacy, it was Corinth which
Athens had injured. For a long time past the city
had cherished a deadly hatred of her neighbour, and
in energy and capacity she was quite the leading
city of Peloponnesus. Ægina and Megara had felt
the weight of Athenian oppression, but they had
taken no active steps to obtain redress, and might
have taken none, had not the Corinthians set the
example.

They invited the injured allies to meet at Sparta
and inveighed against the Athenians, declaring that
they had broken the treaty by their proceedings at

Corcyra and Potidæa. They called on the Spartans
to rescue the cities of the confederacy which looked
to them for help. The Spartans had no special reason for going to war. Athens had in no way injured
them, nor shewn the least inclination to attack the
Peloponnesus. But it was impossible to turn a deaf
ear to the complaints of so important a city as
Corinth. They summoned any other allies, who had
similar charges to make, and calling their own ordinary assembly bade them speak before it. Among
others, the Megarians came forward, declaring that
they had been excluded from dealing in the Athenian
markets, contrary to the provisions of the Thirty
Years' Peace. The Æginetans did not venture to
send envoys openly to the conference, but in secret
they complained bitterly of their lost independence.
Others followed with the story of their wrongs,
and at last the Corinthians, trusting to the indignation which these tales of oppression had excited,
came forward. In the speech which Thucydides
has put into their mouths on this occasion, they
treat the question from a general point of view.
They reproach the Spartans with their inactivity,
which allowed the Athenians to enslave one Grecian community after another. The crimes of the
aggressor were no secret, yet no measures had been
taken to counteract them. Sparta trusted that her
reputation alone would save her allies, but Athens
was active and restless. "Of all the Hellenes,
Lacedæmonians, you are the only people, who never
do anything. Instead of attacking your enemy, you
wait to be attacked." The Corinthians then drew

an elaborate parallel between the Spartan and Athenian character, a comparison which is one of the most famous passages in the history of Thucydides, bringing before us in the clearest light the nature of the two forces which were about to meet in deadly conflict:

"You have never considered what manner of men are these Athenians with whom you will have to fight, and how utterly unlike yourselves. They are revolutionary, equally quick in the conception and in the execution of every new plan; while you are conservative—careful only to keep what you have, originating nothing, and not acting even when action is most necessary. They are bold beyond their strength; they run risks which prudence would condemn; and in the midst of misfortune they are full of hope. Whereas it is your nature, though strong, to act feebly; when your plans are most prudent, to distrust them; and when calamities come upon you, to think that you will never be delivered from them. They are impetuous, and you are dilatory; they are always abroad and you are always at home. For they hope to gain something by leaving their homes; but you are afraid that any new enterprise may imperil what you have already. When conquerors, they pursue their victory to the utmost; when defeated, they fall back the least. Their bodies they devote to their country as though they belonged to other men; their true self is their mind, which is most truly their own when employed in her service. When they do not carry out an intention which they have formed, they seem to have sustained a personal bereavement; when an enterprise succeeds, they have gained a mere instalment of what is to come; but if they fail, they at once conceive new hopes and so fill up the void. With them alone to hope is to have, for they lose not a moment in the execution of an idea. This is the life-long task, full of danger and toil, which they are always imposing upon themselves. None enjoy their good things less because they are always seeking for more. To do their duty is their only holiday, and they deem the quiet of inaction to be as disagreeable as the most tiresome business. If a man should say of them, in a word, that they were born neither to have peace themselves, nor to allow peace to other men, he would simply speak the truth." *

In the face of such an enemy delay was fatal. Let the Spartans at last shake off their lethargy, and go with the stream. They must invade Attica and relieve Potidæa as they were pledged to do. They could not expect loyalty from their allies, unless they came to their help in a time of trouble.

Some Athenian envoys who happened to be at Sparta at the time, on other business, were allowed to reply to the charges of aggression which the Corinthians had made against their city. Their empire, they said, was the growth of circumstances; it was administered wisely, as the Greeks would discover if the Lacedæmonians were placed in a similar position. The ruling power, whatever it was, was always disliked; the Lacedæmonians now en-

* Thuc., i., 70, Jowett.

joyed the good-will of Hellas, but they would lose it,
if they succeeded to the Athenian empire. Let the
matters in dispute be settled by arbitration; war was
a calamity of which the end could not be foreseen,
and all cities should shrink from bringing it upon
Hellas. When the allies had stated their case, the
Spartans bade them retire, and discussed the question among themselves. There was a difference of
opinion. King Archidamus was strongly opposed
to immediate war; he considered that the confederacy
in its present condition was no match for the Athenians. For nearly fifty years Sparta had remained
stationary, while Athens had pressed forward with
rapid strides. Delay was necessary to restore the
balance. Let them send and remonstrate with the
Athenians, and while negotiations went forward, put
themselves in a state of preparation. Such a course
was wise and not unworthy of Sparta. On the other
hand, the ephor Sthenelaidas, who came forward last
of all, was for immediate and open war. The alliance
must be kept together; and the oppressor must be
resisted, not by words but by deeds. The honour
of Sparta demanded prompt and immediate action.
The question was then put to the assembly, whether
or not the Athenians had broken the treaty. It was
the custom at Lacedæmon to decide by acclamation
and not by votes, but on this occasion, under the
pretence that he could not distinguish which was the
louder cry, Sthenelaidas divided the assembly by
directing those who said " Aye " to go to one side,
and those who said " No " to the other. The result
was thus placed beyond doubt. A large majority

voted that the treaty had been broken. The decision was at once communicated to the allies, but
before further steps were taken it was resolved to
summon a general meeting of the confederacy at
Sparta, and ask the allies to vote separately for
peace or war.

Meanwhile the reaction against Pericles at Athens
was becoming more and more powerful. He had
never been without enemies, but they had been
powerless so long as the people were with him, and
the people were with him as long as he courted their
favour. But when he began to control them and resist their will, another feeling prevailed. Pericles was
no longer their idol; they looked round for other leaders who would go further on the path which he seemed
to have deserted. For Pericles had roused a spirit
which he could not quell, without resorting to extreme
measures. This "demos," on which he had risen
to power, was insatiable; and when its demands were
refused, it was ready to turn upon the man who had
hitherto ruled it. Another class of enemies consisted of the old aristocratical party, which viewed
the entire policy of Pericles with dislike, and had
opposed it as long as opposition was possible, first
under Cimon, and afterwards under Thucydides.
Between the two sections, the demos and the aristocrats, there was of course no real sympathy; yet
they were now drawn together by common opposition to Pericles. Without the demos the aristocrats
were powerless; with it they might at least get
rid of the man who had so long kept them in subjection. In this coalition they were also joined by

those who were offended at the presence of Anaxagoras and Aspasia at Athens. Thus, by a momentary
combination of parties, a power was brought to bear
upon Pericles which rendered his position insecure.
He found first his friends, and then himself exposed
to attacks; and in more than one instance the vote
was given against him.

The first attack was made against Pheidias. The
great sculptor had been the adviser of Pericles in
erecting the stately buildings which adorned Athens.
Pheidias therefore was peculiarly obnoxious to those
who had opposed the expenditure of public money
on these objects. If the people could be induced to
condemn him it would be an indication that they
sympathised with the party which had endeavoured
to check this expenditure. The first charge was one
of embezzlement. Some years previously Pheidias
had constructed the famous statue of Athena of ivory
and gold. He was accused of keeping back part of the
materials assigned to him for the purpose by the people. This accusation he was able to repel. On the
advice of Pericles the statue had been so constructed
that the gold and ivory could be removed without in-
jury to the work. It was now taken off and weighed
and no deficiency was discovered. Such evidence was
conclusive, and Pheidias was triumphantly acquitted.
The accusers were foiled, but they were not silenced.
The public mind had already been disquieted by
Diopeithes and his friends on the subject of religion;
a charge of impiety might succeed where the charge
of embezzlement had failed. It was found out that
in the figures which Pheidias had depicted on the

shield of Athena, he had inserted portraits of himself and Pericles. This was interpreted to be an offence against the goddess. Pheidias was at once thrown into prison, and all the efforts of Pericles to procure his release were in vain. Before the day of trial arrived he was found dead. There was a strong suspicion that he had been poisoned, but the truth was never known. Some even suggested that Pericles himself had made away with the man who had been the instrument of his own peculation. Such was the end to which party strife brought the great artist who had made Athens the wonder of the world.*

Another object of attack was Anaxagoras. Of all his associates, this man seems to have exercised the most influence on Pericles. He was a native of Clazomenæ, and belonged to the Ionian school of philosophers. Like Thales of Miletus and Heraclitus of Ephesus, he endeavoured to find a cause for physical phenomena, but, unlike them, he did not seek the cause in any single physical element, but in a guiding and uniting force. This force was Mind or Intellect; " all things were together in confusion, and were brought into order by Intellect," was his maxim. On this principle Anaxagoras sought to eliminate chance from everything, and to substitute natural causes for supernatural. Plutarch tells an amusing story of the different explanations given of a supposed portent by Anaxagoras and his contemporary Lampon, the great soothsayer of the age. A ram with one horn was brought to

---

* This is the story repeated by Plutarch. In another version we are told that Pheidias was acquitted and retired to Elis.

ATHENA PARTHENOS.

The Varvakeion Statuette. (Front view.)

(Bœtticher.)

Pericles. When Lampon saw it, he at once interpreted the meaning of the malformation. As the ram had one horn, instead of two, so would the two parties which now divided the state disappear, and the whole power pass over into the hands of Pericles. But Anaxagoras had the ram's head opened, and shewed that the single horn was the result of natural causes. For the moment the philosopher seemed to have triumphed over the soothsayer, but the subsequent fall of Thucydides created a reaction in favour of Lampon. A man whose mind was ever directed to the search for natural causes was of course raised above many of the fears and superstitions of his time: Among the multitudes of prophets, who swarmed in Greece, he could pursue a calm and even path. From Anaxagoras Pericles is said to have learned much of the stately reserve which was so remarkable a trait in his character. From him also he learned to differ from the common opinion of his day, which was ever on the watch for portents and omens, and was content to be guided in the most important affairs of life by the flight of birds or the monstrous births of animals.

Such a philosophy of necessity came into collision with the cherished religious beliefs of the Greeks. There was no room in it for that gay variety of powers, with which a lively imagination had peopled earth and sea and sky. The sun, in the eyes of the Greeks, was a holy god, a living personal deity, who traversed the heaven daily from east to west in his bright chariot. Anaxagoras openly taught that the sun and stars were nothing more than red-hot stones.

13

To those who held the old beliefs, and entered heart
and soul into all the various forms of worship with
which the old gods were celebrated, such tenets were
" flat blasphemy," and the author was a dangerous
man.

On these grounds Diopeithes, a friend of the or-
thodox Nicias, so well known to us from the pages
of Thucydides, brought forward a proposal that
those, who disbelieved in deities, and passed their
time in discussing the nature of the heavenly
bodies, should be impeached before the assembly.
This general proposition was accepted—but whether
Anaxagoras was attacked personally by Diopeithes
is not known.   A late writer informs us that Cleon
brought an accusation against him for impiety;
or, as others said, Thucydides, who had returned
from his ostracism, attacked him for treachery.
Whatever the precise nature of the charge and the
process, it is pretty certain that Anaxagoras was
condemned.   He was thrown into prison.   In a
short time he either escaped or was allowed to go
free, and a few years later he died an old man at
Lampsacus.

The ferocity of party strife was not satisfied with
attacking two of the most intimate friends of
Pericles.   A still more savage blow was aimed at
one with whom his domestic happiness was inseparably connected.   Aspasia of Miletus belonged
to the class of women whom the Greeks called
Hetæræ, or companions.   We can only describe
them as adventurers, who attached themselves to
any man willing to spend money upon them.

ATHENA PARTHENOS.

The Varvakeion Statuette. (Side view.)

(*Boetticher.*)

Such relations were openly tolerated in Greece—
where society was more masculine than among
us,—but they were not approved. No man could
associate with a "companion" without some loss
of reputation; no thoughtful citizen for a moment
confounded the marriage relation with such con-
nexions. There was no greater outrage on social
feeling than to bring the members of an Athenian
family into the society of "companions." For the
hetæræ themselves we must allow that the tolerance
with which they were regarded saved them from the
degradation into which the outcast of modern society is plunged. Whatever the misery of their
lives might be, they were not hunted or starved
into suicide, and as slaves, for most of them were
slaves, they were too valuable to be murdered or
injured with impunity. For such women it was
necessary to be attractive. They had recourse to
the various feminine arts in order to beautify their
persons, and some at least sought to improve their
minds and conversation. In this last respect more
especially they had the advantage of the Greek
matrons, who knew nothing of society, and were
uninstructed in anything beyond the duties of the
house.

Aspasia then was a "companion," but she was the
first of her class. Ancient writers agree about her
beauty and her intellect. Her circle was the first
circle in Athens. How and when she attracted
Pericles we do not know; we cannot say whether
she drew him from his wife, or whether the short
and somewhat unhappy years of his married life

were ended before he made her acquaintance. What is certain is that he entered into a close relationship with her, which continued for the rest of his days. That she ever became his wife, as recent writers assume, is not asserted by any ancient author of credit ; her son was certainly regarded as illegitimate, and the attacks of her enemies imply that she held a position which was at the best dubious. But whatever her position, the bond which united her with Pericles was very close. The two lived together in perfect harmony ; their tastes and sympathies agreed. In the company of this cultivated woman Pericles found the relaxation which he never so much as sought in ordinary society. Once, and once only, as Plutarch relates, was the great statesman present at an evening entertainment, and even then he went away early. But he never left his house to go to his daily duties without taking a tender leave of Aspasia.

The comedians had long made merry with the character of Aspasia. The worst charges were brought against her. That married Athenian women visited her salon—if we may use the term—was a proof that she corrupted women as well as men. That Anaxagoras and Socrates were seen in her company was a proof that she sympathised with godless and atheistical sophists. Was it not she who in the past had brought on the Samian war, by persuading Pericles to aid Miletus? Was it not she who had procured the Megarian decree, to revenge the loss of two of her shameless women? And now Hermippus, a comedian whose power lay in the coarseness of his satire, weary perhaps of his own

ASPASIA.
From a Bust Found near Civita-Vecchia.
(*Baumeister's "Denkmäler des Klassischen Altertums."*)

abuse, or believing that the ground was well prepared, determined to bring her to trial. In this case
also the charge was impiety, but it was united with a
more odious accusation. Aspasia was represented
to the court as an atheist and a procuress. Her
position as an alien did not give her the right of
appearing at the trial; and she might confidently
leave her cause in the hands of Pericles. He came
forward in person to defend her. For the first time
the Athenians saw their great statesman overcome
with emotion, and pleading as men plead for their
lives, with the entreaties and tears which Greek
manners permitted in a court of law. The judges
were stirred by such an exhibition, and Aspasia was
acquitted.

The attack was no doubt made in the interests of
a party, but it probably commanded the sympathy
of a great many honest citizens. Such a character
as Aspasia was out of place in a Greek community,
and the more out of place, as the relation between
her and Pericles approached the nature of lawful
union. There was no room at Athens for women
educated to live the life which Aspasia lived in
the house of Pericles; and there could be no room,
until the whole structure of society was altered.
Greek society was emphatically a society of men;
as men they met in the assembly or the market-
place; as men they raced, or talked, or fought.
Their homes were isolated; and family life came
into little or no relation with social life. No doubt
Greek society suffered by the absence of women;
and the Greek nature would have been improved

had their women been better educated.   There are
writers who would have us believe that Pericles endeavoured by means of Aspasia to give Greek women
an insight into their true position.   Without admitting this, we may allow that he was conscious of a
great defect in Athenian life.   But it is easier to
detect an evil than to devise a remedy.   Even
Lycurgus was baffled when he attempted to reform
the Spartan women !

The acquittal of Aspasia was merely a concession
to the personal influence of Pericles.   His enemies
were defeated, but the victory did not strengthen
his position.   On the contrary, he had been compelled to appear in open court to defend the mistress of his household from charges which could not
even be breathed against an honest woman.   His
behaviour at the trial had made it clear that he was
sensible to the attacks made upon him, and this
was an additional reason for continuing them.   His
opponents now ventured to bring a direct charge
against the statesman himself.   Dracontides proposed in the assembly that Pericles should give,
before the Fifty Prytanes, an account of his expenditure of the public money, and that in this case
the judges should give their votes in the most
solemn manner on the altar.   The proposal was subsequently altered, and Pericles was to be brought
before a jury of fifteen hundred men, voting in the
usual way by dropping pebbles into an urn.

The proposal probably referred to some extraordinary payments of Pericles ; at least it is difficult
to understand how he could be called upon to give

an account of transactions which had been examined and passed by the financial officers at Athens. Such extraordinary payments were sometimes made for objects which it was not convenient to announce openly; they were in fact secret-service money. In 445 B.C. Pericles had paid away a sum of ten talents, and when required to account for it had merely replied that it was spent "on a necessary purpose." The answer was accepted in the days when he had the confidence of the people, but now a different temper prevailed. Was it so certain that the necessary purpose was a public purpose? In any case it would be difficult for Pericles to prove it. Secret-service money is secretly paid, and without acknowledgment. It is an expenditure in which absolute faith must be reposed in the honour of the man who makes it, and to call for the details of the payments is a breach of the conditions upon which they are made. But the opponents of Pericles had no scruples of this kind, and the people were in a mood in which Pericles could not trifle with them. It was necessary for him to find some answer to the charge or divert the attention of the Athenians into another path. Plutarch tells a story which at least puts the situation in a dramatic form. Pericles was discovered one day by Alcibiades in deep and anxious thought. Alcibiades enquired what was causing him so much trouble. He was thinking, he replied, how he could best render the Athenians an account of the public money he had spent. Would it not be better, rejoined Alcibiades, to think of a plan, by which you need not give them any account at all?

Such was the position of affairs external and internal at Athens in the years 435–431 B.C.   Among
their own allies the Athenians were an object of
dislike, and some were in open revolt.   Among
those of the Peloponnesians who had been brought
in contact with them they were regarded with
hatred; the Corinthians more especially were prepared to go to any extremity in order to bring
about a war between Athens and Sparta.   At the
same time Pericles was losing ground; it was greatly
to his advantage to distract the attention of the
people from the matters which now occupied them,
and to break up the coalition which had formed
against him.   A war with Sparta would accomplish
both these objects.   It would naturally fill the public mind, and it would divide the oligarchs who
clung to Sparta from that advanced section of the
demos who attacked Pericles because he would not
satisfy their demands.   In the next chapter we shall
see that at the last moment the Peloponnesian
confederacy hung back, and endeavoured to avoid
an open breach, while Pericles insisted that no concession whatever should be made.   The guilt of the
final outbreak lies decisively at his door.   Had the
Athenians refused to follow his lead, the war could
have been postponed, if it could not have been
averted.

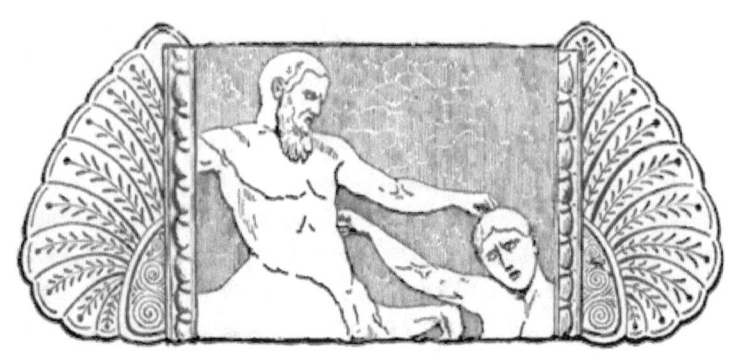

CHAPTER XIII.

THE OUTBREAK OF THE WAR.

Final congress at Sparta—Attempts to put Athens in the wrong—Negotiations between Athens and Sparta—Pericles is firm for war—Attack on Platæa by the Thebans—Preparations for war—Final attempts at negotiation—The invasion of Attica—Pericles' scheme of defence.

AFTER passing the vote in their own assembly that the treaty had been broken, the Lacedæmonians still delayed to enter upon active measures. They consulted the deity at Delphi, who replied that if they did their best in the war they would gain the day, and he would himself be on their side, invited or uninvited; but even this favourable reply did not lead to immediate action. Wishing to implicate the whole confedracy in their policy, they again summoned the allies to Sparta (p. 190), where the question of peace and war was put before them. Here, as everywhere, the Corinthians were most energetic; they did their utmost to excite the allies; and, when all had made their complaints, they came

forward and insisted that immediate war was necessary to put an end to the growing power of the
Athenians. There was every prospect of success.
On land the Peloponnesian confederacy had greater
numbers, superior skill and organization. The
Athenians, it was true, had money and ships in
abundance, but the allies could contribute or borrow
funds from Olympia and Delphi; and when they
had money, it would be easy to build ships and buy
up the foreign sailors who rowed in the Athenian
fleet. Or the allies of Athens might be induced to
revolt. At any rate, the risk must be run, for submission implied slavery. "The tyrant city, which
has been set up in Hellas, is a standing menace to all
alike; she rules over some of us already, and would
fain rule over others. Let us attack and subdue her
that we may ourselves have safety for the future, and
deliver the Hellenes whom she has enslaved. We
are not the aggressors; we have justice on our side,
and the god has promised his help." When all had
spoken, the Lacedæmonians put the question to each
ally—great and small,—and the majority were in
favour of war. But so slow and ill-prepared was the
confederacy; so unwilling, we may perhaps add, were
the Spartans themselves, or at least a large party
among them, to take any active measures—for no
wrong had been done to them by the Athenians—
that nearly a year passed before open hostilities
broke out. In the meantime, embassies went to and
fro between Sparta and Athens in the hope that
peace might still be maintained, or, if this were impossible, that there might at least be a definite cause

for war. For in all the quarrels of the Greeks, whether public or private, each side was at all times eager to prove that he was not the aggressor.

The Spartans were anxious by every means to put the Athenians in the wrong. First they called on them to banish the accursed of Athena—by which were meant the Alcmæonidæ, the great family with which Pericles was connected. Had the Athenians agreed to this demand, Pericles must have gone into exile, and the greatest opponent of Sparta and of peace would have been removed. But so far from yielding, the Athenians retorted by bidding the Spartans expel the " curse of Tænarus " (p. 70), and the " curse of Athena of the Brazen House " (p. 60). In a second demand the Athenians were asked to raise the siege of Potidæa and restore Ægina to independence. They could reply that the allied states of Sparta had already agreed to the principle that each confederacy should deal as it chose with its own allies; and the position of Ægina was precisely what it had been when the Thirty Years' Peace was concluded. Once more, the Spartans insisted that the decree which excluded the Megarians from trading in the markets of Athens and the Athenian empire, should be rescinded. To this the Athenians answered : first, that the Megarians had tilled the border-land between the two countries, and received Athenian slaves ; secondly, that there was no agreement in the terms of the peace stipulating that the Megarians should trade with Athens ; and that the Spartans were in the habit of expelling strangers from their own city. A final embassy came with a de-

mand which swept away these small differences in one
general stipulation : The Lacedæmonians, they said,
desire peace, "and peace there will be if you restore independence to the Hellenes, if not, there will be war."

This broad demand appealed to the sympathy of
Hellas. It enabled the Spartans to call on their confederacy for help, and supplied a common motive for
war. Allies might ask: Why should they go to war
for the interests of Megara, or Ægina? What was
the siege of Potidæa to them? But if the Athenians
refused to restore independence to the Hellenes, their
empire was placed in its most odious light, and the
danger threatened all alike. On the other hand, such
a request was calculated to strengthen the hands of
Pericles at Athens. He could now point out what
the design of Sparta really was. It might seem pre-
posterous to enter upon a great war merely to keep
the Megarians out of Athens, but now it was clear
that the existence of the empire was at stake. The
form in which the demand was thrown was even
worse than its substance. The Spartans were in
no position to dictate to Athens, and Athens could
not accept such orders without admitting the claim
of Sparta to act as a sovereign city. All the hatred
and suspicion which for years past Pericles had
been labouring to implant among the Athenians
against their great rivals would be called into new
activity by this sweeping demand.

Pericles at once availed himself of the situation,
and employed to the utmost his powers of eloquence
to induce the Athenians to be firm for war. He
pointed out that the Spartans enforced their de-

mands by the threat of arms; there was no talk of
arbitration. But in the treaty it was arranged that
any differences which arose were to be settled by
arbitration, each side in the meanwhile retaining
what it possessed. The Megarian decree was a
mere pretext, veiling further claims, and, even if it
were not, concession was impossible. No matter
how small the point at issue, the principle involved
was the existence of Athens. For "any claim, the
smallest as well as the greatest, imposed on a neighbour and an equal, where there has been no legal
award, can mean nothing but slavery." Such arguments were sufficient to prevail with his audience;
but they could hardly have prevailed with Pericles
himself, if he had not wished to make peace impossible. The Spartans had declared that there would
be no war, if the Megarian decree were cancelled;
was it not worth while to try the experiment?
Fourteen years before, Pericles had purchased peace
by enormous concessions to Sparta, without in the
least injuring the position of Athens in the Delian
confederacy. Why was concession so fatal now?
There was, as Pericles well knew, a powerful peace
party at Sparta. Had he acted in concert with
Archidamus, his own personal friend, in this matter,
a better feeling might have prevailed between the
two cities. As it is, we see the greatest statesman
of the day putting logic in the place of policy; and
if he does not drive his nation into war with the
rude brutality of a Spartan ephor, the reason is that
as an Athenian he has learnt the art of calling in
general principles to support his views.

Pericles gave the Athenians ground for hoping that they would be successful in the war. And here again his love of a principle misled him. The wealth of Athens was doubtless an enormous advantage, which enabled her to keep control of the sea; and so long as she was mistress of the sea, the Spartan confederacy could not touch her. The walls of Athens were impregnable; whatever damage the Peloponnesians might do to Attica, they could not enter the city or break the communication with the Peiræus. But on the other hand ships will wear out, and money is quickly spent. A very few years of war served to empty the Athenian treasury, and she was thrown back on her yearly income, no less than the Spartans and their allies. It is true that she received the contributions of her subjects, but these could not be collected without a force; and there was the constant fear that they might revolt. From these defects the Peloponnesians were free. Their soldiers were citizens who fought without pay; if there was any want of action, it was not for want of money, but for want of leisure. Their operations were limited, no doubt, but they were effective as far as they went. Pericles himself was driven to confess that on land the Athenians could not risk an engagement with the Peloponnesians. The indomitable spirit of the citizen-soldier is something which money cannot buy, and it was with this spirit that Pericles was going to war. He might destroy the Corinthian navy, but what hope had he of ever conquering the Bœotian and Spartan infantry? His treasures would be exhausted long

HEAVY-ARMED WARRIOR.
Bronze from Dodona.
(*Baumeister.*)

before the spirit of his enemies was broken. At the best, such a war as that which he contemplated would go on indefinitely, each side being superior to the other on its own element, but neither able to inflict irreparable damage. Only when one or other struck out a new line or committed a fatal mistake, could the end come.

The Athenians were persuaded by Pericles, and answered the Laconian envoys as he wished. They would do nothing upon compulsion, but were ready to settle the differences by arbitration upon fair terms according to the treaty. The ambassadors returned ; the treaty was practically suspended ; but neither party would commence hostilities.

Suddenly, in an unexpected quarter, a decisive step was taken. The Thebans were in no way concerned in the dispute which had brought about the suspension of the treaty, but they were allies of the Spartans, and for three-quarters of a century they had cherished a deep-seated hatred of the Athenians. About the time when the Pisistratidæ were expelled from Athens, the inhabitants of Platæa, a city on the northern slopes of Cithæron, had applied to Cleomenes, the king of Sparta, for protection against Thebes. Afraid of the aggression of their neighbour —Thebes is six or seven miles to the north of Platæa, beyond the Asopus—they wished to break loose from the Bœotian confederation, of which Thebes was now the head, and attach themselves to Sparta. But Cleomenes pointed out that his city lay at a great distance from Platæa ; before assistance could arrive from the Peloponnesians, the Thebans

could lay waste the Platæan territory and enslave
the city twice over. He recommended the Platæans to apply to Athens, their next neighbour,
who would be able to protect them. The Platæans
acted on this advice, and, finding a ready response,
placed themselves under Athenian protection. A
quarrel with Thebes was the immediate result, and
though the Corinthians, who were called in to decide
the matter, decided that Platæa should choose her
own alliance, the Thebans never acquiesced in the
arrangement. They looked on Platæa as a part of
Bœotia, and only waited for an opportunity to assert
their claim.

Such an opportunity seemed now to have arrived.
At the beginning of spring, in the year 431 B.C.,
a force of over three hundred Thebans, under the command of two of the Bœotarchs, as the officers of the
Bœotian confederacy were called, entered Platæa by
night. No watch had been set, for as yet war had
not been openly proclaimed, and the Platæans had
no reason to apprehend an attack. But the Thebans
did not stand on ceremony, and here, as was always
the case in Greece, treachery had been at work.
There was a party in Platæa which hoped, by detaching the city from Athens, to get the chief power
into their own hands. With this view they negoti-
ated with an eminent Theban for the despatch of
the force, and, when it arrived, they opened the
gates and received it into the city. Their desire
was to cut down their enemies at once, and so clear
the ground for their own advancement; but the
Thebans took a more conciliatory course. Ground-

ing their arms in the market-place of the city, they called on those who wished to return to the ancient constitution of Bœotia to join them, and become their allies. It was not in the interests of a party, but in the interests of Bœotia, that they wished to recover Platæa.

The delay was fatal. At the first entrance of the Thebans, in the darkness of night, the Platæans were panic-stricken; they could form no estimate of the number of the enemy, and, in the belief that they were much more numerous than they really were, they listened to their proposals. By degrees they discovered that the force was not overwhelming, and as the Platæan people were strongly attached to Athens, they resolved to attack the invaders, and drive them out. They reflected that the Thebans were strangers in the city, of which every street, house, and gateway was familiar to themselves. It was easy to surprise them, if the attack was made in the dark. The plan was carried out. Just before daybreak a furious onset was made, and though for a short time the Thebans were able to resist, they were soon driven in confusion along the streets, seeking their way out of the city. All the gates save that by which they entered were closed; the Platæans met them at every turn. Even the women from the house-tops threw tiles and stones upon them, and when day returned, the force which had entered so easily, was annihilated; one hundred and eighty Thebans, including the leader, were taken captive; of the rest, the majority had been killed.

It had been arranged that the main body of the Theban army should march out in support of the attack. But a heavy rain had caused the Asopus to rise in the night, and it could not now be crossed without difficulty. Before the Thebans reached the Platæan territory, they were met with the news of the disaster which had befallen their countrymen. They pressed on, hoping to seize men and property as a compensation for their own citizens, who were in the hands of the Platæans; the Platæans, however, warned them by a herald that, if any damage were done to their property, the Theban captives would be put to death; if they retired, the captives would be given up. On this the Thebans went back into their own country.

The Platæans at once set about bringing in their property from the fields, and, as soon as all was secured, they slew the whole of their prisoners. News of the attack had been at once conveyed to Athens, and a second messenger had reported the capture of the Thebans. The Athenians at once arrested all the Bœotians who happened to be in Attica, and despatched an envoy to Platæa, requesting that the prisoners should be kept for further instructions. The request unhappily came too late. The prisoners were already dead when the envoy arrived, and the Platæans were busy preparing their city against further attacks.

Such was the first act in the great drama. It forms a striking instance of the insecurity of Greek life, and the furious passions to which this insecurity naturally gave rise. In Platæa there is a party of

traitors, waiting for an opportunity to cut the throats
of their opponents; the Thebans attack a city secured by treaty, without waiting for any formal
declaration of war; the Platæans, in spite of the
promise by which the Thebans were induced to
retire, put all the captives to death. The question
was indeed debated whether the promise was or was
not confirmed by an oath. Their cruelty and perfidy
the Platæans could not deny, but they resented the
charge of perjury; a refinement which merely proves
the superstition and sophistry in which the Greeks
of the time were sunk. A hundred years had still
to pass; Platæa had twice to be levelled to the
ground before this neighbourly quarrel was finally
settled by the utter destruction of Thebes at the
hands of Alexander.

The Thirty Years' Truce had now been openly
broken. Had the Platæans preserved their prisoners
alive, the Thebans might have been brought to
terms; Sparta might have disowned the action of
her ally in violating the treaty. But the murder of
one hundred and eighty Thebans made it impossible
to draw back. On both sides preparations were made
for immediate war. The enthusiasm was great,—the
greater because it was intended that the struggle
should be final. The Peloponnesians, aware of their
deficiency on sea, requested their allies in Italy and
Sicily to build additional ships and contribute money;
in their ambition they dreamed of a navy of five
hundred vessels! The Athenians sent to their allies
in the Ionian Sea, Corcyra, Acarnania, and Zacynthus, with whose assistance they hoped to enclose the

Peloponnesus and cut off all communication with the
west.   There were doubtless many who hailed the
outbreak as a relief from an intolerable tension ; many
more who, from mere ignorance and love of change,
were weary of peace.   " The youth of Peloponnesus
and the youth of Athens were numerous, and neither
of them had ever seen war." Prophecies and oracles
passed from mouth to mouth, and the ingenuity of
diviners was tasked to the utmost.   Every uncommon phenomenon of nature was noticed and recorded.   The Delians announced that their sacred
island had been " shaken " for the first time in the
memory of man.

Whatever the faults of the Peloponnesian confederacy, it seems to have answered to the ideas
which the Greeks formed of federation.   The allies
had the right of making themselves heard at Sparta,
they were not harassed by constant requisitions ;
and though Pericles asserts that Sparta insisted on a
form of government among her allies which was
suitable to her own interests, it is difficult up to this
time to produce an instance of any interference on
her part with the politics of her allies.   She had of
course reduced Laconia and Messenia to submission,
but this was accepted by the rest of Greece with the
same acquiescence as the union of Attica, or the
federation of Bœotia.   These were changes which,
whether the result of just or unjust dealing, were
regarded as final.   But Athens was a conquering
state, engaged at the moment in consolidating an
empire, and exposed to the bitterness now present
in the hearts of men who were conscious of lost in-

dependence. Some longed to be delivered from her control; others were afraid of falling under it.

The Athenians had taken no very active part in the incident of Platæa; no additional complaint could be brought against them on this ground, except the arrest of the Bœotians in Attica, which was merely a measure of precaution. Sparta was still without any clear and well-defined *casus belli*, so far as she herself was concerned. But the spirit of war had been aroused, and even those who deeply regretted the outbreak of hostilities were compelled to go with the stream. Immediately after the affair at Platæa, the ephors of Sparta, who were practically the executive of the confederacy, sent round to the allies bidding them furnish troops equipped for a foreign expedition; and at the time appointed, a little before midsummer, the various states met at the Isthmus of Corinth, each with two-thirds of her whole force, for the invasion of Attica. Each contingent was commanded by its own generals, but the whole expedition was under the command of Archidamus, king of Lacedæmon.

Archidamus, as we have seen, had attempted to dissuade the confederacy from open war; even now he cherished the hope that the last and irrevocable step might be avoided. He impressed his army with the necessity of caution in attacking so powerful an enemy, who might at the last moment be stung into desperate resistance; and even despatched a Spartan envoy to Athens, in the hope that some concession might yet be made. But the Athenians were resolute. The envoy was not even admitted

into the city, for Pericles had induced the people to
refuse to listen to any overtures, so long as the
Lacedæmonians were in the field. He was sent
away without a hearing, and told that he must cross
the frontier before sunset; if the Lacedæmonians
wished to negotiate with the Athenians, they must
disband their army and go home. When he arrived
at the frontier, and was about to take leave of the
escort which had accompanied him, the envoy, impressed with the greatness of the struggle which was
now inevitable, uttered these words of melancholy
prophecy : " This day will be to the Hellenes the beginning of great calamities." On learning that no
concessions would be made, Archidamus gave the
final order and prepared to enter Attica.

Meanwhile Pericles had taken measures for the
safety of the Athenians. He was well aware that
he could not meet the Peloponnesians in the field,
or prevent them from laying waste as much of
Attica as they chose. He must place his city in a
state of siege, and concentrate Attica in Athens.
Within the walls of the city, and Peiræus, and the
long walls which connected the two, the whole population of the country could be secured; and the
damage which might be done to the country would
be a trifling matter so long as the city retained her
ships, her money, and her allies.

His authority prevailed; the country people left
their pleasant homes, and cultivated farms, and
came to Athens with their wives and children, their
household goods, and even the woodwork of their
houses, which in Attica was far more valuable than

stone or brick. But the removal was not accomplished without much discomfort and vexation.
Many families had lived in the country for generations; the town and town life was quite strange to
them; they were leaving the tombs of their race, the
temples where they worshipped. And when they
arrived in the city, there were no houses to receive
them. They had to obtain such shelter as they
could in vacant spaces, or temples and shrines, or
the turrets of the walls. Afterwards they spread
down the long walls, and into Peiræus, but for a
time the sudden influx of so large a population
caused the greatest disorder. The sanitary conditions created by the change must have been little
less than revolting. That Pericles should have contemplated the removal of such numbers into the
city without making due provision for them was of
course a gross oversight,—an oversight of which no
shrewd practical man would ever have been guilty.
He could discuss physical phenomena with Anaxagoras, and arrange with Pheidias and Ictinus for
the construction of beautiful buildings, but the
prosaic details of life were forgotten. The day of
vengeance was not long in coming.

At the same time that he called on the Athenians
to make this great sacrifice, he cheered them with
hopes of victory. Still insisting on his old maxim
that war was mainly an affair of money, he pointed
to the large revenues and accumulations at the disposal of the Athenian state. From the allies the
income was 600 talents (£120,000) a year; in the
treasury of the Acropolis there was a reserve of 6,000

talents of coined money (£1,200,000). The offerings and sacred vessels and the like were worth 500 talents more (£100,000), and in a great extremity the gold, 40 talents in weight, could be taken from the statue of Athena, and converted into money (£100,000 or more). Sacred as many of these objects were, it was proper to use them in self-defence on the understanding that they would be replaced at a future time. Then he passed in review the forces of Athens. Her heavy-armed soldiers amounted to 13,000, besides the 16,000 engaged in garrison duty at Athens or in the various fortresses of Attica. The cavalry numbered 1,200, including mounted archers; of foot archers there were 1,800; the triremes were no fewer than 300. Such an array of forces was imposing, and Pericles left it for others to point out that the heavy-armed soldiers were of little use, if they could not be put in the field, while the constant desolation of Attica by the Peloponnesians must inevitably impoverish the class from which the trierarchs, so necessary for the equipment of the fleet, were taken. Nor did he make it clear how Athens, even if she obtained the most brilliant victories by sea, could ever keep a hold on the Peloponnesus. That was impossible without a large army of soldiers, strong enough to occupy a number of fortresses in Laconia and Elis. If the Spartans were in perpetual fear of the Helots, whom they had held in subjection for two centuries, what would have been the position of the Athenians with rebellious Spartans round them? In their dreams of empire they never spoke of restoring Messenia to independence. Yet such a restoration, and perhaps the entire extirpation of the whole Spartan race, would have been the only conditions on which Athens could have ruled the Peloponnesus. Nevertheless, the Athenians were full of spirit, and set about preparing a fleet of one hundred ships, with which to sail round the Peloponnesus, and make reprisals for any damage which might be inflicted on Attica.

GREEK WARRIOR.

CHAPTER XIV.

FIRST YEAR OF THE WAR—THE FUNERAL SPEECH.

First invasion of Attica—Archidamus at Œnoe
and Acharnæ—The Athenians remain in their
walls—A fleet sent round the Peloponnesus and
to the Euripus—The Athenians at Ægina and
Megara—Alliance with Sitalces—Public funeral
at Athens—Speech of Pericles.

IXTY-THREE days had now elapsed
since the Thebans entered Platæa.
Even Archidamus could delay no
longer. Leaving the Isthmus, he
led his forces over Mount Geraneia
into the territory of Megara, where two routes
lay before him: he might turn to the right, and
pursue the coast road to Eleusis; or he might
continue his march in a north-easterly direction
till he reached the confines of Bœotia, and then
strike into the direct road which connects Thebes
and Athens. He chose the second, and when we
next hear of him, he is besieging Œnoe, the fortress
which secured the communication of Athens with
Platæa. In taking this course he may have acted
on the advice of his Bœotian allies, for, if this for-

tress were in his hands, the Thebans would not only be able to pass in and out of Attica as they pleased, but Athens would be prevented from coming to the aid of Platæa. At the same time he would open a more easy and convenient road between the northern and southern halves of the Peloponnesian alliance, than the usual route by Ægosthena and Creusis.

The fortresses which commanded the various passes into Attica were held by garrisons formed chiefly of young men in the earliest years of military service. Of the fortifications of Œnoe we know nothing, but, whatever they were, they were sufficient with the natural strength of the place to enable such a garrison to bid defiance to the whole strength of the Peloponnesian army. After a waste of time, which brought on him the suspicion of intentional delay, Archidamus found himself compelled to leave the fortress in his rear. Descending down the valley of the Eleusinian Cephisus, he ravaged Eleusis and the Thriasian plain, from which he advanced over the ridge of hills to Acharnæ, the largest of the "demes" of Attica, and barely seven miles from the city. Here he encamped for some time, ravaging the immediate neighbourhood, but not entering the central plain.

In thus holding his hand while within sight of the city he sought to draw the Athenians out of the walls. He had hoped, though in vain, that they would come to meet him at Eleusis, and when he encamped within sight of Athens, in a town which furnished no fewer than 3,000 heavy-armed soldiers to the Athenian army, he confidently expected to

reap one of two advantages. Either he would
exasperate the enemy into fighting in the open
field; or the Acharnians, knowing that their own
property was destroyed, would be less eager to fight
for that of others, and Archidamus would be at
liberty to ravage Attica as he pleased.

His plans were not ill-laid, but they were frustrated by the strong personal ascendancy of Pericles.
So long as the Peloponnesian army lay at Eleusis,
the Athenians still cherished the hope that the rest
of the country would escape. Those who knew the
history of the past would call to mind that Cleomenes, the famous king of Sparta, had once led
a Peloponnesian army as far as Eleusis, only to see
it disperse. And many would remember that fourteen years before the present invasion Plistoanax
had reached the Thriasian plain, and then retired.
But when the invaders were actually in sight, and
the fairest possessions of Attica were at their mercy,
the situation seemed intolerable. The whole people,
and more especially the younger men, were eager to
go out and put a stop to it. The sight was new to
them, and they had little experience of the Spartan
soldiers' courage and skill. Men gathered in the
streets, abusing Pericles and his cowardly policy;
the excitement was increased by all kinds of oracles
invented or remembered for the occasion. The
Acharnians, as was natural, were in the last stage of
exasperation. They were a hardy race, the colliers
of Attica, who got their living by manufacturing
charcoal, "hearts of maple," stiff and sturdy as the
logs they burned. Forgetting all the counsels of

Pericles, the whole people called on him to do his duty as a general. The situation was difficult, but Pericles did not flinch. He seems at this time to have enjoyed an extraordinary degree of authority, and in virtue of this power he abstained from summoning any public meeting at which the popular excitement might find expression. He did what he could to soothe the prevailing irritation; and meanwhile sent out parties of horse to prevent the invaders from coming too close to the city walls. The Thessalians, true to their old alliance, had sent cavalry to the aid of Athens, and these with the native horse proved themselves at least a match for the Bœotians in the Peloponnesian army.

These measures seem to have had some effect upon Archidamus. It is at any rate remarkable that when he broke up from Acharnæ on finding that the Athenians would not come out against him, he directed his course to the north, and contented himself with ravaging the country between Mt. Parnes and Mt. Brilessus. Here his provisions began to fail, and he found it necessary to retire. Passing through the coast land near Oropus, to the north-east of Parnes, and wasting the country as he went, he entered Bœotia by the route past Tanagra. The invasion had lasted about five weeks.

The successful defence of Œnoe had shewn that the army of the Peloponnesus was powerless against an insignificant fortress. Athens, therefore, was absolutely safe behind her walls, and though the Athenians suffered severely by the invasion, Pericles found means in the course of the year to compensate

many of the sufferers. In spite of opposition he
held on his way. His plans for the war were still
accepted as the best, and in the conviction that
Athens, and not Attica, was the vulnerable point of
the state, a decree was passed that a thousand talents
should be set apart out of the reserve in the treasury, and a hundred of the best triremes selected
every year, with trierarchs appointed for each, to be
ready for use in case an attack was made on the
Peiræus. So earnest were the people in the matter,
that the proposal to use the money or ships for any
other purpose was made a capital offence. Measures
were also taken for securing the safety of the country from unexpected attack by establishing guards
on the frontiers.

While the Lacedæmonians were still in their
country the Athenians took steps to revenge themselves. A fleet of a hundred vessels was despatched
to ravage the shores of the Peloponnese. They
were joined by a contingent of fifty ships from
Corcyra, and a combined attack was made on
Methone, a fortress on the coast of Messenia, a little
to the south of Pylos (Navarino), which, in the days
of Tolmides, had been captured and again abandoned
by the Athenians. Had the attack succeeded, the
Athenians would have anticipated in some degree
the position which they obtained six years later by
the capture of Pylos. They would have established
a support in Messenia for any Helots who could find
an opportunity of joining them, and a convenient
station for the union of the contingents coming from
east and west. But the attempt failed. In this,

their very first landing on the shores of the Peloponnesus, they were confronted by a Spartan, whose
courage and genius were more than a match for the
plans of Pericles and the power of Athens—Brasidas,
the son of Tellis.   He happened to be on guard in
the neighbourhood—for the Spartans sent out parties of their citizens to keep watch on the out-lying
districts of their dominions,—and knowing the weakness of the place, he came to the rescue with a hundred men.   Without a moment's delay he broke
through the scattered troops of the Athenians, and
secured the town for Sparta.   Thus repulsed the
Athenian fleet sailed on to Elis, where it was joined
by a few ships from Naupactus.   Some successes
were gained at Pheia, near the mouth of the Alpheus,
but on the approach of the Elean army the Athenians re-embarked.   More important by far was the
conquest of Sollium, a Corinthian town near Leucas,
and the acquisition of the whole of the island of
Cephallenia for the alliance.   This success was
achieved without a single blow, and not long afterwards the fleet returned home.   No attempt appears
to have been made by the Peloponnesians to intercept the progress of the Athenians or to meet them
on the seas ; but after their return the Corinthians
ventured out as far as Astacus in Acarnania.   The
town had been captured by the Athenians, who had
expelled Evarchus the reigning tyrant, and added
it to their confederacy.   It now fell back into the
hands of Corinth, and Evarchus was restored to
his throne.   An attempt to recover Cephallenia
turned out a complete failure.

While thus engaged on the shores of the Peloponnesus, the Athenians were able to send a smaller
fleet into the Euripus, to cruise off Locris and keep
watch over the island of Eubœa. The expedition
was successful ; the Locrian coast was ravaged, the
town of Thronium was captured, and the Locrians
defeated in an attempt to relieve it. To secure their
good behaviour a number of hostages were taken,
and the island of Atalante, which had hitherto been
uninhabited, was fortified and held by an Athenian
garrison. By these measures any designs which the
Locrians or Phocians may have had upon Eubœa
were entirely frustrated.

These successes were accompanied by others nearer
home, from which the Athenians reaped a more definite and tangible advantage. Soon after the return
of the Peloponnesian army from Attica the Athenians crossed over to Ægina, and, on the plea that
the Æginetans had been the main cause of the war,
entirely expelled the inhabitants from the island. The
long quarrel between the cities was drawing to a close,
though unhappily even this severe punishment did
not fill up the measure of Athenian hatred. Most of
the Æginetans were received by the Lacedæmonians
and settled in the Thyreatis—the beautiful coastland on the western shore of the bay of Argos,
which so long formed a bone of contention between
that city and Sparta. From this point they continued to sail out and harass the Athenians, until
at last, in 424 B.C., a descent was made on the country and they were cut down to a man. After expelling the inhabitants from Ægina, the Athenians

divided the farms, houses, and other property in the island among their own citizens, who now occupied the island as colonists (cleruchs).

Later in the summer, Pericles led out the entire force of the city into the territory of Megara to ravage the country. The army was joined by the fleet, which had just returned from Western Greece, and by this union of forces, the largest force which Athens ever had in one place, was occupied in devastating the fields of an unresisting and insignificant adversary! The same display, though on a smaller scale, was repeated twice a year for the next seven years. The exasperation of Athens against Megara was extreme, even beyond the measure of neighbourly hatred in Greece. It was no doubt vexatious to find so small a state so obstinate in its attachment to the Peloponnesian cause; the more so as Megara had once been the friend of Athens. Her forts had been garrisoned by Athenian soldiers; her long walls had been built by Athenian citizens, even before Athens had long walls of her own. While Megara was the ally of Athens the route from the Peloponnesus to Attica was closed, and Pericles was not likely to forget that in the day of danger Megara had thrown Athens over and opened the Isthmus to Plistoanax. Indeed his feeling towards the Megarians amounted to a personal animosity. Not only had he refused to cancel the decree which excluded the Megarians from Athenian ports, even at the cost of a war with Sparta, but at his instigation a second decree was passed on the motion of Charinus, declaring truceless and eternal

war against Megara. Every Megarian found on
Athenian soil was to be put to death at once ; and
twice in every year the Athenian generals were compelled to invade the country. These savage measures were excused by historians on the plea that the
Megarians had murdered Anthemocritus, a herald
sent to them from Athens, while protected by the
sanctity of his office ; and explained by comedians as
the vengeance demanded by Aspasia for the loss
of three courtesans who had crossed the border!
From Megara, where no defence could be offered,
the army returned home with such spoil as the country afforded, and this, like the property of the Æginetans, was no doubt consumed in soothing the
irritation of the Athenians at their own losses and
privations.

In addition to these expeditions Athens had been
sustaining for the whole year the burden of the siege
of Potidæa, where no fewer than three thousand of
the citizen soldiers were permanently encamped,
besides a large additional force, subsequently despatched under the command of Phormio. The
invasion of Attica had not caused the Athenians to
withdraw a single man, and nevertheless, in spite of
strenuous exertions, the city itself held out, and not
one of the revolted Chalcidic towns returned to its
allegiance. In these circumstances it was tempting
to try what could be done by negotiation with the
princes of the Barbarian nations in the neighbourhood. Could they be induced to assist the Athenians
against their rebellious subjects? With this object a
citizen of Abdera, Nymphodorus by name, whose

sister Sitalces, the king of the Odrysian Thracians, had married, was appointed by the Athenians their representative at Abdera, and invited to Athens in order to negotiate an alliance with his brother-in-law. Sitalces was willing enough to avail himself of the support of the Athenians in extending and strengthening his kingdom; the Athenians were not less willing to obtain his alliance against Chalcidice. Their expectations were fulfilled. Nymphodorus not only brought about the desired alliance, but also set on foot a peace between Athens and Perdiccas, the king of Macedonia, a crafty and unscrupulous barbarian, without courage or honour, whose sole guide was the advantage of the moment. For some time past he had been at war with the Athenians, but now he joined Phormio, the Athenian general, in fighting against the Chalcidians. That the alliance with Sitalces might be the more lasting, the Athenians gratified the wish of Sadocus the son of Sitalces, by making him a citizen of their city. Further and more brilliant promises which Nymphodorus held out during his stay at Athens—that Sitalces would send forces to Chalcidice, and bring the war to an end—were only partially fulfilled.

So the year ended, the first year of the terrible conflict in which Pericles had involved his city. The Athenians had acquired some distant and uncertain allies; they had secured the shores of Euboea from attack; they had repulsed the Peloponnesian army at Œnoe; they had acquired Cephallenia for the alliance, and they had gained some successes at the mouth of the Corinthian gulf. On the other hand

the Peloponnesians had defeated the attack on Methone; they were in as good a position at the end
of the year as they had been at the beginning; and
they had desolated a great part of Attica.   We
can imagine with what bitterness the country people
revisited their ruined homes and desolate fields.
Their vexation was the greater when they reflected that the same thing would happen from year
to year without any end.   What was gained, they
asked, by such a sacrifice?   The empire must be
maintained, no doubt, but why force matters to such
an extremity with Sparta?   The two cities had
drawn together in old days; why should there not
be mutual concessions now?   Sparta had shewn a
great desire to avoid war; why should Athens insist
on it?

The custom of the Athenians furnished Pericles
with an opportunity of stating at length his view of
the issues which were really at stake.   The bones of
those who perished in the service of their country
were always brought home to be buried at the public expense, in the Ceramicus, or Potter's Field, the
most beautiful suburb of the city, and a day was appointed in the winter, when military operations were
over, for the funeral.   The strictness of Athenian
habits was relaxed on the occasion; the funeral procession was accompanied by anyone who chose,
whether citizen or stranger, and the female relatives
of the dead were present at the sepulchres to make
lamentation.   When the remains had been laid in
the earth some man " of known ability and high
reputation" was chosen by the city to pronounce an

oration over those who had fallen in her cause. In accordance with this custom Pericles was chosen to speak over those who were first buried in the war; and Thucydides has availed himself of the opportunity to put into his mouth a sketch of Athenian life and institutions, which the world accepts as the ideal description of democratic government.

He began with deprecating the custom which demanded a speech on such an occasion. Those who had acted nobly should only be honoured by noble acts—such as were the funeral rites paid by a grateful country. Their glory should not be risked upon the eloquence of one man, who might speak well or ill, and who would certainly be thought to say too much or too little. But such was the law, and he must obey it.

Then he spoke of those who in past days had been brought to their rest in the Ceramicus. Their ancestors had possessed the land from immemorial antiquity, handing it down from generation to generation unstained by foreign conquest, the home of freedom. Their fathers had beaten back the tide of foreign and Hellenic war, and after many a struggle had transmitted to their sons the great empire which they now enjoyed. And those who were assembled there, most of them men in the prime of life, had improved their inheritance and endowed the city with all that she needed to enable her to stand alone in peace or war. "Let me dwell," he continued, " on the principles of action by which we rose to power ; on the institutions and manners which have brought our empire to this pitch of greatness. Such thoughts are a fitting prelude to the praises of those who have died for Athens; and there is no one here, whether citizen or stranger, who will hear them without profit.

"Our institutions are not borrowed from those around us; they are our own, the creation of Athenian statesmen; an example, and not a copy. In the political language of the day we are called a democracy; and the name is true and not true. It is true, because the administration of our city is in the hands of the people; and there is one law for rich and poor; it is not true, because, above all states, we recognise the claims of excellence. In this sense we are an aristocracy; not of birth, for among us there is no privilege; not of wealth, for poverty is a bar to none; but of merit; a state in which every one who *can* benefit the city *may* do so without let or hindrance.

"Such is the freedom of our political life, and in society we are equally without constraint. Everyone does what he pleases, without suspicion or offence. There is nothing modish, nor exclusive, in our habits; we do not banish a man from our company because his ways are different from our own. But along with this unconstrained liberty there goes a spirit of reverence, which pervades every act of our public life; authority is maintained; the laws are obeyed, not from fear of punishment, but from principle; and of all ordinances the most sacred in our eyes are those which protect the injured, who cannot retaliate; and the unwritten laws, which, though enforced by no legal penalty, bring reproach to the transgressor.

"First, then, we have striven to be free, and
we seek to be happy.   We have provided ourselves,
in a greater degree than any other city, with festivals and public games, to be a rest and refreshment
after toil; in our own homes we are surrounded by ele-
gance and refinement, as a charm against melancholy;
and owing to the greatness of our city, to which the
produce of all the earth is brought, we are as familiar with the gifts of the most distant regions, as we
are with the fruits of Attica.

"In the same spirit we approach the severer duties
of the citizen's life.   Our resources are not a mystery
to be concealed from every eye, but anyone may
visit our city and learn from us what he can.   We do
not afflict ourselves with laborious training, and yet,
in the hour of trial, our courage does not fail.   Free
and light of heart, trusting to habit rather than law,
we are yet as ready for action as those who spend
their lives in anticipating danger and preparing to
meet it.   So much the greater is our gain.

"Once more: we dare to think as well as act; we
live for ourselves, while living for the state.   With
us a love of what is beautiful is consistent with
economy, and a man is a man, though he cultivates
his mind.   Yet we do not separate the citizen from the
statesman; when a man has no time to give to state
affairs, we do not merely say that he is minding his
own business, but we call him an unprofitable servant.
If we cannot always set a policy on foot, we can form
a good judgment about it, for we look on discussion
as the best preparation for action; our courage is
not due to ignorance, or stupidity, but we go into

..ger with our eyes open, and counting the cost. And yet our policy is not a mere calculation of self-interest. More than any other nation, we have drawn our friends to us by kindly actions, and we have assisted others, without hope of advantage, in the confidence of freedom. From such a city the Hellenic world may take a lesson. Of all men, the Athenian citizen is the most accomplished and versatile; his parts are many, and he is admirable in each. Of all cities, Athens alone is even greater than her fame. She needs no poet to sing her praises; every land and every sea can furnish proofs of her enterprise and success. Her enemies, when defeated, are not disgraced; her subjects confess that she is worthy to rule them.

"Such is the city for which these men have given their lives, whose obsequies we have met to celebrate. Her praises are theirs, for it is they, and such as they, who have made her what she is. What can be more glorious than such a fate as theirs, which, whether early or late, the first indication or the final seal of virtue, is the 'true assurance of a man.' Neither hope of the future, nor desire to redeem the past; neither wealth, nor poverty, checked them in their noble race. Their hearts were set on vengeance and honour, and when the final moment came, it was in the glory of victory, not in the terror of flight, that they fell.

"Let us, who remain, endeavour to follow their example, while praying that our days may be longer in the land. I will not stir your hearts by speaking of the blessings which are secured to those who defeat their country's enemies, for we have other and higher reasons for our devotion. Look round on this glorious city; think of her mighty empire. Let the love of her beauty sink into your souls, and when you contemplate her greatness, remember that it was by the daring deeds of her citizens, done in the cause of duty and honour, that she was raised to this glorious height. Even when their efforts failed, they remained faithful to the death, giving their lives, when nothing else was left to give. Their reward is worthy of them. Their glory shall never die; the whole wide world is their sepulchre; their epitaphs are written in the hearts of mankind; and wherever there is speech of noble deeds, their names are held in remembrance.

"To men who fall as they have fallen death is no evil. And therefore, while I sorrow with the parents of the dead, I will also remind them of the changes and chances of life, in which his lot is fortunate whose days, though short, are days of happiness and honour. I know that the lesson is hard to learn, especially for those who see others in the enjoyment of blessings which they have known and lost. Still I say: Be not broken-hearted, but endure. With some of you other children will take the place of the dead, filling the void at home, and making good the loss to the city. And those to whom this hope is denied may comfort themselves with the thought that their years are drawing to a close. The better part of life has been the longer part; and for the brief remainder they will enjoy the honour and reverence which are at once the solace and the glory of old age.

" For those of you who are the children or brothers of the dead an arduous struggle is in store. While men live they are but men ; but when they die their deeds become superhuman. What a task for you to emulate virtue, which is beyond the reach of malice and calumny !

" To the wives, who will henceforth live in widow-hood, I will speak, in one short sentence only, of womanly virtue. She is the best of women who is most truly a woman ; and her reputation is the high-est whose name is never in the mouths of men for good or evil.

"There is nothing more to be said, and what remains to be done will be the care of the city, which will bring up to manhood the orphans of those who have fallen in her defence, for this is the prize, with which, as with a garland, she crowns the virtues of her citizens. Wherefore, when your lamentations are ended, you may depart." *

* Thuc., ii., 34–46. See Jowett's translation.

ATTIC FUNERAL URN.

CHAPTER XV.

THE LAST YEAR OF PERICLES.

Second Invasion of Attica—Surrender of Potidæa
—Death of Pericles.

ITH the return of spring (430 B.C.) the
Peloponnesians were again in Attica.
After desolating the central plain they
passed on towards Sunium, laying waste the coast
land on either side of the promontory; but before
many days had passed they received the news that the
plague had broken out at Athens, and it is said that
their invasion was cut short on this account. However this may be, they remained not less than forty
days, the longest stay they ever made, and ravaged
the entire country. During the whole of the time
the plague was raging in the ill-fated city.

This new and terrible disaster, the like of which
is not recorded in Grecian history, came, as such
disorders commonly do, from the East. It first appeared in the Peiræus, from which it spread rapidly
to the upper city. For a time it was supposed that

the Peloponnesians had poisoned the water-tanks, but the disease was soon discovered to be of an infectious nature, utterly unknown to the Greek physicians, and beyond the reach of help, human or divine.

Athens was ill prepared for such a visitation. The city was crowded with the inhabitants who had been brought in from the country, and, as they had no houses of their own, the new-comers were closely packed together in stifling huts, among which the disease raged with terrible effect. The dead lay in heaps; the dying wallowed in the streets or crawled round the fountains. The very temples were filled with corpses. There was no organised service for the removal of the dead; each man buried his own as he could, and often the survivors, overcome by the number of the corpses, made use of burial-places not their own, or threw the dead on funeral pyres which were burning for others.

Great and terrible as were the physical evils of the plague, the moral evils which it wrought were greater still. There were men at Athens, as there are every-where, who found it convenient to conform to the decencies of life, though without moral principle; there were still more who were only deterred from crime by the fear of punishment. Of both these classes of men the conduct was now entirely changed. Those who had concealed their pleasures threw the veil away, and the criminal was no longer terrified by any fear of God or man. The divine law was disregarded, when good and evil perished alike, and the human law was superseded by the terrible sentence which seemed to be passed on the whole city.

BASSÆ (PHIGALIA), TEMPLE OF APOLLO.

From the N. W. with Mt. Eira in the Distance.

(From a Photograph by Mr. Clark.)

In the Peloponnesus the plague did little harm. That it appeared in the peninsula we know from the statement of Thucydides, but we do not hear of it in any of the great cities. Only in the remote town of Phigalea, in the south-west corner of Arcadia, have we any record of its presence. Here, in the glen of Bassæ, surrounded by rocks and old knotted oaks, stands the temple of Apollo the Healer,—the most perfect ruin in Greece next to the "Theseum" at Athens,—which was built as a thank-offering for the assistance rendered by the god when the plague raged at Phigalea.

The horrors with which he was surrounded did not turn Pericles from his purpose. Even in the early days of the invasion, before the Peloponnesians had left the central plain for the coast, he equipped a fleet of one hundred vessels, on which were placed no fewer than four thousand Athenian hoplites. A number of old ships were also converted into transports, for the conveyance of three hundred horses, a new feature in the naval equipment of Athens. The armament was then joined by fifty vessels from Chios and Lesbos. At the head of this imposing force, Pericles set sail for the Peloponnesus to make reprisals for the damage done to Attica. From the coast land, into which they had now moved, the Peloponnesians would see the enormous fleet standing out across the bay, a convincing proof that Athens was not yet crushed by her misfortunes.

Arriving off the coast of Argolis, the fleet attacked Epidaurus, but, though the country was laid waste,

the town could not be taken. Similar descents were
made at Trœzen, Halieis, and Hermione, cities on
the same coast, which were allies of Sparta, and
with a similar result. At Prasiæ, an insignificant
place on the coast of Laconia, the expedition was
so far successful that it took and destroyed the
town, besides ravaging the country round, but no
attempt at permanent occupation seems to have
been made. The fleet then returned to Athens,
whence it was immediately sent out again, under
the officers who had served with Pericles, to take
part in the siege of Potidæa. It had hardly arrived
at its destination before the plague broke out among
the troops, spreading from the new-comers to the
soldiers previously engaged in the siege, and as
every attempt to take the city failed, the fleet
returned to Athens, after a stay of forty days, with
a loss of more than a fourth of the four thousand
hoplites.

No wonder that a change came over the spirit of
the Athenians. In the city the plague was raging;
and no one could deny that its effects were greatly
increased by the policy which kept the Athenians
confined within the walls. Had they been scattered
over Attica, the danger of infection, at any rate,
would have been greatly reduced. Outside the walls
the whole of Attica from Athens to Sunium, from
Sunium to Marathon, from Marathon to Eleusis,
was utterly laid waste. Every proprietor and farmer
was cut off from the income which his lands might
have brought him. At the same time, the richer
men, on whom the chief burdens of the navy and

cavalry fell, had been called upon to furnish an enormous force, which cannot have been at sea for less than two months. And what had the force accomplished? A few patches of coast-land had been ravaged in Argolis; a Laconian hamlet had been destroyed. At Potidæa the expedition had not only failed, but had carried the plague into a healthy army.

The first effect of the change of feeling was seen in the despatch of envoys to Sparta with proposals for peace. But the Spartans, who probably had received very exaggerated accounts of the plague, and looked on Athens as hopelessly ruined, would listen to no overtures. Or they may have distrusted proposals which did not come to them with the authority of Pericles. Whatever the reason, the envoys entirely failed in their mission. The greater was the exasperation against the author of the war. Pericles found himself the object of a furious outbreak of popular odium. He had hitherto done his utmost to prevent the people from meeting for the discussion of public affairs, but he now found it necessary to summon an assembly, and endeavour to bring them into a better mood. He had no confessions of error to make; it was the people, not himself, who had changed; with the exception of the plague, which was beyond human foresight, nothing had happened of which they had not been forewarned. If they had been right in resolving upon the war, they were wrong in wishing now to discontinue it. The change was indeed unworthy of them, and more unworthy still was the determination to make

one man responsible for a policy to which all were
pledged. War was a great evil, which no city would
bring upon herself, if it could be avoided, but loss of
independence was a greater evil by far, and, when
the choice lay between the two, there could be
no room for hesitation.

Pericles then pointed out that the evils which
had overtaken the Athenians, however disastrous to
individual citizens, left the strength of the city
unimpaired. Their chances of victory were as good
as ever. Their navy was still the greatest in the
world; they were absolute masters of the sea; and
not even the Great King could prevent their vessels
from sailing wherever they chose. What was the
loss of houses or lands to men who possessed such a
power? So long as they preserved their freedom,
they could quickly recover what had been lost; but
if they became the servants of others, they would
lose not freedom only, but all that freedom brings
with it. Their ancestors had won a great empire,
were they unable even to maintain it? Far be such
a disgrace from them!

It was the possession of this great empire which
made the position so critical. "Do not imagine,"
Pericles said, "that you are fighting for a simple
issue, freedom or slavery. You have an empire to
lose; you are exposed to the hatred into which your
imperial policy has brought you. Your empire is a
tyranny, which in the opinion of mankind has been
unjustly acquired, and which you cannot safely surrender. It is too late to play the honest man; and
those who advise such a policy will bring the state
to ruin."

"No! we must hold on our way, and tread the path of glory. Our city has the greatest name in all the world because she has never yielded to misfortunes, but has sacrificed more lives and endured severer hardships in war than any other; wherefore also she has the greatest power of any state up to this day, and the memory of her glory will always survive. Even if we shall be compelled at last to abate somewhat of our greatness (for all things have their time of growth and decay) yet will the recollection live, that of all Hellenes, we ruled over the greatest number of Hellenic subjects, that we withstood our enemies whether single or united, in the most terrible wars, and that we were the inhabitants of a city endowed with every sort of wealth and greatness. The indolent may indeed find fault, but the man of action will seek to rival us, and he who is less fortunate will envy us. To be hateful and offensive has ever been at the time the fate of those who have aspired to empire. But he judges well who accepts unpopularity in a great cause. Hatred does not last long, and, besides the immediate splendour of great actions, the renown of them endures forever in men's memories. Looking forward to such future glory and present avoidance of dishonour, make an effort now and secure both. Let no herald be sent to the Lacedæmonians, and do not let them know that you are depressed by your sufferings. For the greatest states and the greatest men, when misfortunes come, are the least depressed in spirit and the most resolute in action."*

---

* Thuc., ii., 64, Jowett's translation.

16

We cannot but admire the undaunted spirit of the man who, in the teeth of a powerful opposition, amid the ruin and desolation of Attica, with the groans of the dying almost sounding in his ears, could present such a front to his enemies. Of such stuff the rulers of the world are made. And yet this last speech of Pericles is a terrible speech—breathing in every line a love of domination which threatened the freedom of Greece. Beyond the walls of Athens such words would be received with fierce denunciation; and within the city they nourished the most selfish passions of the Athenian people. The Athenians had long been taught to regard the money of the allies as their own, and the Delian confederacy had been reduced to submission by the contributions which were made to ensure its freedom. Now they were taught that Athens was a tyrant city, hated like a tyrant, and compelled like a tyrant to rely upon force for protection. " Necessity, the tyrant's plea," was laid upon her; and glory, the conqueror's idol, was held out as the final goal of ambition. Not only were the interests of Hellas regarded as subordinate to the interests of Athens, but honesty was confessed to be a ruinous policy. Such was the dangerous eminence to which Athens had been raised by the policy of Pericles, a policy which he sought to defend by sophistry and exaggeration. It was an exaggeration to say that peace with Sparta involved the slavery of Athens, for even at the close of the war, Athens was not enslaved. It was sophistry to separate the misfortunes of Athens from the misfortunes of her citizens. What sort of spirit was likely to arise in men who were bidden to " die like sheep " behind the city walls, rather than face their enemy in the field ? What was the value of an invincible fleet, when it failed at Epidaurus and Potidæa?

The Athenians were so far moved by the advice of Pericles, that they sent no more embassies to Sparta, and resumed with eagerness the prosecution of the war. Yet the opposition was not only strong enough to secure the deposition of Pericles from his post of general, but also his condemnation in a court of law, on a charge of embezzlement. He was sentenced to a fine of fifty talents. As we find his old opponent Cleon among the leaders of the prosecution, we may assume that the extreme democrats, who were in favour of the war and yet opposed to Pericles, proved stronger than the oligarchical party, who would have combined his overthrow with negotiations for peace. The inhabitants of the country, who were the worst sufferers by the plague and the war, seem to have been unable to turn the scale. The condemnation was of course a party stroke, for embezzlement was of all offences the one which could not be proved against Pericles. But it was an offence readily believed of all public men at Athens, and that was enough.

For the first time for fifteen years Pericles was without public office ; he was compelled to look idly on while the management of the state passed into the hands of others. The bitterness of his fall was rendered more acute by the private misfortunes which gathered thick upon him. In his youth he had married the wife of Hipponicus, who seems to have been transferred to him from her husband by some arrangement, which caused neither a scandal nor a feud. By her he had two sons, Xanthippus and Paralus. Xanthippus had long been on bad terms with his father owing to his own worthless character, and that he fell a victim to the plague was perhaps no reason for regret. So much the deeper was the affection lavished on Paralus, and when he also was carried off by the remorseless pestilence, Pericles was entirely crushed by the blow. As he placed the funeral crown on his son's head, he broke into loud lamentations at the doom which had left him desolate. The Athenians were so greatly moved by his calamities that a decree was passed, under which his son by Aspasia, Pericles the younger, was made an Athenian citizen, and by this expedient his house was saved from extinction.

From July 430 to July 429 B.C., Athenian policy was not controlled by Pericles. The war went on as before. The operations were chiefly in Western Greece. The Lacedæmonians endeavoured to make reprisals for the Athenian expedition round the Peloponnesus, by sending a hundred ships against Zacynthus, the ally of the Athenians, but though the island was ravaged, the Zacynthians could not be brought to terms. Later on in the year the Ambraciots summoned a force of Chaonians and other barbarians to their aid for an attack on the city of Amphilochian Argos, with which they had been on bad terms for years, but in this case also the city could not be taken, and after ravaging the country the army dispersed.

These movements naturally attracted the notice of the Athenians, who were allies of the Argives and Acarnanians. An expedition of twenty ships was despatched to Naupactus under the command of Phormio, one of the generals of the year. The appointment was a most happy one. Some years before, Phormio had delivered Argos from the aggression of the Ambraciots ; he was well known in the West, and was soon to prove himself the ablest naval officer at Athens. In the North affairs were favourable to the Athenians. A number of envoys from the Peloponnesus with Aristeus of Corinth at their head—a man whom the Athenians considered to be the cause of all their troubles in Chalcidice— had been despatched to Asia in the hope of persuading the king of Persia to take part in the war. On their way they went to the court of the Odrysian king, Sitalces, thinking that he might be induced to throw the Athenians over, or at least to convey the envoys across the Hellespont. The visit proved a fatal mistake. Two Athenians who happened to be with Sitalces at the time persuaded his son Sadocus to seize the envoys as they were about to cross the straits and deliver them into their hands. The captives were at once carried to Athens, where they were put to death on the very day of their arrival, without any trial, and their bodies thrown down precipices. This savage act—which might not have occurred had Pericles been in power—was justified as a retaliation on the Lacedæmonians, who, at the beginning of the war, slaughtered every one captured at sea, whether he was an ally of the Athenians or a neutral. A bad act cannot justify a worse, but it was certainly a gain to the Athenians to have got rid of Aristeus and to have put a stop to Spartan negotiations with Persia. The alliance with Sitalces was not without results.

More important was the surrender of Potidæa, which took place towards the end of the year 430 B.C. For more than two years the heroic defenders had held out against the utmost efforts of Athenian skill and energy. But the invasions of Attica, from which so much was expected, had brought no relief, and at last supplies ran short. Even then the city held out, and it was not until the extremity of famine, "even to the eating of human flesh," had been endured, that the final overtures were made. On the other hand, the besiegers had suffered much, and they had before them the prospect of a third winter in their exposed situation, while the expenses of the siege had run up to £400,000 of our money. On both sides, therefore, there was an eagerness to bring the long drama to an end, and the terms proposed were accepted by the Athenian generals. The Potidæans with their wives and children, and even the foreign troops, came out of the city, the men with one garment, the women with two; besides which they received a certain sum of money for their journey. They dispersed among the cities of Chalcidice or wherever they could find a home, and Potidæa was henceforth occupied by Athenian colonists.

In the spring of the following year (429 B.C.) the Peloponnesians did not invade Attica. They may have been afraid of the plague, or they may have left so little behind them in the previous year that invasion was useless. At the request of the Thebans, they marched upon Platæa, and endeavoured to detach the city from Athens, or at least to insure its neutrality. On applying to Athens for advice, the Platæans were urged to hold out, the Athenians declaring that they never had forsaken them and never would, but would assist them to the utmost of their power. On this assurance they refused to enter into any negotiations with Archidamus, and prepared to resist his attack. All the resources of engineering skill were brought to bear upon the city, but in vain; when a huge mound was raised against the wall, the Platæans rendered it useless, partly by raising the wall, partly by removing the earth through a mine, but most of all by building a second wall within that part against which the mound was raised, so that, if it were captured, the city would still be defensible. When battering-rams were brought up, they broke off the heads by dropping heavy beams upon them. The Peloponnesians then attempted to set the town on fire, but the plan failed of success, owing to the stillness of the weather and an opportune storm of rain. Finding his efforts useless, Archidamus was driven to invest the city; a double wall was built round it, and garrisoned partly with Peloponnesian, partly with Bœotian soldiers.

These operations occupied the Peloponnesians from May to October. During the whole of this time Athens took no steps whatever to deliver those who had allowed their country to be ravaged in reliance on promises of Athenian help. For these promises Pericles was not himself responsible, but those who gave them must have been aware that they could not assist the Platæans without meeting the Bœotians, at least in the open field—a policy which had been renounced in the very beginning of the war. The abandonment of Platæa to her fate, for so we must call it, was the inevitable result of the line taken by Pericles since the peace of 445 B.C. Nothing but an effective Athenian army could have saved the town, and the Athenian army in the hands of Pericles became eminently ineffective. Some years after his death, the Athenians tried their strength against Bœotia in the battle of Delium (424 B.C.), but only to meet with a most disastrous overthrow.

While their faithful friends and allies were being shut up to destruction on the borders of Attica, an Athenian army, which had been sent out to Chalcidice, was severely defeated at Spartolus. The victory was chiefly due to the superiority of the Chalcidic horse and targeteers, or light-armed troops, who now appear for the first time as an efficient force against heavy-armed soldiers. About one-fifth of the Athenian force and all the three generals in command were slain.

The news of this defeat seems to have caused a reaction at Athens in favour of Pericles. At the next election of generals he was chosen into his old place, and "all things were put into his hands." But the reaction came too late. At the time when he returned to office he was already perhaps stricken with the disease which in two or three months brought him to the grave, and under such circumstances he can hardly have taken any very active part in public affairs. Nevertheless, his last days were cheered by reports of the most brilliant exploits ever achieved by the Athenian fleet.

Though the Ambraciots had failed to take Argos Amphilochicum in the preceding summer, they had not abandoned their designs on the city. On the contrary, they now came forward with a plan for subjugating the whole country of Acarnania, and detaching it from the Athenian alliance. A combined attack was to be made by land and sea, so that the Acarnanians might be unable to unite their whole forces for resistance. With this view, the Ambraciots called upon the Lacedæmonians to send them a fleet, with a thousand hoplites on board. On their own part, they would bring into the field their army, and also obtain the help of the barbarian tribes of Epirus. If the plot succeeded, Zacynthus and Cephallenia, and perhaps even Naupactus, would fall into the hands of Sparta, and it would no longer be easy for the Athenians to cruise round the Peloponnesus.

The scheme was eagerly taken up at Sparta. Cnemus, the admiral who had conducted the attack upon Zacynthus in the previous year, was at once despatched with a thousand hoplites in a few ships to Ambracia; a larger contingent of vessels from Sicyon and Corinth, which, as the mother-country of Ambracia, warmly espoused her cause, was to follow as soon as ready. When he reached Leucas,

Cnemus was joined by the ships furnished from Leucas, Ambracia, and Anactorium, with which he at once crossed the sea, unperceived by Phormio, the Athenian officer at Naupactus. On landing, Cnemus found a large force of Chaonians and other barbarians ready to obey his orders, and as he felt himself sufficiently strong to open the game without waiting for the ships from Corinth, he at once began his march. His route lay along the eastern edge of the Ambracian gulf, through the territory of Argos, to Stratus, on the Achelous, which was the largest city in Acarnania.

The Acarnanians at once sent to Phormio for help; but as Phormio was daily expecting to see the Corinthian fleet sail down the gulf, he could not leave Naupactus. Meanwhile the combined forces were approaching the town. They came on in three divisions, of which the barbarians formed the centre. The Hellenic soldiers marched in good order as they had been trained to do, but the barbarians rushed on at full speed, thinking they had only to be first on the scene to capture the town. The Stratians saw their opportunity; if they could destroy the barbarians before the Greeks came up, the whole expedition would receive a very sensible check. They placed some of their soldiers in ambuscades outside the city, and when the barbarians were close to the walls, a combined onset was made from the city and from the ambuscades. The Chaonians were at once seized with a panic; many were slaughtered; the rest, carrying the other barbarians with them, rushed back to the Greeks, who received their first news of

the battle from the defeated fugitives. Here a stand was made for the remainder of the day, but when night came on Cnemus began his retreat to Œniadæ. The invasion was at an end before the Acarnanians could assemble all their forces, and the plan which promised so fair turned out an utter failure.

And this was not the worst. Almost on the very day of the battle of Stratus the fleet from Corinth, which should have co-operated with Cnemus and the land army, was utterly defeated by Phormio at the mouth of the gulf. From his station at Naupactus the Athenian commander saw the ships moving along the Peloponnesian shore; they had no intention of attacking him, for they were not equipped for a battle, but for the conveyance of troops, and that Phormio would attack their forty-seven vessels with his twenty never occurred to them. Suddenly they saw the Athenian ships moving along the opposite coast of Ætolia, and when in the dim light of morning they attempted to cross over from Patræ in Achæa towards Acarnania they were met by Phormio bearing down upon them from the mouth of the Evenus. It was impossible to avoid an engagement.

The Corinthian commanders knew that their seamen were not a match for the Athenians in point of skill. To be forced into an engagement was bad enough; to be attacked in the open sea where there was room for every manœuvre was still worse. They resolved to arrange their fleet in such a manner that the ordinary tactics of sailing through the lines of vessels and then charging from the rear would be

impossible. With this object they drew up their ships
in a circle, turning the prows outward, and keeping
them sufficiently close to avoid any inlet. The
smaller craft were gathered in the central space,
where also were placed five of their swiftest triremes
ready to run out at any point, which the enemy
attacked.

On seeing this formation Phormio at once took his
measures. Arranging his vessels in a single line, he
bade the sailors row round the enemy's fleet in ever
narrowing circles. By this means he brought their
ships into the smallest possible compass, and kept
them in constant expectation of an attack. He continued this manœuvre till the moment when the
morning breeze came down from the Corinthian gulf
—as he knew that it would—and made it impossible
for the Peloponnesian vessels to remain steadily in
their places. Ship began to dash against ship; the
attention of the sailors was occupied in keeping them
clear of each other, the more so as the rough water
made rowing difficult for the unpractised oarsmen.
Then Phormio gave the signal for attack. The first
vessel sunk was one of the admirals, but soon the
havoc was universal; no resistance could be made;
in wild disorder the whole fleet ran for the Achæan
coast, hotly pursued by Phormio, who captured
twelve vessels with most of their crews. The rest
escaped to Cyllene in Elis, where they were joined
by Cnemus and the ships from Leucas.

At the news of this disaster the Lacedæmonians
were highly indignant. They did not indeed recall
their admiral and condemn him to death, as the

Athenians would have done under similar circumstances, but while sending him orders to fight again,
they also sent three commissioners, one of whom was
Brasidas, to advise with him. They could not understand how a few ships could defeat so many, or
recognise that their own fleet was so vastly inferior to
the Athenian, as the battle had proved it to be.
When the commissioners arrived at Cyllene, Cnemus
sent round to the Peloponnesian allies for more
vessels and refitted those which had been damaged
in the engagement.

Intelligence of their movements was conveyed to
Phormio. He at once sent to Athens for reinforcements ; a battle might take place any day, in which
he would have to meet the whole Peloponnesian
fleet with only twenty vessels. From Corcyra,
whose fleet was to be of such advantage to Athens
in operations in Western Greece, not one vessel had
been sent, either to the aid of Argos or Acarnania or
Phormio, who was left entirely to his own resources
or help from Athens. The greater is our astonish-
ment to find that the reinforcement decreed at
Athens amounted only to twenty vessels, and that
even these, though every day was of great importance, were bidden to sail to Crete before they went
to the west! Who was responsible for this extraordinary order we do not know ; the Athenians could
have gained nothing by the most brilliant success in
Crete—which, so far as we know, they never revisited
in the course of the war ; while on the other hand
the position of Athens in Western Greece was in
peril. It was a grave blunder, and nothing but the

wonderful skill of Phormio saved Athens from irre-
trievable disaster.

When all was ready the Peloponnesian fleet left
Cyllene for Panormus in Achæa, where the land
forces were assembled to support it. Phormio meanwhile, who was resolved not to fight in the narrow
channel, if he was compelled to fight at all, sailed
from Naupactus to the promontory of Antirrhium,
where he anchored. The Peloponnesians, who were
as anxious to fight in the gulf as Phormio was to
fight out of it, met him by moving to a point exactly opposite, where the gulf was not more than a
mile broad. The number of their vessels was seventy-
seven, while Phormio had no more than his original
twenty. For six or seven days the two fleets lay
opposite each other. At length Cnemus and Brasidas, finding that Phormio would not return within
the strait, determined to draw him into it. Forming
their vessels four deep, they fronted north-east or
east and sailed along the Achæan shore into the
gulf, twenty of their fastest vessels leading the way.
Phormio at once saw the danger; he had left Naupactus without any guard, for even the Messenians
of the town had followed him on shore, to support
his vessels, and if the Peloponnesian fleet got ahead,
they would reach the place before he could save it.
He at once embarked, and bidding the Messenians
follow sailed in single file along the coast with all
speed for Naupactus. This was exactly what Brasidas wished; the Athenian ships had now no room
for any exhibition of their dreaded skill. Changing
front, he suddenly brought his whole line, four deep,

upon the flank of Phormio's vessels. It was an excellent manœuvre, and well carried out; but owing to the superiority of the Athenians in rowing, it was only partially successful. Eleven of Phormio's vessels escaped the swiftest Peloponnesian ships; the remaining nine were forced aground, and one ship was already taken with its crew, when the Messenians dashed into the water and saved the rest.

So far, the victory was on the side of the Lacedæmonians, who might reasonably have thought that they had redeemed their previous failure. But half the Athenian fleet still remained. Of the eleven ships which escaped the attack, ten reached Naupactus and ranged themselves in a position of defence should the enemy attempt to force them to shore. One remained behind, unable to keep up in the race. In their wake came the twenty Peloponnesian vessels, of which one, far in advance of the rest, was chasing the Athenian laggard. It chanced that in the deep water off Naupactus a merchantman lay at anchor in the line of pursuit. The Athenians saw their opportunity. Quick as thought they sped round the anchored vessel, and bearing down on the ship by which they were themselves pursued, struck her amidships and sent her to the bottom. Such a splendid feat of audacity and skill filled the Peloponnesians with dismay. They had come on in loose order singing the pæan of victory, but their temper changed in a moment, and checking their pursuit, they waited for the body of the fleet to come up. The delay was fatal; the Athenians, cheered by the brilliant success of their ship, and seeing the disorder

of the enemy, sailed out and fell upon the Peloponnesian fleet, which was without any settled plan of
battle. Some of the sailors, ignorant of the locality,
had run their vessels ashore ; all were expecting the
fate of the Leucadians. After a short resistance the
whole fleet fled to Panormus, whence they had
started, with the Athenians after them, eleven ships
in chase of more than seventy ! On the following
night the Peloponnesians stole away to Corinth.

This was perhaps the last event of which the news
was brought to Pericles. It was a great and decisive
victory won by an old comrade of his own—a victory which confirmed his policy and proved the incomparable superiority of the Athenians on the sea.
But the eye which in days gone by would have
brightened at such achievements was growing dim ;
the eloquent voice which would have bestowed on
them their due reward of praise was silent. Though
Pericles had escaped the first virulence of the plague,
he was seized by the disease in an insidious form, and
in the late summer of 429 B.C., two years and a half
after the outbreak of the war, he lay on his death-
bed. The misfortunes of the year had broken him,
and when the final illness came, there was little
strength of body or mind to resist it. The master
spirit was laid low ; half conscious of his weakness,
he would shew to the friends who visited him the
amulets, which the women of the household had tied
about his neck in the vain hope of checking the
progress of his sickness. Yet something of the old
Pericles remained ; a few days before his death,
when friends were praising his deeds, thinking per-

haps that he was unconscious of their words, he murmured that in all the past nothing gave him so much satisfaction as the thought that no Athenian had by any act of his put on the robe of mourning! The boast was true. Himself the constant object of calumny and attack, he had never abused his power to pursue an enemy to the death.

He died in the sixty-fifth year of his age.

17

HEAD OF THE NIKE.
West front, Parthenon.

CHAPTER XVI.

THE ATHENS OF PERICLES—THE GOVERNMENT, HOME AND FOREIGN.

Change in the Athenian democracy—The Law-courts—The Assembly—The Council—The Generals—The Archons—Checks on public officers—The Delian league—The Cleruchies or colonies—The allies.

ROM the days of Solon Athens had been a democracy, and from the days of Clisthenes the people had been conscious of their power. But the democracy of Pericles was widely different from that of Solon or Clisthenes; and the change was partly in form and partly in spirit.

During the Persian wars, and for some time afterwards, the influence of the great families, or at any rate of the great men among them, was still dominant at Athens. However deeply attached to the blessings of freedom and "equal speech," the Athenian people had not yet cast aside the habit of deference

——y were also the only power capable of enacting new laws. We are very ill informed about the process by which new laws were passed at Athens in the time of Pericles, but we may certainly affirm that the power of making them rested with the jurors, and not with the Assembly. The utmost that the Assembly could do, except in rare and exceptional cases, was to pass a decree, which, if it was not contrary to any existing law, was valid for the current year. The Assembly was competent to change the whole constitution of Athens; it could decide whether the laws of Solon should be maintained or superseded by a new code; it could close the law-courts; it could give permission for new laws to be passed, or withhold it, but it had not the power, by a mere resolution, to add to the statute-book.

Lastly, an Athenian juror was both judge and juryman. Though an archon presided in the courts, he merely introduced the case; he did not explain the law to the jury or check the contending parties in their statements. It was indeed forbidden under pain of death to quote the law falsely in a court, but the interpretation of the law, on which so much depends in the administration of justice, was within the competence of the juror. It was also for him to decide whether he would insist on the letter of the statute, or allow himself to be moved by pathetic appeals and extenuating circumstances.

The technical name for the whole body of jurors was the Heliæa. It is probable that a Heliæa existed in some form at Athens, from the time of Solon onwards, and that appeals could be made to it from the sentence of the archons, who in those days had a good deal of judicial power. But it was not till the time of Pericles that the Heliæa acquired the position which we have described. So long as the Areopagus retained its extensive powers, the Heliæa could hardly be more than a court of law in the stricter sense; and until the jurors were paid, their functions could not be very engrossing. It was Pericles, as we have seen, who overthrew the Areopagus; it was he who caused the jurors to be paid. With him, therefore, the reign of the Heliæa must have begun. We cannot indeed trace the steps by which the system was built up, but we know from the plays of Aristophanes that it was in full working order before the death of Pericles. For good or for evil, the Heliæa, as we find it in the "Wasps," is his contribution to the public institutions of Athens.

By the development of these courts at the expense of the Areopagus, he withdrew important functions from a section of the community and conferred them on all Athenians of full age, who could prove that they were fit to receive it. Above all, he established the majesty of law, and claimed for it the support of the whole nation. Every Athenian had now a direct reason for knowing what the law was, and for helping to maintain it. The reign of the Heliæa was the reign of law. The Athenians, as a body, had probably a better acquaintance with their laws than the citizens of any other state, equally large; and even in moments of the greatest political excitement, they were to an unusual degree a law-abiding nation. The laws were simple and clear, and lay within the comprehension of every citizen. There was no "bar" at Athens, nor indeed anything which could be called a legal profession, though a few men of a special aptitude wrote speeches for their clients to deliver, and others, owing to their special knowledge of law and custom, were able to advise men in difficult circumstances. Every man was his own lawyer. In none of the great cities of the world has the interpretation of the law occupied so small a space as at Athens; and in none has the administration of it occupied so large a space.

Other results which followed from the change were by no means so satisfactory. In the first place, Pericles destroyed a time-honoured institution, and erected in its place an arrangement which had nothing dignified or majestic about it. This was in itself a great evil. In all departments of government, customs and institutions are needed which arouse a sense of awe and reverence; and in the administration of law such customs and institutions are peculiarly necessary. The ermine robes, the black cap, the antique foppery of wigs and gowns, are not without a real value. They awake wonder, and shew that something unusual is going on. In the jury-courts of Athens these elements were wanting, and the respect for the administration of justice suffered in consequence. Of the same sort was another evil, inseparably connected with the institution. The jurors could not be the best and most influential citizens at Athens. No man living in the country could be a juror, for the duties demanded his constant presence at Athens; no one engaged in any occupation, even moderately remunerative, would care to spend his time in a court for a payment of about 4*d.* a day; no one serving in the army, no senator, no public officer, could spare time for the duties of a juror. There remained two classes of men: the old or infirm, who could sit in a court, when they could do nothing else; and the idle or nefarious person, for whom the court offered amusement or occupation.

The spirit of litigation, to which such courts gave rise, was in itself a great evil, but it became worse when the courts were composed of men who looked to them for a living. We are told that speakers sometimes warned the courts that if they were slow in the work of fining and confiscating, the funds out of which their payments came would fall off; and whether this be true or not, it is obvious that the rich offered the most tempting victims to courts largely composed of the very poor. The establishment of such courts was a step onwards in the development of class-hatred, ranging the rich and poor on opposite sides; for though the law was the same for all, the administration of it was now as entirely in the hands of the poor, as it had once been in the hands of the rich. And along with this inequality went the degradation of moral sentiment, which could not fail to arise in men who were engaged from morning to night not only in listening to legal quibbles, or falsehoods, but in deciding for hire on the lives and properties of others without the least responsibility or control.*

For a time these evils did not appear. Cimon lived for eleven years after the fall of the Areopagus, and his party survived his death; a party which preserved old traditions, and looked back on the past with reverence. Pericles, too, though he established the courts, stood aloof from them. He kept up the majesty of the state, partly by his own reserved and dignified habits, partly by the splendid buildings with which, following the policy of Cimon, he adorned the city. But when Pericles had passed away, the orators of the law-courts came to the front, and the tone of political life was changed. Unhappily for Athens, the change came at a time when a captious sophistry was destroying the intellectual no less than the moral fibre of the nation.

In all that concerned the administration of the state, home or foreign, the supreme authority was vested in the Assembly, or Ecclesia, as the Greeks called it. Every Athenian of full age—that is, every Athenian who had attained his eighteenth year, was a member of the Assembly, and could record his vote on any question brought before it. He had also the right of addressing the Assembly and proposing any measure he pleased on the subject under discussion; but in practice the younger citizens were expected to wait till the elders had said their say, if indeed they spoke at all. Yet even a young man, if he possessed the gift of persuasive speech, quickly became a power in the Assembly;

---

* See Aristophanes, "Wasps," *passim.*

his friends and supporters would gather round him
to applaud what he said, and cry down everything
which came from the opposite side. In earlier times,
and down to the death of Pericles, the general was,
as a rule, the politician, and the Assembly trusted for
information and guidance to those who were chiefly
responsible for carrying its wishes into effect, but
after his death the "speaker" became almost
synonymous with the statesman. This was more
especially the case when sophists and rhetoricians
had established themselves in the city, teaching men
how to "make the worse the better cause," and
reducing the management of politics to general
rules, to the great disparagement of experience and
knowledge.

There were four stated meetings of the Assembly
in each of the ten divisions into which the civic year
of the Athenians was divided; and, if occasion
required it, extraordinary assemblies could also be
summoned. Early in the morning a flag was raised
at the place of meeting; the people gathered from
all parts, and took their seats, without any order or
division of tribe or demes. Here they remained in
eager expectation till the Councillors appeared and
opened the business of the day. Before they entered
on their duties, the blood of sucking-pigs was carried
round the assembled people as a purification; and a
solemn curse was pronounced upon any one who
should seek to mislead the Assembly for private
ends. Then the Councillors brought forward their
proposals on the subject of the day, and the people
were invited to discuss them. After the motion of

the Council, which was always brought in in writing, had been read, the herald first asked if any citizen over fifty years of age wished to speak; and when these had given their opinions, the turn of the younger men came. The resolution of the Council might be rejected and replaced by a new one, or it might be amended, or simply accepted. The people gave their votes by holding up their hands, and the chairman pronounced on which side the majority lay. For this reason no sitting of the Assembly could be prolonged till an hour at which it was no longer possible to see the hands held up. And if any untoward sign occurred which seemed to indicate the displeasure of the gods, such as an earthquake, or thunder or lightning, or even rain, the sitting broke up at once.

In his play of the "Acharnians," Aristophanes has given us a picture of a meeting in the Ecclesia. Dicæopolis, an honest farmer, who has been driven into Athens by the war, is discovered in his place in the Pnyx, where the meetings were held, in the early morning, waiting impatiently for the arrival of the Prytanes, or presidents.

Dicæopolis.   Ah there!
       The presidents at last; see, there they come!
       All scrambling for their seats—I told you so!
Herald.
       Move forward there!   Move forward all of ye!
       Further! Within the consecrated ground.
Amphitheus.
       Has anybody spoke?
Her.   Is anybody
       Prepared to speak?
Amp.   Yes, I.

Her.	Who are you and what?
Amp.	Amphitheus the demigod.
	The gods moreover have dispatched me here
	Commissioned specially to arrange a peace,
	Betwixt this city and Sparta—notwithstanding
	I find myself rather in want at present
	Of a little ready-money for my journey.
	The magistrates won't assist me.
Her.	Constables!
Dic.	You presidents, I say! you exceed your powers;
	You insult the assembly, dragging off a man
	That offered to make terms and give us peace.
Her.	Keep silence there.
Dic.	By Jove, but I won't be silent.
	Except I hear a motion about peace.
Her.	Ho there! the Ambassadors from the King of Persia.
Dic.	What King of Persia? What Ambassadors?
	I'm sick of foreigners and foreign animals.
	Peacocks and coxcombs and Ambassadors.

*   *   *   *   *   *   *   *

Amp.	We've brought you here a nobleman, Shamartabas
	By name, by rank and office the king's eye.
Dic.	God send a crow to peck it out, I say.
	And yours the Ambassador's into the bargain.

*   *   *   *   *   *   *   *

Her.	Silence there! Keep your seats!
	The council have invited the King's eye
	To feast with them in the Prytaneum.
Dic.	There—
	Ain't it enough to drive one mad? To drive one
	To hang himself? To be kept here in attendance,
	Whilst every door flies open to these fellows.

*   *   *   *   *   *   *   *

Her.	The Thracians that came hither with Theorus
	Let them come forward!
Dic.	What the plague are these?
Theorus.	
	The Odomantian army.

Die.   The Odomantians !
               Out, out upon it !   I 'm a plundered man,
               I 'm robbed and ruined here with the Odomantians.
               They 're seizing upon my garlic.
               You magistrates, have you the face to see it
               With your own eyes—your fellow-citizen
               Here, in the city itself, robb'd by barbarians?
               —But I forbid the assembly.   There 's a change
               In the heaven !   I felt a drop of rain !   I 'm witness !
Her.   The Thracians must withdraw, to attend again
               The first of next month.   The assembly is closed.

                                                              —*Frere.*

Thus the sovereign power of Athens rested with a
gathering which might be composed of the whole, or
of but a small portion, of the citizens, and the votes
were given under the immediate influence of the
speeches made on the occasion.   By the Assembly
the whole of the executive officers of Athens were
immediately and directly controlled.   It is characteristic of democracies, at any rate of city democracies, to be exceedingly jealous of their servants:
either they allow them to hold office for a very short
time, as at Florence; or they retain the right of
discharging them at a moment's notice.   At Athens
the magistrates held office for a year, but once in
every prytany—*i.e.*, ten times in the year—the
question was put in the Assembly whether they
should be continued in office or superseded.   If
anyone among them was held guilty of any offence,
he was at once superseded and delivered over to the
mercies of a law-court.   By the Assembly also war
was declared, expeditions sent out, and conquered
states reduced to slavery; and if a general was
sometimes trusted so far as to carry out the details

of a campaign, he often received minute and precise
instructions to guide his conduct. Any change in
the constitution of Athens, such as the restriction of
the powers of the Areopagus and the admission of
the fourth Solonian class to office, could only be
made in the Assembly.

This sovereign power, so comprehensive and yet
so minute in its operation, could not be left without
checks upon its action. Of those which existed in
the time of Pericles some dated from the days of
Solon, while others must have been introduced, or at
any rate increased in force, by Pericles himself.
Solon established the law that the Assembly could
only discuss and decide on business brought before
it by the Council. It had not the power of simple
initiation. No citizen could get up and propose a
measure without regard to the action of the Council.
The utmost latitude allowed, if indeed so much was
allowed, permitted him to suggest a measure for the
consideration of the Council, and the measure thus
suggested was included by the Council in the pro-
gramme of business at the next meeting. Or a
clause might be inserted in a decree, compelling the
Council to bring forward the business to which it
referred, or to introduce envoys within a certain
time. In the settlement with Chalcis (p. 131), the
prytanes are pledged to bring any envoy from Chalcis before the Council and people within ten days of
his arrival. And in another decree, concerning the
first-fruits at Eleusis, Lampon the seer is to report
to the Council in the ninth prytany, and the Council *nolens volens* must bring the matter forward be-

fore the Assembly. The insertion of these clauses shews that it was in the power of the Council to delay, or even to quash, at least for their year of office, any measures to which they were opposed, and the only safeguards against an abuse of this power, except such peremptory orders, were the numbers of the Council, and the " scrutiny " at the close of the year of office.

Another check or limitation of the power of the Assembly was the separation of the judicial and legislative from the administrative functions. The Assembly was indeed a sovereign power, but, as we have said, it could not, except in peculiar circumstances, make a law, or pass a legal sentence. Nor could it revoke a sentence when passed by a law-court. In its own sphere it was absolute; it could bring forward for discussion a matter on which a vote had been taken; it could cancel a previous decree; it refused, in fact, to be bound by its own acts; but over it was the law, and the administration of the law. This limitation—which is honourable to the Athenian democracy—was so strictly observed that on the few occasions when the Assembly became a court of law, it met, as a rule, under peculiar conditions. The place of meeting was the market-place, and not the Pnyx; the citizens voted by their tribes, and not promiscuously; the votes were given by ballot; and in order to be valid, the decision must be supported by no fewer than six thousand votes.

The supremacy of the law over the Assembly was probably maintained by the Areopagus, so long as that court was in possession of its ancient privileges. With the development of the paid juries a peculiar form of process replaced the supervision of the Court. It was open to any citizen in the Assembly to declare that the motion brought forward was contrary to the law of the land, and by pledging himself to indict the proposer for " illegality," he at once secured the suspension of the motion. The case was then tried in a court. If the proposal was found to be illegal, the mover was punished more or less severely ; if the attack turned out frivolous, the accuser was fined one thousand drachmæ (about £35). This process was the " Graphe Paranomôn," the great engine by which the daily working of the constitution was kept in harmony with its established principles. So long as this was in force, the decrees *(psephismata)* of the Assembly could not over-ride the laws *(nomoi)* or institutions *(thesmoi)* of the State.

Once more, it seems that the presiding officer in the Assembly had the power to refuse to put a motion to the vote, if he considered it to be plainly illegal. On the famous occasion, when it was proposed to condemn six Athenian generals to death by a single vote in the Assembly, instead of trying them separately, Socrates was the chairman for the day, and he refused to put the proposal to the vote. As it was carried in spite of him, the opposition must have been in some way overcome ; but unfortunately our meagre information does not allow us to explain how this was done.

It was also a limitation, not on the power of the

Assembly, but on the use of it, that anyone who
came forward with a proposal was regarded as responsible for what he proposed, even when he was
strictly within the law. In all states, and under all
forms of constitution, treachery and corruption are
the just objects of severe punishment, but the
Athenians went further than this. They brought
to trial for " misleading the people " anyone
whose advice had caused disaster to the state.
The evil of the custom was as great as the good,
and perhaps greater. For if on the one hand it
checked any inclination to make reckless proposals
in the Assembly, it tended on the other to make a
single individual suffer for acts done with the approval of a majority. We find Pericles himself
more than once speaking in severe condemnation of
this unwillingness of the Assembly to accept the
responsibility of its own acts ; and after his death
the mischief became worse. Successful orators knew
how to turn the indignation of the people at the
failure of measures, which they had proposed, on
the heads of the unfortunate generals who had
failed to execute them.

The Council, whose preliminary action was necessary to legalise any decree passed by the Assembly,
was an institution founded by Solon, but altered and
developed by Clisthenes. In the time of Pericles it
consisted of five hundred members, fifty from each
of the ten tribes. They were men of thirty years of
age or more, chosen by lot to hold office for a year.
Before admission each candidate had to undergo a
public examination, touching his life and character,

18

at which every Athenian was at liberty to put what questions he pleased. If approved, the Councillors entered on their office with solemn ceremonies, binding themselves by a vote to discharge their functions honestly, and at the end of the year of service the whole Council and each member of it were held responsible for their conduct. During their year of office the Councillors were relieved from certain burdens, which fell upon the ordinary citizen; they could not, for instance, be called upon to serve in the army. They received a drachma (8*d*.) a day as payment for their services—a payment which, like the half-drachma of the jurors, was probably established by Pericles.

The Council met daily, with the exception of festivals and days of ill omen. In times of great distress or excitement it sat continuously, ready to act at a moment's notice. A special chamber in the market-place was known as the Council-chamber, but this did not prevent the Council from assembling at any convenient place. If, for instance, they had naval business in hand, they assembled at the dock-yards; if the subject concerned the Mysteries, at the Eleusinium. The meetings were so far open to all that the public were only separated from the Council by a cord drawn round the meeting, and could easily hear all that was said, though private persons could not communicate with the chamber unless permitted to do so by a decree of the Assembly or the Council. Nothing would have created greater alarm and suspicion than a sitting of the Council with closed doors.

Besides its duties as a preparatory assembly, the Council was the great agent in carrying out the decrees of the people. It formed the connecting link between the Athenians gathered in the Assembly and the individual officer or magistrate. The details of measures were often left to the Council, which was empowered to supplement what was wanting in the decree of the Assembly by decrees of its own, or it received authority to investigate any matter of public importance, such as the famous mutilation of the Hermæ, which took place just before the Sicilian expedition. It was especially charged with the maintenance of the fleet;—a Council which during its year of office had not built a single trireme, would not venture at the close of it to ask for the crown which it was usual to bestow as a mark of honour for a proper discharge of its duties. To it also were brought all matters concerning foreign policy and the league. Above all, the Council managed the finances of the state, receiving money, and confirming by its presence the acts of the financial officers.

It is obvious that so large a body as five hundred men could not be kept constantly at work. However important it might be to have the whole number at hand when wanted, it was necessary for practical purposes to subdivide it. For this object the fifties elected from each of the ten tribes were kept apart; and the Greek year of 354 days was also divided into ten periods of 35 or 36 days. Then one of the ten tribes was allotted to each of the ten periods, to be in office constantly during that time. The periods were called " prytanies " or presidencies; the tribe in office was the "presiding tribe"; and the members of it were the "presidents." Out of the fifty presidents, one was chosen by lot to be the chairman for each day and night in the term of office, and, as the same person could not be chosen twice, thirty-five or thirty-six out of the fifty would hold the office of chairman. During the day of office, the chairman "took the chair," as we should say, in the Council and the Assembly, if an Assembly were held ; he also kept the state seal and the key of the state archives. To the presidents all business of immediate importance was at once conveyed, and the generals and the officers chiefly responsible for the peace of the community were in constant communication with them. In the "Knights" of Aristophanes, Cleon, who is one of the generals of the year, attempts to forestall the attack of the Sausage-Seller by hastening to the Council :

> " I 'll set off this instant to the Council,
> To inform them of your conspiracies and treasons,
> Your secret nightly assemblies and cabals,
> Your private treaty with the King of Persia,
> Your correspondence with Bœotia,
> And the business that you keep there in the cheese press,
> Close pack'd, you think, and ripening out of sight."
> —*Frere.*

Of the numerous officers at Athens the Generals were the most important. In the earliest times the third archon, or Polemarch, was the commander-in-chief of the Athenian army, but after the reforms of Clisthenes, ten Strategi, or generals, were elected, one for each tribe, with whom the polemarch was associated. This was the system in existence at the time of the battle of Marathon. On that famous occasion each of the ten tribes of Athens furnished a contingent to the army, and each contingent was commanded by a general, who in his turn became commander-in-chief of the whole army, the polemarch retaining a nominal control and commanding on the right wing, but with little real authority. Each general belonged to the tribe which he commanded, but he was not chosen by the tribe ; the election was the work of the whole Athenian people assembled for the purpose in the Pnyx, under the control of the archons. In the next ten years we find a great change taking place in the duties of the generals ; one of the body was chosen commander with full powers, and the rest were subordinated to him, while the polemarch disappears entirely. In this capacity Themistocles commanded at Salamis, Aristides at Platæa, and Xanthippus at Mycale. Under these circumstances the generals could not any longer be the commanders of their tribes, and we sometimes find two generals belonging to the same tribe. The tribes were now commanded by the Taxiarchs, the generals being set free for executive functions of a higher nature. They were, in fact, the chief executive officers at Athens. Not only the management of the army, whether on land or sea, but the management of public business generally, was in their hands. They were, as we have said, in constant communicat꜀ with the Council, to which they conveyed inf꜀ tion and made proposals for meeting any eme꜀ which arose.

As the office was one which required special knowledge and capacity, the generals were chosen by show
of hands, not by lot. For the same reason an efficient officer was often re-elected; Pericles, for instance, was a general for fifteen years after the peace
of 445 B.C. Such constant re-election was of course
the strongest proof of popular confidence; a man so
favoured was not only the most influential member
of the board of generals, but he was the foremost
man in the city. In order to retain such a position
it was necessary that he should be something more
than a good captain and a clever administrator; he
must also be a clear and eloquent speaker, able to
explain his policy to the people, and convince them
of its merits. Such a combination of qualities was
rare, especially when rhetoric became a passion with
the young Athenians who haunted the Assembly.
The orator and the general then parted company;
one was supreme in the Assembly, the other in the
field; and nothing delighted the Athenians more
than a passage of arms between the two.

It is not necessary here to go into the working of
the board of ten generals. That they could not
always act together is obvious. As a rule they
were sent out in such numbers as the importance
of the expedition required, and possibly one of the
number was placed in some sort of authority over
the rest. At the end of the year they, like all other
officers at Athens, had to give an account of their
; more especially of the money which passed
their hands. Very often the Athenians,
waiting for the end of the year, condemned

their generals to death, or exile, for failing to carry out in a satisfactory manner the instructions given them. In fact the position of a general was by no means an easy one; his conduct was judged, not by a committee of experts, who could form a sound opinion of the extent to which there had been a want of honesty or of capacity, but by an irresponsible mob, led by an orator who was only too anxious to make good the position of his party, or to throw the blame of mistakes made by the people on those who had to carry them out.

As we have seen, the Athenians deposed Pericles from the office of general in the year 430 B.C. But in the years 431 and 429 B.C. he seems to have occupied a position of extraordinary authority. Thucydides informs us that he prevented the Athenians, when shut up in Athens, from meeting together to express their discontent at his plans, " being still general "; and that after his re-election, " all things were committed into his hands," expressions which imply a far greater power than was commonly exercised by a general.

Among the civic magistrates of Athens, the archons held the first place. They were nine in number, elected annually, like the generals, but elected by lot. The office was one of the oldest in the city, the archons being in fact the successors to the power of the kings who had once ruled the people. But the creation of the board of generals detracted largely from their executive powers, and when the law-courts were established—if not earlier—their judicial functions were confined to a preliminary examination of the cases brought before them. The first archon gave his name to the year; he was also in a sense the *pater patriæ*, under whose care were all orphans requiring protection, and other matters connected with family rights and duties. The second was the King archon; he was in charge of the religious observances of the city, and before him were brought, in the first instance, all charges of murder and homicide. The third archon was the polemarch, or general-in-chief, of whom we have already spoken. The remaining six were called the Thesmothetæ, or "makers of ordinances"; they were concerned with the administration of justice, and in old days, when there were no written laws in existence, they must have been to a large extent the administrators and repositories of law, in all those cases which did not come under the Areopagus. When the law-courts came into vogue, the thesmothetæ were occupied in allotting the juries and bringing cases before them. Their functions in this respect were purely formal. They were not judges, and they gave no votes. They merely provided that the proceedings of the courts should be legal and orderly.

Before entering office the archons had to be approved as fit and proper persons for the duties which fell upon them, and at the end of the year they had to undergo the usual "scrutiny." When this was satisfactorily passed they took their seats in the Areopagus, where they continued for the rest of their lives. No citizen could be elected archon a second time.

Besides these officers there was a host of others, some charged with keeping order in the market-place, others with the care of the public buildings, others with the exportation of corn, etc. There were stewards and treasurers and collectors and clerks, all of whom were only elected after a formal approval, and only released from office after a formal scrutiny; liable at any moment to be suspended by a decree of the Assembly and brought to trial before a law-court. Most of these officers were united in boards, usually of ten, for it was the exception to trust anything to the care of an individual. Never, we may say, was there a state more suspicious of her public servants than Athens; never was there a state which held them responsible for their actions with greater severity. Where other governments, perhaps too blindly, have trusted to personal honour and *corps d'esprit*, the Athenians insisted on a public approval of character before entering office, and a formal discharge on leaving it, and the ever present fear of punishment for misconduct. And never, we are compelled to add, was there a state in which the belief in the corruption of public servants was more universal.

We turn now from Athens to the Athenian empire. The sovereign power was of course the same in both, but we have to examine the manner in which that power acted upon the allies and subjects throughout the wide dominion where it was the ruling force.

In the fourth chapter we have pointed out the causes which tended to transform the Delian league

into the Athenian empire. The subjugation of
Naxos, the first act of aggression which brought
home to the confederates the true nature of their
position, was followed by the splendid victories of the
Eurymedon, whereby the limits of the league were
widely extended, and the management of Athens
was justified, so far as success could justify it. Not
long afterwards, twelve years at the latest, the chest
of the league was brought from Delos to Athens,
and whatever the reasons for the change may have
been, the result was inevitable. The last vestiges
of the Delian synod disappeared ; Athena, and not
Apollo, became the presiding deity of the league,
and the management of the common fund, which
had from the first been collected by Athenians, now
fell wholly under Athenian control. It was no longer
the representatives of the allies, of whom we never
hear, but the Athenian Assembly, which decided on
the outlay of the accumulated treasures.

From the year 454 B.C. onwards, the evidence of
inscriptions enables us to speak with some certainty
about the arrangements of the league, or of the
empire, as we might more justly call it. We see
that the payments made by the cities were frequently
revised ; sometimes they were raised, sometimes they
were lowered. The amount was generally fixed by
the Council, after consultation with certain officers
called "Assessors"—who were sent, when necessary, to visit the various cities, — but any city
could appeal from the decision of the Council, if
it appeared unjust. The case was then tried in a
law-court, whose award was final. Other cities

are registered in inscriptions as fixing their own tribute; in others the amount seems to have been fixed by private persons on the part of the community. The assessment took place at the Panathenæa at the beginning of the Attic year, but the payments were brought to Athens at the time of the great Dionysia in the following spring. They were received by the Hellenotamiæ in the presence of the Council, and, after one sixtieth had been deducted as the share of Athena, the residue was paid over to the public chest of the city.

The three great islands of Lesbos, Chios, and Samos never paid any tribute. Chios to the last, and Lesbos till the revolt of 427 B.C., continued to be independent allies, who furnished ships and crews to the service of Athens. After the great revolt of 440 B.C., Samos was deprived of her fleet, and compelled to pay an indemnity for the expenses of the war. She was reckoned among the subject and tributary allies, but her name never appears in the tribute lists.

Beyond this great distinction, that a few supplied ships as independent states and the majority paid tribute as subjects, we cannot lay down any general rules about the relations prevailing between Athens and the allies. They differed in each case. In some instances Athens fixed the constitutions of the subject cities, as at Erythræ and Chalcis; in others they were left very much to themselves. But the system of *laissez-faire* extended only to their internal politics; in the administration of law, Athens interfered to a considerable extent. Not only were the allies compelled to come to Athens to answer any charge touching their allegiance to the league, but any cases involving the life of a citizen were tried at Athens; even civil suits, if the amount at issue exceeded a certain sum, were brought before Athenian courts. This was doubtless regarded as a great burden and expense; men would much prefer to fight out their own quarrels, than to feel that their lives and properties were at the mercy of the Athenian jurors. But these regulations, which seem to us so extraordinary and even tyrannical, were not an invention of the Athenians. In very early times, when the island of Ægina was a dependency of Epidaurus, the inhabitants were compelled to take their suits to Epidaurus for settlement.

If we attempt to balance the good and evil, the justice and injustice, of the conduct of Athens in the Delian league, we must admit that the Athenians delivered the allies from the power of Persia, and that they kept the Ægean free of pirates; the amounts which they exacted from the cities were not large, and, so far as we know, they imposed but few restrictions on their trade. We must also allow that Athens was elected to be president of the league by the voluntary choice of the allies, and that it is the duty of a president to keep a league in order and prevent it from falling to pieces through the inactivity or carelessness of the members. Nor can we justly blame the Athenians for the decay of the Delian synod, or for acceding to the wish of the allies to pay money instead of sending ships. These changes were indeed fatal to the equality of the league, but they were not

fatal to its efficiency. Nevertheless, when the
allies found themselves the helpless subjects of a
tyrant, instead of equal allies led by a president,
they could not fail to resent the change ; they felt
that their contributions, though small, amounted in
the aggregate to a sum which in Athenian hands
maintained a fleet sufficient to overpower their
utmost resistance. Their contributions were no
longer voluntary, but exacted whether they would or
no ; the expenditure was beyond their control, and
not less so the disposition of the forces which they
were compelled to supply. The necessity of carrying their law-suits to Athens was a proof that their
independence was gone, and in some cases the loss
was made more evident by the presence of Athenian
garrisons and overseers in their cities. The growth
of Athens, the adornment of the city out of funds
intended for other purposes, while it tended to make
the city more and more the centre of the Grecian
world, attracted thither an ever increasing amount of
trade to the detriment of other ports in the Ægean.
The allies could not but feel that the interests of
Athens were distinct from their own, and often opposed to them ; and Athens did nothing to soothe
the irritation. As she felt her greatness depending
on her empire, she resolved to maintain it at all costs;
and for this purpose it was easier to employ force
than policy. Indeed a Greek statesman would never
have attempted to form an United State on the
only basis on which it could last—by destroying the
political isolation of the units and fusing them into
a larger whole. Had Pericles proposed to make all

the members of the alliance citizens of Athens, the
Athenians would not have permitted it, and the
allies themselves would have resisted to the death.

Besides the members of the confederation, the
Athenian empire included all the various cleruchies,
or colonies composed of Athenian citizens. These,
as we have seen, were part and parcel of the
Athenian state, and pledged to support her interests
to the death. They were chiefly founded by
Pericles, and were intended to support the power of
Athens in Euboea and the Ægean, especially in the
northern part of it. The Lemnian and Imbrian
troops fought in the Athenian armies, and the
colonists were in fact Athenians, members of
Athenian tribes. But the gain was counterbalanced
to some degree by the suspicion which these
colonies excited in the rest of Greece; they were
evidence of an appropriation of territory, which was
neither forgotten nor forgiven.

Lastly, Athens had a number of allies outside the
circle of the league, through whom her influence
was extended to the remoter parts of Hellas. She
was on friendly terms with Thessaly in the North
of Greece, though we must admit that on more than
one occasion the Thessalians shewed themselves
to be untrustworthy allies. The reigning monarch
of Macedonia, Perdiccas, was so perfidious that
it was difficult to say whether he was a friend
or foe, for he became one or the other as it
suited his immediate policy. The alliance with
Sitalces, the king of the Odrysian Thracians (p.
227), was of more value, chiefly because it prevented

any attacks by the natives on the Athenian possessions in the Chersonese. More important still,
from a commercial point of view, were the relations
which united Athens and the powerful princes in
the Greek cities on the northern shore of the
Euxine. These cities were the granaries of Athens,
from which, even in the beginning of the fifth
century, Greece was supplied with corn, and with the
increase of the city Athens became more and more
the centre of the corn trade.

With the remote east Athens had little connexion. Egypt was, of course, wholly in the hands
of Persia. We have seen that Pericles refused to
send aid to the rebellious king, though he accepted
the cargo of corn which was given in the hope of securing Athenian assistance. Of Cyprus we hear little
or nothing after the victory of 449 B.C. Relations
were kept up with Crete, but they led to no result.
The island was once visited by the Athenian fleet
during the Peloponnesian war, and we hear of Cretan
mercenaries in the Athenian army; but Crete was
never connected, even remotely, with the Delian
confederacy.

In the west, Athenian influence was widely felt.
An Athenian general, Diotimus, is said to have
instituted a torch race at Naples, and traces of
Athenian pottery are abundant in Campania. Of the
colony of Thurii we have already spoken (p. 146), and
of the alliances with Rhegium and Leontini. It seems
to have been a part of the Periclean policy to develop
the connexion with the west, and by every possible
means to raise the condition of the Ionic cities

of Sicily and Italy as a counterpoise to the Dorian power in Tarentum and Syracuse. Of the relations of Athens to Carthage, we can say nothing but that she traded with the Etruscans, either directly or indirectly, is proved by the Athenian vases found in Etruria. The day of Rome was not yet come.

Nearer home Athens was on friendly terms with Acarnania, which looked to her for help against the aggression of the neighbouring city of Ambracia. Corcyra was received into alliance in 433 B.C., and Cephallenia was gained in the first year of the war. In the Peloponnesus she could count in the neutrality of Argos and Achæa.

Thus at the time of her greatest power, the influence of Athens extended from the Crimea to Crete, from Miletus to Sicily and Naples; and she could place upon the sea a fleet incomparably superior to any force which could be brought against her. It was a great empire, and it was the greater because it included within its circle the most active and civilised states in the world. But from the first it was doomed to failure. The Greeks could never be induced to accept the principle on which it was founded. At the moment when the Delian synod ceased to exist, the Athenian empire became a *tyrannis*, and the strongest sentiment which could animate a Grecian breast—the love of independence —was aroused against her.

CHAPTER XVII.

THE ATHENS OF PERICLES : ART AND LITERATURE.

HE early stages of civic freedom, the attempt to found an empire in the most civilised people of antiquity, the methods by which a democracy sought to govern itself and carry on a vigorous foreign policy, will always have an interest for mankind, however small may be the scale on which these events took place, but no one will deny that it is the Art and Literature of the time of Pericles which have won for it the title of the "Golden Age of Athens." In his treatise on the "Glory of the Athenians," Plutarch endorses the criticism of the Laconian who declared that the Athenians spent on amusement the funds which ought to have gone to more serious objects. "If we were to calculate," he says, "the cost of the various plays, we shall find that the Athenians laid out more on "Bacchæ" and "Phœnissæ," on "Œdipuses and Antigones," on the woes of Medea and Electra, than was spent on the wars which they waged against the barbarians for empire and freedom." Time has justified the Athenians in their expenditure; the money which they lavished on amusements has turned out an imperishable investment, a source of instruction and delight thoughout the civilised world.

When the Persians retired from Athens in 479 B.C., they left behind them a ruined city. The walls and houses were destroyed; the temples blackened and burnt. Fifty years later, at the death of Pericles, Athens was incomparably the most strongly fortified and the most beautiful city in Greece. It is indeed true that the houses even of the richest inhabitants were of a modest size and appearance, and the streets were narrow and irregular owing to the haste and disorder in which the city was rebuilt. This defect could not be remedied without a reconstruction of the city. But the walls were impregnable, those of the port were stronger still, and the two were connected by the Long Walls, or " Legs," and the Phaleric wall. The new town of Peiræus was laid out with straight and spacious streets by Hippodamus (p. 146); while the spoils of Persia and the contributions of the allies were lavished on the adornment of the ancient city.

The probable direction and extent of the city walls in the time of Themistocles are shewn in the accompanying map. From Thucydides we learn that the circuit of the city, excluding the space between the Phaleric wall and the outer of the two " Legs," was somewhat more than five miles. Of the walls subsequently built, the Phaleric wall was

more than four miles long; the Peiræic, five, the total circuit of Peiræus and Munychia was about seven miles and a half. Thus, without counting the inner of the two "Legs," or the length of the city wall between the Phaleric and the outer "Leg," we have no less than twenty-one miles of fortification. Of part of these walls we are told that, though the height was only half that intended, the width was such that two wagons could pass each other, and the whole wall was made of large stones hewn square and clamped together on the outer faces with iron and lead.

In the most ancient times the city of Athens included the Acropolis and the land to the south as far as the Ilissus, and to the last, the shrines and sacred places, with the exception of the Areopagus and one or two others, lay in this district. In the citadel itself were the temples of Athena and Poseidon, who were said to have striven for the possession of the place. In the low lands by the banks of the stream was the temple of Dionysus, and farther to the east the temples of Zeus and Apollo. Here, too, was the fountain of Callirrhoë, the water of which was always used "on great occasions, at marriage rites and other ceremonies." But long before the fifth century, the city had spread to the west and north of the citadel, and by the time of Themistocles a part of the Ceramicus, or Potter's Field, was included in the circuit of the wall. This was in fact the busiest part of the town, lying as it did between the great western gate of the city and the market-place; and when Cimon began to adorn the city with the spoils of

his great victories, it was still possible to make
alterations in this quarter. Outside the large double
gate (Dipylon) by which the city was entered, a
road ran in a north-westerly direction, to the groves
of the Academy, where amid shady recesses the
waters of the Cephisus preserved a verdure even in
the glare of an Attic summer. In this pleasant
place a gymnasium was built, at which the Athenian
youths ran and wrestled, or sat beneath the plane-
trees which Cimon had planted. To the west from
the gate ran the " Sacred Way," along which processions passed to Eleusis at the time of the Mysteries, and towards the south a broad road carried
the traffic between the city and Peiræus. On either
side of these roads were placed the monuments,
which reminded the Athenians of the mighty dead
who had fallen in the service of their country (p. 228);
the district was in fact the public cemetery of the
city, where even in the second century A.D., Pausanias the traveller could still see the tombs of
Pericles and Phormio. Within the gate a broad
road—the Dromos or Corso—led to the market-place,
in which were grouped the public buildings of the
city, the offices of the archons, the Council-Chamber,
and the Dome or Rotunda, in which the Prytanes
were to be found during their term of office. The
eastern end was occupied by the Painted Porch,
which was erected by Peisianax, a friend of Cimon,
and adorned with pictures by Polygnotus and others;
on the northern side, where the Dromos entered,
were Hermæ or pillar-statues, some of which were
erected by Cimon, and inscribed with records of his

THE ERECHTHEUM.
From the South-East,
(*Boetticher.*)

victories in Thrace; the centre was made shady
with trees, which also were due to the care and
liberality of Cimon.   In the neighbourhood was the
Theseum, a shrine built to receive the bones of
Theseus, and on a terrace to the west rose the
beautiful temple—whether sacred to Heracles or
Theseus is uncertain—which now remains the most
perfect among the ruined temples of Greece.

The east of the city presented a strong contrast to
the west.   Here all was quiet and seclusion, for the
overland traffic from Eubœa was carried past De-
celea and Acharnæ to the northern gate of the city.
Outside the walls, near the Ilissus, were two gym-
nasiums, one at the Lyceum, which was built by
Pericles, the other at the Cynosarges (p. 24).   Within
the city, on a low terrace, rose the pillars of the
temple of Olympian Zeus, a temple which was begun
by Pisistratus on a scale far exceeding that of any
other, but which was never finished, perhaps because
the memory of the tyrant was too closely connected
with it.

On the south-east slope of the Acropolis was the
great theatre of Dionysus, at which dramas were
acted twice a year, in the winter at the Lenæa, or
festival of the wine-press; in the spring at the Great
Dionysia, the festival at which the allies came to
Athens with their tribute.   The theatre was not begun by Pericles, nor was it finished till long after his
time, but we cannot doubt that he carried on the
work, and did much to adorn it.   Not far from the
theatre Pericles built an Odeum, or Music Hall,
which is said to have been a copy of the tent of

Xerxes, and some writers add that the woodwork
was made out of the masts of the ships which
fought at Salamis.

' But the adornment of the Acropolis was the highest object of Athenian ambition.' The rugged rock,
precipitous on all sides but the west, rises to a height
of 156 metres from the sea level; in length it is
about 300 metres; in breadth at the broadest, 140
metres. As the level of the orchestra in the theatre
of Dionysus is 91 metres, and the level of the Ilissus
about 40 metres above the sea, we get a rise from
the river to the lowest part of the theatre of about
150 feet; and again from the theatre to the summit
of the citadel, of about 200 feet. The surface of
the rock is far from being level, rising considerably
towards the eastern end, and being higher in the
centre than at the sides, for which reason sub-struct-
ures of considerable extent were required before
the temples could be erected. In the sixth century B.C. the Acropolis was the fortress of Athens;
the place which was always seized, as a first step, by
anyone who wished to obtain control of the city. So
far as we can ascertain, a wall ran round the summit,
along the edge of the rock, and a second wall round
the base, at some little distance from the foot of
the precipitous rocks. This second wall was called
the "Pelasgic fortress," because it was supposed to
have been built by Pelasgians, and the name spread
to the space between the precipices and the wall.
Pisistratus, and his sons after him, had their palace
on the citadel, and in the final struggle, when the
Spartans came to expel him from Athens, Hippias

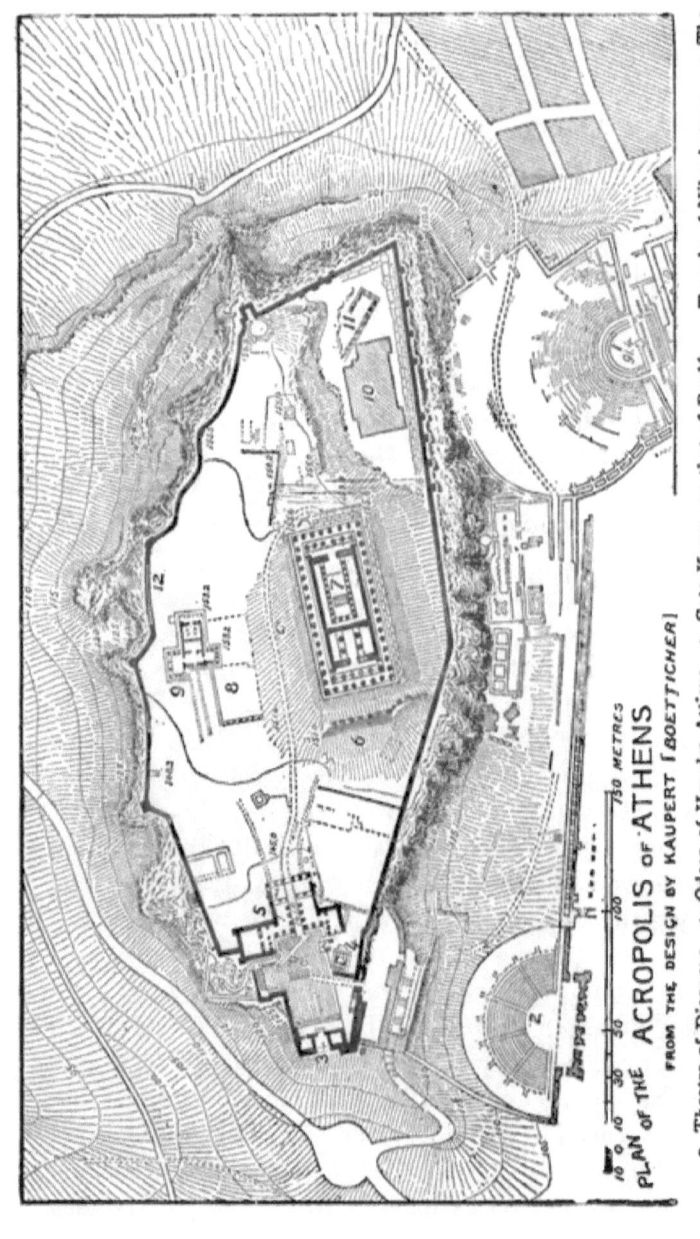

PLAN of the ACROPOLIS of ATHENS

FROM THE DESIGN BY KAUPERT [BOETTICHER]

1. Theatre of Dionysus. 2. Odeon of Herodes Atticus. 3. Gate known as that of Beulé. 4. Temple of Nike Apteros. 5. The Propylaea. 6. Terrace Walls. 7. Parthenon. 8. Foundations of an Old Temple of Athena. 9. Erechtheion. 10. Museum of the Acropolis (Modern). 11. Old Unknown Building 12. Columns in the Wall. [The heights and contours are given in metres.]

prepared for a siege in the "Pelasgicum." The entrance to the Acropolis was then, as always, at the western end, which was, no doubt, secured by fortifications. At this time there were two temples in the citadel—the ancient Erechtheum, at the northern edge, and a larger temple, apparently built by the tyrants, which occupied the centre.

In the Persian invasion of 480–479 B.C. all the buildings on the Acropolis were utterly swept away; the Pelasgic wall was entirely destroyed; the temples were levelled to the ground. For a time the ruins were allowed to remain as mute evidence of the outrages of the impious foe, or perhaps because Themistocles urged the imperative duty of securing the city from attack; but when Cimon brought home the spoils of Persia from the Eurymedon he resolved to spend a part of them in rebuilding the shrine of the guardian goddess. As the whole city was now surrounded by an enormous wall, it was no longer necessary to treat the Acropolis as a fortress. No attempt was made to restore the Pelasgic wall. But in order to obtain a sufficient area for the new temple which he contemplated, Cimon not only rebuilt on a larger scale the southern wall of the citadel, but he carried substructures over the depressions in the native rock for the support of his heavy pillars and walls. But the work was never carried out as Cimon planned it. When Pericles became leader of the city, the matter passed into his hands, and it was under his authority that the great temple, which is the wonder of the world, was carried out by Ictinus the architect (aided by Callicrates) and Pheidias the sculptor.

The form and position of the Parthenon will be best understood from the plan of the Acropolis, which is taken from that of Dr. Kaupert.

The Doric pillars rose on a base of three receding steps ; at each end there were eight, on each side seventeen, counting the corner pillars twice. The total length was 69.51 metres; the width, 30.86 m., a proportion of 9 to 4. Each pillar was 10.43 m. in height, and 1.905 m. in diameter; the distance between them was 2.4 m. The pillars were channelled in the Dorian manner, each with twenty grooves.

The lines of the temple were not rigidly straight. The "stylobates," *i.e.*, the courses of stones on which the pillars were placed, were higher in the middle than at the corners, and the pillars were slightly diminished as they rose; they also inclined inwards.

Within the rows of pillars was the temple in the stricter sense, consisting of four parts: the Pronaos, fronting east; the Cella; the Parthenon; and the Opisthodomus. The Pronaos and Opisthodomus were porticoes. The Cella (also called the Hecatompedos because it was just one hundred Attic feet in length) contained the great chryselephantine statue of Athena. It was divided by two rows of pillars into three "naves," of which the central nave was closed at the end opposite the entrance by pillars, and separated from the Parthenon chamber by a wall, without any door, so that the temple was really divided into two parts, one entered from the west, the other from the east. The Parthenon chamber was the treasure-house of Athena, in which a part

of the furniture and sacred vessels belonging to the
temple were kept.*

Within and without the whole temple was adorned
with sculptures and ornamentation and colour. The
sculptures are of three kinds: those contained in the
"pediments," or triangular spaces formed by the
gables of the roof at either end of the temple; those
on the "metopes," *i.e.*, on the flat slabs which, alter-
nating with grooved slabs (or "triglyphs"), ran *outside* the temple between the architrave, which immediately rested on the pillars, and the roof; and the
"frieze," which ran round the whole of the wall of
the inner temple above the architrave.

In the pediments the sculptor had to deal with a
triangular space in which the figures must be arranged
according to their size. In the centre there was room
for figures standing erect; towards the angles the
figures must appear as sitting or recumbent. The
subjects represented were the birth of Athena, which
was depicted in the eastern gable, and the strife of
Athena and Poseidon for the possession of Attica,
which occupied the western gable, looking towards
the Propylæa.

The figures of these sculptures were removed
from their places and brought to England by Lord
Elgin, but drawings have been preserved, which
enable us to realise their position before removal,
though even then the eastern gable had suffered
severely, the central group being destroyed. At the
left or southern corner of this pediment the horses

* The name "Parthenon" was never given to the whole temple
till long after the time of Pericles.

of the sun were seen rising from underground; at
the right or north they sank down again into the
darkness. In the centre was a group which represented Zeus, Athena, and Hephæstus; between the
two were the seated sisters or " Fates," and the
reclining figure which is sometimes called Theseus
and sometimes Olympus, statues which are the *ne
plus ultra* of the sculptor's art. The figures on the
western gable are not so striking, and the identifica-
tion of them is very doubtful.

All the figures in these pediments were of colossal
size, but each, without exception, was finished with
the most minute accuracy. Even those parts which
were hidden from view by being turned to the surface of the pediment were worked out with the same
finish as the parts turned to the spectator. Man
has here striven with nature to produce perfect
work regardless of the eye which sees it.

Of the metopes each contained two figures, which
were represented in conflict; and they were so
arranged that the figures on the four sides of the
temple formed four separate groups. Originally there
were ninety-two metopes in all, fourteen at each end
and thirty-two on each side. A great number were
destroyed in the explosion of 1687, but fifteen have
been brought to London, one is at Paris, three in
the Museum at Athens, and some fragments of others
remain in their original position. The metopes at
the eastern end represented the contest of Athena
with the Giants; those at the western end, the contest of Theseus and Heracles with the Amazons;
on the north was depicted the capture of Ilium;

on the south, where the sculpture has been best preserved, the conflict of the Lapithæ and Centaurs.

The frieze is not less than 159.42 metres in length. The whole of this splendid work, strange to say, received no direct light whatever; it was only illuminated by the reflected light which, streaming through the pillars, struck the white marble floor beneath. The sculpture represents in all its details the great Panathenaic procession, which took place every fourth year in the month of July. The frieze at the western end, which exhibits the preparation for the procession, is still in its original place; of the remainder, fifty-three slabs are in the British Museum and one at Paris.

The Parthenon and all the sculptures upon it are throughout of Pentelic marble, obtained from quarries in the north of Attica, a stone distinguished by its fine grain and the yellowish tinge which, deepening with time, has contributed in no slight degree to the almost magical colouring of the glorious temple.

The crowning work of the genius of Pheidias at Athens was the statue of the goddess, of gold and ivory, which was placed in the Cella of the temple in 438–437 B.C. The oldest statues—and often the most sacred—in Greece were rude idols of wood. Then stone and bronze were adopted, and, finally, in the hands of the great artists of the fifth century, gold and ivory—ivory being used in the parts where the flesh was allowed to appear, while the robes and attributes were of gold. Of course no relics of these costly and perishable materials have come down to us, and our ideas of the statue of Athena must be

derived from copies of the great original. In 1879
a marble statuette was found at Athens which is
thought to be a copy of the Parthenos, more accurate
than any hitherto known. The goddess, who is
heavily draped in chiton and diplois, wears her helmet and ægis; on her right hand, which is supported
by a pedestal, rests a winged Victory; her left hand
holds the upper rim of her shield, within which coils
a serpent, the emblem of Erichthonius. From this
copy we may gain some idea of the outward form of
the work of Pheidias, but it will always be difficult
to realise the difference between the marble and
the more delicate material. Moreover, the statue
of Pheidias was coloured. "It was a supreme work
of art, the pride of the temple and the city, representing the goddess in all the majesty of complete
victory. All strife is now ended; peaceful and powerful she protects the nation which has built the glorious shrine for her use.

Besides the Parthenon, there was another temple
on the Acropolis—the Erechtheum, which Athena
shared with Poseidon. This was the older and more
sacred temple of the two; in it was preserved the
wooden block, which in the minds of the Athenians
was the most holy idol of their goddess. The
central parts of the shrine seem to have been
restored and enlarged not long after the Persian
war, and before the building of the Parthenon
(447–438 B.C.) it was perhaps the treasury of the
Athenians; but the beautiful colonnades on the
north and south, which form the chief attraction of
the Erechtheum, were not finished till after Pericles's

death. The temple differs from the Parthenon in
being very small; it is also built in the Ionic, not in
the Doric style. Though it has suffered severely at
the hand of time, it is sufficiently perfect to allow us to
judge of its beauty. The slender Ionic pillars are in
their places, though the gable and pediment are gone.
The porch of the Caryatides, *i.e.*, the porch looking
to the south at the western end, and furnished with
draped female figures instead of pillars, cannot fail to
attract peculiar attention owing to the beauty of the
statues and the boldness of the design.

As we have said, the Acropolis can only be entered
at the western end. Here, therefore, were the great
gates or Propylæa, which Pericles began to build after
the completion of the Parthenon. The architect
was Menecles. The entire plan was never carried
out, owing perhaps to the enormous expense which
it involved, but what was done was executed in a
manner worthy of the site on which the gateway
stood.

The entrance was formed by two porticoes, facing
east and west, and separated by a wall. The western
portico was, of course, that which first met the eye of
the Athenian who was about to ascend the hill. He
saw before him six massive Dorian pillars, three on
each side of a broad path, surmounted by a gable.
The pillars were approached by steps, but the path was
perhaps merely smoothed, in order that horses and
carriages might ascend by it. On either side of the
approach, at right angles to left and right, were other
porticoes, each with three Dorian pillars. The portico on the left (north) was large, and formed a kind

of picture-gallery; the portico on the right (south)
was contracted in order to leave room for the temple of Wingless Victory, which occupied the south-
west corner of the Acropolis. On entering the
portico, by the path, the traveller found three Ionic
pillars on either hand, supporting a decorated marble
roof, and before him was a wall pierced with five
openings, one large central door which received the
path, and two smaller on each side confronting the
spaces between the great Dorian columns of the
portico. Passing through the door he found himself
in the inner portico, which was a repetition of the
outer, but not so deep, and without the Ionic pillars
on either side of the central path.

When he passed beyond the pillars he was on
sacred ground. Before him was the Erechtheum, and
a little to the right the Parthenon. Immediately in
front, raised aloft on a high pedestal, was the colossal bronze statue of Athena Promachus, the work of
Pheidias, which was said to have been furnished by
the spoil of Marathon. On every side were offerings
dedicated either by the state or by individual citizens: the Bull dedicated by the Areopagus; the
Chariot and Four, which commemorated the victory
over Chalcis; the Perseus of Myron; the Aphrodite
of Calamis. On every side were inscriptions testify-
ing to the wealth and power of Athens: lists of the
tribute, catalogues and inventories of the temples,
treaties with foreign states, records of her anger
against traitors such as Arthmius of Zelea, who first
brought Persian gold into Greece, and of her grati-
tude to patriots; portrait statues set up in honour

of distinguished citizens, of Xanthippus, of Phormio the great sailor, and of Pericles himself.

The Acropolis was indeed the centre of the life of Athens. If the Erechtheum was the home of the guardian deities of the city, the shrine which reminded the Athenians more than any other of their legendary past, the Parthenon was the symbol of the city and empire of Pericles. It was not intended in the least to replace the older temple; it was not regarded as a dwelling-house of the goddess, but rather as her treasury. There was no priesthood connected with the Athena of the Parthenon, as the Praxiergidæ, for instance, were connected with Athena Polias, and no organised provision for worship. The Parthenon was, if the expression may be used, the palace of the goddess, where she received her worshippers on the day of her great festival.*

It would be tedious to continue the description of the works of art which adorned Athens at the time when Pericles fell a victim to the plague, and no description can give anything but a very inadequate idea of the splendour, strength, and beauty which met the eye of the Athenian, whether he walked round the fortifications or through the broad streets of the

---

* Since this was written, Miss Jane Harrison's work on the mythology and monuments of Athens has appeared. Her views on the topography of the " market-place," and on the temples of the Acropolis differ widely from those expressed in the text. With regard to the existence of a third temple on the Acropolis in the fifth century, I fear that she has not yet proved her point, though I feel very strongly the force of her remarks on the state treasure-chamber (pp. 465, 505). And in regard to the " Ennea-krounos episode," I cannot think that Thucydides gave the name to a spring near the Areopagus

Peiræus, or along the Long Walls, or in the shades
of the Academy, or amidst the tombs of the Ceramicus; whether he chaffered in the market-place, or at-
tended assemblies in the Pnyx, or loitered in one of
the numerous porticoes, or watched the exercises in
the gymnasia, or listened to music in the Odeum and
plays in the theatre, or joined the throng of worshippers ascending to the great gateway which formed
the front of the Acropolis. And this magnificence
was not the result of centuries of toil; it was the
work of fifty years. In 479 B.C. Athens was a heap
of blackened ruins; in 429 B.C. all the great works of
the Periclean age had been accomplished except the
Erechtheum. Athens indeed became a vast workshop, in which artisans of every kind found employment; all in their various degrees contributing to
the execution of the plans of the master-minds—
Pheidias, Ictinus, Callicrates, Mnesicles, and others.
Their productions aroused the wonder of the Grecian
world hardly less on account of their excellence, than
on account of the rapidity with which they were
carried into execution.

When we reflect on this great achievement, we
naturally ask: How did it become possible that,
within the lifetime of one man, such a series of
masterpieces could be created? Attica could supply
marble in plenty; the surplus of the treasury of
Athena could be spent in the purchase of gold and
ivory, and in paying for the services of artists and
workmen; but genius cannot be so easily procured;
the wealth of a kingdom may be offered in vain for
a Pheidias. We must allow that Pericles was in this

A CARYATID FROM THE ERECHTHEUM.

(*Müller.*)

respect peculiarly fortunate. His life fell at a time
when artistic genius was abundant ; a wave of inspiration seemed to pass over the sculptors and
architects of Greece, and through the liberality of
Cimon and Pericles that inspiration reached its highest level at Athens. It is true that some of the artists
employed were not Athenians at all, and that others
were trained in foreign schools, but their best work
was done at Athens, and by their efforts the city
became the centre of the art of Hellas.

The greatest painter of the age, Polygnotus, was a
native of Thasos, and may have come to Athens with
Cimon after the reduction of his native city (p. 73).
We hear of his work at Delphi and Platæa ; but he
seems to have settled permanently at Athens. He
founded a school, and in conjunction with his contemporaries and pupils, he adorned the Painted
Porch at the eastern end of the market-place, the
Theseum, and the chamber in the northern wing of
the Propylæa. Among the artists who came after
him, there were perhaps some who were as great, or
greater, masters of technique ; but no one ever attained the elevation of his style. He was the great
painter of character or " morals," an artist who could
depict men as " they ought to be." It was good for
the young to look at his paintings, for, like the
greatest of the Italian masters, he idealised human
nature, and impressed on the spectator the combination of beauty, grace, and virtue.

Before the time of Polygnotus, the pictorial art of
Greece was mainly employed on the decoration of
vases, which, however delicate and beautiful, were

productions for private use. It was otherwise with
sculpture. This art was from the first employed in
the service of religion or for the commemoration
of great events and persons. Even in the sixth century B.C.—under the rule of the tyrants,—the sculptors of Athens had attained some eminence, as we
know from the statues recently dug up in the Acropolis (pp. 16, 34). These statues are of marble, and as we
might expect in early work in that stubborn material,
they are massive and rigid, with a good deal of con-
ventionality in the more difficult parts, such as the
hair, eyes, and mouth. About the end of the century
a new impulse was given to the art by the use of
bronze, a material which admits of greater lightness
and mobility than stone. It was in the Peloponnesus that the great artists in bronze arose: Canachus
at Sicyon, Onatas at Ægina, and Ageladas at Argos.
And not only were they famous for their success
in metal, but the skill with which they were able to
treat the human and animal forms in that material
exercised a strong influence on work in marble.
Following their example, artists sought to produce
something more vigorous, life-like, and graceful,
and pupils trained in their schools carried plastic
art to its greatest height.

Among the pupils of Ageladas at Argos were the
Athenians Myron and Pheidias. The works of Myron were to be seen throughout all Hellas. Like
Polycleitus of Sicyon, he was a great master of the
art of casting bronze: his Ladas expiring at the
moment of victory in the Olympic race, and his
Quoit-thrower (Discobolus), were perhaps his most

THE DISCOBOLUS OF MYRON.
(Statue in the Villa Massimi.)
(*Müller.*)

signal triumphs with the human body; hardly less excellent, in another region, was the famous cow which Cicero saw in the market-place at Athens. Pheidias, on the other hand, from the time that he returned from Argos to his native city till his departure for Olympia after the completion of the Parthenon, was almost exclusively employed at Athens and in Attica. Among his earliest works were the statues which commemorated the battle of Marathon, and before the death of Cimon he had cast the great statue of Athena Promachus. When Pericles succeeded in acquiring the supreme direction of affairs, the decoration of the Acropolis became a part of his public policy. He did not dedicate a statue or build a temple as a private gift or thank-offering; he determined to use the services of art in order to bring before the Athenians in visible form the position of their city, and unite the whole empire under the protection of the guardian goddess. The Acropolis was to be a fortress no more, but a sanctuary, and Pheidias was at hand to assist in carrying out the plan.

To Pheidias, therefore, these great achievements were mainly due. But he was well supported by his architects; and even in the decoration and plastic work he must have been able to secure the services of a number of admirable artists. The sculpture in the Parthenon, amounting, it is said, to four thousand square feet of frieze and metopes, besides fifty colossal statues, cannot have been the work of Pheidias's own hand, and yet it is all finished with the same perfect skill. We must assume that he was able to breathe his spirit into those around him, and inspire them with the devotion which alone can produce such masterpieces of art. When the great work was done and the temple with the statue of the goddess was presented to the eyes of the astonished Greeks, it was inevitable that Pheidias should be regarded as the foremost of the sculptors of his time. As such he was summoned to Olympia, in order that he might do for Hellas what he had done for Athens. On a larger scale and with still greater magnificence, he created an image of the supreme Hellenic deity, which, by its superhuman majesty, filled every beholder with wonder and awe.

From art we turn to letters. In two departments of literature, the drama and history, the achievements of the age of Pericles have never been surpassed, and in a third, the department of philosophy, the foundation was laid for triumphs not less splendid. The dialogues of Plato, which remain without a rival in their beauty of form and language, belong to the generation after Pericles; but they are due, both in manner and matter, to the influence of Socrates, whose strange figure and still stranger habits were known throughout Athens for some years before the beginning of the Peloponnesian war. Of course these were not the only forms of literature produced at this period. Epic poetry was indeed a thing of the past, but elegiacs were still used for inscriptions, and the lyric poetry of Pindar and Simonides, if less passionate and personal than the poems of the Æolian school, was distinguished by a greater dignity and sweetness. The songs in which Pindar celebrated the Olympian victors of his day still remain to attest the almost superhuman glory achieved on the banks of the Alpheus; the "epigram" of Simonides on the Spartans who fell at Thermopylæ is felt to be a tribute not unworthy even of their devotion; and the fragment of his "Danaë" leaves in every reader the memory of a tender and delicate grace which can never be forgotten.

But neither Pindar nor Simonides stands in any close relation to Pericles and Athens. Neither poet was an Athenian; their poetry is Hellenic rather than Attic; it has little or nothing in common with the spirit which created the new democracy, or the Athenian empire; it would have been what it is if the theatre of Dionysus had never been built, or the Peloponnesian war had never been fought. In these respects it differs widely from the plays of Sophocles and of Aristophanes.

It is not worth while to trace the dramatic literature of Athens back to its earliest sources. It is sufficient to say that at the beginning of the fifth century B.C., Æschylus was twenty-five years old. Now Æschylus is the Homer of Greek tragedy, and though there is enough evidence to shew that the Athenians were devoted to the drama before his time, there is also enough to shew that the drama, as we know it, was his work. Of the ninety plays which he wrote, seven only have come down to us; the earliest in date being the "Persæ," which was brought out in 472 B.C., eight years after the famous battle of Salamis, which it commemorates, and the

last, the "Orestea," a group of three plays, acted in
458 B.C. These dates shew us that Æschylus was
a poet of the Cimonian rather than the Periclean
Athens, and indeed we cannot read his plays without
feeling that the spirit by which they are pervaded is
the spirit of the Persian rather than the Peloponnesian
war.

Like every dramatic poet the Greek tragedian
attempted to please his audience, and in his case
this feeling was the stronger because his plays were
brought out as part of a contest, just as much as the
tunes played, or the races run, at the Panathenæa.
Whatever his theme, this object must be kept in
view. His plays were acted at the festival of Dionysus, but he was not compelled to make the acts and
sufferings of the god his principal theme; it was
enough that in addition to the three plays, which
he brought out as tragedies, he provided a satyric
drama, in which the chorus was composed of the
attendants of Dionysus. For the rest, he might
choose a historical subject as Æschylus did in the
"Persæ," or he might take a plot from the myths of
Theban and Trojan story.

On the other hand there were limitations. The
tragedy of the Greeks, though arising out of the
worship of the god of wine, became so severe and
elevated in tone that there was no room in it for
comic or humorous scenes. It was grave and solemn, dealing indeed with the passions of men, but
dealing with them in reference to human destiny; it
was religious, in the sense that it carried the mind
beyond the limits of visible life, and attempted to

trace the working of a divine power in the great scenes which it depicted. The characters which it presented were intended to be typical and ideal, far removed from the life and individuality of the common world. Even in the " Persæ," where events are described in which the audience had participated, the realism is softened, partly by the use of general terms—no Greek is ever mentioned by name in the play—partly, by placing the action in Persia, and partly by bringing on the stage the shade of the great Darius, a device which at once lifts the drama above the level of a merely human victory of Greeks over Persians.

In none of the Greek dramatists is this elevation more conspicuous than in Æschylus. The spirit of the great scenes in which he took a part passed into his soul, and received from his lips an expression not unworthy of it. The experiences of the sixth century B.C.,when the strongest thrones had crumbled to dust, and tyrants had been hurled from the height of power and luxurious enjoyment into the deepest abysses of ruin, had impressed on the Greeks a deep distrust of human prosperity. That the anger of the gods was provoked by the violent deeds of men was an old truth, but a feeling now began to spread abroad that mere prosperity, if it exceeded a certain limit, was regarded with jealousy by the gods and brought down their vengeance upon men. From the first—even from Homer's time—the Greeks were wont to take a far from cheerful view of human existence, and as time went on the shadows deepened. Man's capacity for happiness was never sat-

isfied, and if at one moment he seemed to have
triumphed over his evil fortune, and laid up goods
for many days, in the next, he was an outcast in the
world. This view of man's condition, which is constantly dwelt on by Pindar and Herodotus, received
an immense support from the failure of the great
armament of Xerxes. The ruin of that mighty host
was a signal instance of the humiliation of those
who deemed themselves exalted above the lot of
mankind. After the battle of Salamis the insta-
bility of human greatness and the punishment of
"insolence" echoed as an undertone through all
Greek thought.

But while other writers were content to speak of
the gods as jealous beings, who cut down the mighty
things of earth, simply because they were mighty,
Æschylus took another view : he insisted on the justice of the divine dealings with men ; on eliminating
anything like caprice or favour. The evil which fell
upon men never came without some provocation.
The race of the just is at all times prosperous ;
their happiness is abiding, and passes from father to
son ; but if prosperity leads to evil and impious
words and acts—as in Greece it often did—it is
never so great that it can resist the vengeance which
it provokes. Sooner or later, in this generation or
the next, the sentence pronounced will come to pass,
and if man will only consent to look at human nature, as it appears

> "in those pure eyes
> And perfect witness of all-judging Jove,"

the sentence will be found in every case to agree with
the highest conception of divine justice.

In the light of such thoughts Æschylus composed his tragedies, reading anew the lessons of the old mythology for his purpose. Even when the material was most untoward, as in some of the legends of Zeus, he endeavours to harmonise it with his central thought of justice. In the "Prometheus Vinctus," which is the most commonly read of his plays, we see the friend of man, to whom he owes his rise from a condition lower than that of the animals, waging an unequal contest with the youthful god, who has built up his throne on the ruins of ancient dynasties. It is a strange allegory which the poet presents to us; an allegory of which we hardly know the meaning, but expressing perhaps a consciousness of the ceaseless strife raging between human intellect and a superhuman power, whose ways are not as our ways. Whatever the interpretation may be, Æschylus makes it clear that the conflict of human aspirations with divine ordinances will find a reconciliation in the decrees of a justice which reigns supreme over gods and men. It is only when Zeus becomes the highest minister of justice that his power is supreme.

In a similar spirit the poet muses over the stories of Thebes and Troy. What was the meaning of the curse, he asks, which rested on the sons of Œdipus and the house of Atreus? Was it a blind impulse driving the innocent on to ruin? He allows that it was an impulse, but it was not irresistible; and only when reinforced by other passions, did it carry men on to the appointed end. The passages in which the poet describes the passions which drive Eteocles on to meet his brother Polynices at the gates of Thebes, and those which impel Agamemnon to sacri-

fice his daughter, are masterpieces of subtle analysis.
Personal ambition and inveterate hatred are blended
with the sense of an inherited curse and divinely appointed purpose. Crimes must be punished, yet in
the punishment a new crime is committed; and so
the tragedy goes on from generation to generation,
bringing down the great and noble, whenever they
allow their ambition or rage to lead them astray.

Thus the drama becomes with Æschylus an attempt to interpret the conditions and limits of
human life. As much as any prophet or philosopher, he strives to establish a firm basis upon which
a man may act and think; delivering him on the one
hand from superstitious fears, and warning him on
the other against self-assertion. It was a noble conception of poetry, and it was nobly carried out. The
grandeur of his characters has never been surpassed:
the proud defiance of Prometheus; the dauntless
courage of Clytemnestra, who seems lifted by her
very crime into an avenging spirit; and above all the
prescient frenzy of Cassandra, in which every element of pathos is rendered more pathetic by a helpless fore-knowledge of death—are among the immortal productions of human genius. And the language
of Æschylus is unlike the language of any other
poet, ancient and modern. The lines of Marlowe—
the so-called "master of the mighty line,"—are fal-
tering and feeble when compared with the large and
ample utterance of the old Greek poet. Gods and
heroes move before us in his scenes, and god-like
are the tones in which their words are conveyed
to our ears.

The long life of Sophocles nearly fills the whole of the fifth century. He was born about 495 B.C.; his first victory was won over Æschylus in 469 B.C., and his last play was brought out just after his death in 405 B.C. In that long space of time the spirit of the Greek drama was entirely changed, for there can hardly be a greater contrast than the contrast between Æschylus and Euripides, and, to a certain degree, Sophocles participated in the change. He made improvements in the scenery and added a third actor, for hitherto no more than two had been allowed to appear on the stage at the same time, thus attaining a greater degree of variety in his situations and a more vivid contrast of characters. He made each of the three plays which, in obedience to custom, he brought out at the same time a separate piece, unconnected with the rest; a change which enabled him to gain a separate interest and a more rapid movement in each of the dramas. No one who reads the " Orestea " of Æschylus can resist the feeling that the " Agamemnon " is more than half of the whole. The plays which follow want variety and incident; the movement grows ever weaker as it approaches the close. This error Sophocles sought to avoid. He perceived that concentration and unity were among the advantages which dramatic possessed over narrative representation, and that these advantages could not be fully realised if a single theme were spread over three plays.

There is also another change to be observed when we compare him with his great predecessor. Though

his dramas are filled with a religious spirit, and rest
to a large degree on the contrast of the divine and
human will, they are not conceived in the high pro-
phetic tone of Æschylus. He is nearer the common
thought of his time. He accepts the inevitable, and
muses over the strange sad destiny of man. What
a wonderful creature is man! he exclaims in a chorus
of the "Antigone"; how infinite in art and invention! what victories has he not won! victories over
bird and beast; over earth and sea; over his own
unsocial temper. Yet his wilfulness and pride bring
him to nought. And when a race is once doomed
to ruin, the evil passes on from generation to generation, and there is no release. With Æschylus he
agrees that insolence or rebellion is the worst of
crimes; it is the root from which the tyrant springs,
the destruction of the high laws which govern the
host of heaven—yet he sees clearly that the passions
of men are the chief agents in their undoing. The
spirit of love holds an equal empire with the most
solemn ordinances—that is, it is as powerful a motive
in the actions of men. Love is invincible in battle,
and none may win a match from Aphrodite. The
same deep sympathy with the passions of life is seen
in his abhorrence of old age—a truly Greek feeling
—and in the part which he assigns to women in his
dramas. In two of them the *denouement* is brought
about by the love of youth and maid, of wife and husband; a motive which never appears in the extant
plays of Æschylus. We observe the same tendency
in the situations in which we can compare him with
his rival. Æschylus keeps the relations of Ægisthus

SOPHOCLES.
From the marble statue in the Lateran Gallery.
(*Baumeister.*)

and Clytemnestra steadily in the background; Sophocles brings them vividly to the front. Æschylus makes little of the sisterly devotion of Antigone for Polynices; in Sophocles it is the first motive of the play. But we must not think of Sophocles as wanting in force, or dependent on love for a tragic situation. In the "Ajax" the love of Tecmessa merely adds a tender grace to the rugged hero, whose noble spirit cannot survive the death of his honour, and in the "Philoctetes" there is no female character at all. Nor is there any want of sterner stuff in his plays; he never shrinks, when necessary, from the terrible resources of his art. Ajax slays himself on the stage in the presence of the spectators; Œdipus staggers into sight, with his bleeding eyes, crying for some one to support and guide him; Philoctetes sinks down in a swoon of intolerable anguish; we are allowed to hear the appeal of Clytemnestra to Orestes: "My son, have pity on the breast that nursed thee!" and from the lips of Electra, standing watchful at the door, falls the crushing answer: "Pity she had none, for thee or for thy father."

Yet terrible as these scenes are, we never close a play of Sophocles with feelings shocked or distressed. A perfect master of his art, he knows how to give the pleasure which tragedy ought to give—the pleasure of elevated feeling passing beyond the limits of individual nature to be engaged on high and solemn themes, and so returning with renewed strength and patience to the everlasting puzzle of human existence.

In his language Sophocles is less simple and also less grandiloquent than Æschylus. The majestic lines, which fall on our ears as " thunder-drops fall on a sleeping sea," have disappeared, and in the place of the splendid wealth of metaphor in which the older poet clothes—and sometimes veils—his meaning, there is a striving after subtle combinations which often ends in obscurity—at least for us. Nevertheless there is a beauty in the songs and a pathos in the speeches of Sophocles which Æschylus has not surpassed; he has written lines in which we seem to come near to the utmost limits of human expression. Such are those with which Electra closes her lament over the urn of Orestes; such, too, are those in which the poet has chosen to paint the beauties of his own birthplace, Colonus.

There are scenes in Æschylus more striking than any scene in Sophocles, but, on the other hand, almost any play of Sophocles, taken as a whole, is a more perfect work of art than the best play of Æschylus. There is a better connexion of the scenes, a more even balance of the parts. This superiority, as we have said, was partly attained by the limitation of the subject to a single play, but it was also due to the consummate skill of the poet in arranging his plots. In this respect the " Œdipus Rex " has always been regarded as the model of a perfect play.

Euripides, who, by common consent, stood third in the list of Greek tragic poets, was a contemporary of Sophocles, both poets dying in the same year.

But he was a much younger man, and the difference of age coincided with a remarkable difference of nature and development. It is perhaps hardly too extreme to say that the difference between Shakespeare and Euripides is scarcely greater than the difference between Euripides and Sophocles. The conception of tragedy is changed ; and human nature is regarded from an entirely different point of view. The old submissive attitude, in which man is taught to think human thoughts, and walk in reverent humility towards higher powers, whose laws, however inscrutable, are nevertheless righteous and form the foundation of human society, is cast aside in favour of a criticism which shrinks from nothing, however sacred and sublime. The old myths, so simple and stately, are dragged down to the level of a case at law ; the old heroes appear as stupid, brutal, or contemptible men ; the great dames of story scold like fish-wives. Every illusion of epic art is dispelled ; we are brought face to face with the absurd facts, or the gross passions which underlie them. The very worship of the gods is shewn to be an occasion of ruin to those who cherish it. In the excitement of the Dionysiac possession Agave tears her son to pieces, and Artemis cannot protect her votary from the implacable wrath of Aphrodite. Or the politics of the day are allowed to influence the characters of Trojan legend. Agamemnon and Menelaus are Spartans, as an Athenian thought of Spartans in the Peloponnesian war ; Helen and Hermione are such women as Aristotle in a later generation declared that the Spartan women were

—imperious, proud, and licentious. The strife of man with destiny, which gives such elevation to the earlier drama, has passed away; man is now shewn contending with the base passions of his own nature. Lying, treachery, malice, uncleanness, jealousy, rage, vengeance, envy,—these are the instruments with which Euripides works to bring about a tragic situation. He deals with no ideals; he is misled by no illusions; he is softened by no pity; he will not spare us a line of the picture; in his merciless analysis of human motives, he tears away the tender coverings which contrition or hope or pity have spread over the weakness of human nature; and proclaims aloud, often in the name of the gods, the triumph of what is evil and base.

Such is Euripides on his sterner side—the author of the "Hippolytus," "Medea," and "Bacchæ." But there is also another Euripides—the author of the "Alcestis," the singer of sweet lyric songs, the magician at whose touch the common things of life become radiant with an eternal beauty,—the master of description, telling his tale at one time with matchless simplicity and grace, at another with a splendour of rhetoric, unsurpassed in any literature. The dignity and graciousness of the dying Alcestis; the glad, eager, stainless youth of Ion, who knows no home but the temple of Delphi, no parent but Apollo; the songs of the "Hecuba" and "Electra," the description of the Bacchants, the appeal of Iphigenia to her father—these will always exercise a charm even over those who turn from the darker

EURIPIDES.

From a Bust in the Museum at Naples.

(*Baumeister.*)

scenes. And even in the darkest, it must be admitted that the expression is almost perfect. The fury of Hecuba crying to Agamemnon to avenge her murdered son is sublime, and not less so the wild declamation of Cassandra, when foretelling her own and Agamemnon's death. The pathos of Medea's soliloquy is a commonplace, and even more pathetic are the simple lines :

> ἔτικτον αὐτούς· ζῆν δ' ὅτ' ἐξηύχου τέκνα,
> εἰσῆλθέ μ' οἶκτος, εἰ γενήσεται τάδε.

A poet so wide in his range and so daring in his departure from the antique solemnity of his art must needs have friends and enemies. Euripides was hated and worshipped in his own day, and the division of opinion exists to this hour. The comedian Aristophanes condemned him as immoral, holding up to scorn his Phædras and Sthenobœas, and caricaturing his sophistry and rhetoric. On the other hand, he was the favourite poet of Socrates, and not of Socrates only, but of the Athenians of his time, and even of those who lived far from Athens. A story was current in antiquity that, of the Athenian prisoners cast into the stone quarries at Syracuse, every one was allowed his liberty who could recite a verse of Euripides. The charm has not vanished with time. Milton and Goethe, Coleridge and Browning, have left a record of their admiration of this " most tragic of poets." Of criticism, which takes a different view, there is enough and to spare ; and even the most devoted admirers of Euripides must admit that his work is very unequal. Fate, which has

21

given us only seven plays of Æschylus and Sophocles, has given us nineteen of Euripides. Had the
same severe selection been exercised in his case, and
nothing left but his " Alcestis," " Medea," " Hippolytus," his " Bacchæ," " Ion," and " Iphigenia in
Tauris," the judgments of his readers would be more
consistent.

The difference which divides Euripides from Sophocles must not be ascribed merely to his personal
character or genius. The two men were indeed widely
different ; Sophocles was at once a poet and a man
of the world, the charm of the society in which he
moved, and now and then employed in the public
business of the city ; Euripides was retired, solitary,
studious, a reader of books, which in his day were still
perhaps a suspicious novelty. Under any circumstances the two would have taken different views of
life. But when Euripides was growing up to manhood, at the time at which the imagination is not
yet controlled by experience and new ideas are most
powerful to sway the mind, a great change came
over Athenian thought. The " spirit that denies "
made itself felt in every department of life, and
questions which had never yet been raised—questions touching the foundation of society and morals
—were matters of every-day discussion.

It was in the Ionian cities of Asia that the movement first began, and it began with enquiries into
the phenomena of nature. What was the cause of
existence and growth ? How did the sun and moon
and stars and earth arise ? How were their motions
regulated ? Numerous answers were given to these

questions. The elements were distinguished from their composite forms, and sometimes one and sometimes another was thought to be the cause of the rest. Various processes of rarefaction and condensation, of attraction and repulsion, were supposed— one philosopher inventing a system which may fairly be called evolution. As thought became stronger the causes of existence became more abstract: one teacher would find the key to the puzzle of the universe in number; another postulated constant change as the condition of existence; a third demanded unity and self-existent Being as the basis of all things. But one and all agreed in denying truth and reality to the changing phenomena of the outward world. By degrees the same criticism was applied to politics and ethics. The various forms of government were discussed, and with them the object and purpose of all governments. In connexion with such enquiries it was natural to ask what was legal and what was illegal. A contrast was established between "nature" and "ordinance," between universal and particular laws. It was but a short step to pass on to ethical truths, and ask: What was the measure of right and wrong? What was the value of custom? To what degree was a man a law to himself? Is truth the same for all, or does it vary according to the circumstances and temperament of each?

Questions such as these cannot be raised under any circumstances without a considerable degree of danger, and the danger was unusually great in a civilisation like that of Greece, in which morality and

religion were by no means in close harmony with
each other. But so long as they are raised in an
honest desire to get at the truth, and establish the
laws of conduct and government upon a firmer basis,
the good which attends the discussion is greater
than the evil. Unfortunately, this was by no means
the case in Greece. For a time, it is true, the
"sophists" and the philosophers were the same,
and both were thoroughly in earnest in their speculations. The great names of Thales, Anaximander,
Heraclitus, and Pythagoras are never to be mentioned without respect. But when politics and
ethics came within the sphere of criticism; above
all, when the Ionian spirit of enquiry was allied with
Sicilian rhetoric, a different spirit prevailed. Sophistry and philosophy parted company; and while the
more disinterested seekers after truth pursued their
researches into Change and Being, there were others
who made discussion a profitable profession. They
travelled through Greece as teachers, imparting for
pay their secrets of logic and dialectics, and making
"the worse appear the better reason." Their wan-
dering life emancipated them from the traditions of
any state, and though we cannot deny to them the
credit of great ability and great knowledge, we must
allow that they made an ignoble use of both. It is
true that they stimulated the intellects of those
who came to them, but the stimulus was all in one
direction—towards the removal of restraint and
the development of personal ambition. Or they
taught the art of making speeches, which, though
they would not bear examination, were brilliant

enough to carry away the feelings of a great audience.

It was in this atmosphere that the youth of the age of Pericles grew up, and Euripides among them. From the " sophists " he learned to question every thing, bringing the deepest feelings of man to the touchstone of a formal and ill-developed logic. From them he learned to turn outwards the " seamy side " of Greek mythology and religion.

The same change was present everywhere, and to many it was a change wholly evil. We have seen how sensitive the Greeks became at this time to attacks upon religion, bringing charges of " impiety " against those of the Periclean circle who seemed in any way favourable to the new intellectual movement. More especially were the comedians filled with antipathy to the sophists and their followers. They looked on them as the corrupters of youth, whose pernicious doctrines were calculated to destroy moral conduct and civic patriotism. Cratinus, the first great comic poet at Athens, had a fling at the " prying rascals " in his play of the " Panoptæ "; and in one of his earliest plays, brought out immediately after the death of Pericles, Aristophanes contrasts the young man, as the sophists had taught him to be, with the youth of an earlier age. In the " Clouds," which appeared in 423 B.C., he selected Socrates, as the most prominent sophist of the time, for the chief object of his ridicule. In this he was partly right and partly wrong; he was right in pointing to the evil wrought in the minds of the young by a crude emancipation from old beliefs and customs; he was

wrong in confounding Socrates with those who
sought to make the worse the better cause.

Socrates availed himself of the instruments which
the sophists put into his hands to destroy sophistry.
From morning to night his strange figure might be
seen in the market-place, or at some other centre of
public resort; there he stood, regardless of poverty,
incapable of fatigue, asking questions of all around
him in the endeavour to find some general principles
of action, and awaken others to an interest in such
questions. What was the relation of virtue to
knowledge? Could a man know what was right and
do what was wrong? Could virtue be taught, and,
if so, who were the teachers and where could they
be found? Was political government an art like
medicine, and what was the aim of the art, as health
is the aim of medicine? It often happened that his
questions led to no result beyond the negative result,
that the common practice and customs of men were
irrational; often they were raised on absurd analo-
gies, in which vital distinctions were overlooked, as
the analogy of men and animals, but they never
carried him astray from the position of a good man
and an honest citizen. While the professional
sophists wandered far and wide in search of profitable employment, he remained within the walls of
Athens, or only left them to fight in the service of
his country. And though many of his numberless
disciples by no means followed in his steps—on the
contrary, it was owing to the conduct of such men
as Alcibiades, Critias, and Charmides that he was
finally brought to trial for corrupting the youth of

SOCRATES.
From a bust in the Villa Albani (near Naples).
(*Baumeister.*)

Athens,—there was one among them on whom his spirit descended in a double measure. Through the dialogues of Plato the name of Socrates has become a symbol for a life passed in the service of truth and wisdom.

Aristophanes did not see this side of the life of Socrates; and even if he had seen it, his business as a comedian was not to say what was true, but what was amusing. The "Old Comedy" of Athens, that is, roughly speaking, the comedy of the fifth century, presents us with a picture of Athenian life and manners; but the picture is far from being true, and it was not meant to be true. We cannot judge of Athenian politics and society, of Athenian statesmen and philosophers, of Athenian men and women, from the descriptions given by the comedians, without being unjust both to the poets and the people.

Attic comedy was essentially a creation of the age of Pericles; it was about the middle of the century when the earliest comedians of any note came forward. It had its root in the merry-makings at the vintage, when the hamlets of Attica worshipped the wine god with indecent rites and riotous glee. The Greeks had a passion for dramatic representation, and their religious worship, like their poetry and even their history, tended to take a dramatic form. Hardly any deity was worshipped without some sort of miracle-play, or at least a procession. The village wits took the opportunity of the festival to form themselves into a band and amuse the audience, who gathered round, with tales of village scandal, or by

imitating the dress, style, and language of anyone
who had earned the aversion of his neighbours.
With the growth of democracy these amusements,
which were essentially amusements of the people, attracted more attention, until at length they too, in a
more developed form, found a place among the
dramas brought out in the great theatre at the foot
of the Acropolis. The old village stories and scandal were of course dropped, in order to make room
for scurrilous attacks on the conduct and character
of men well known in the city, but the old buffoon-
ery and extravagance, by which the attention of the
village had been caught, the old indecency, which
symbolised the worship of the productive power of
nature, were still permitted.

Of the comedies acted in the lifetime of Pericles,
we have nothing but fragments ; but there is no reason to suppose that they differed from the comedies
of Aristophanes, which began to appear in 427 B.C.
The fragments which have been preserved, and the
little that we know of their history, allow us to assert that from the time that comedies were acted
as part of the great festival of Dionysus, they were
distinguished by three characteristics : the direct
attacks on public characters ; the extravagant forms
assumed by the choruses ; and the nakedness of their
indecency.

We have already spoken of the attacks made by
the comic poets on Pericles and Aspasia. Even as
early as 444 B.C., Cratinus, in the "Thracian Women,"
spoke of Pericles as going about with the Odeum on
his head,—a sarcasm on his habit of wearing a helmet

ARISTOPHANES.
From a Bust Found Near Tusculum.
(*Baumeister.*)

to conceal the shape of his head, and on the recent erection of the music-hall. In another play of the same author, Pericles is " the new Zeus born of Faction and of Cronos," enthroned, like Zeus himself, on the destruction of ancient order; and in yet another fragment, Hera-Aspasia is spoken of in language of untempered vigour. Even after the death of Pericles, Aristophanes had no hesitation in repeating the scandal which declared that Aspasia and her runaways and the embezzlements of Pheidias were the real cause of the Peloponnesian war. The same measure was dealt out to others: to Cleon, the ferocious opponent of Pericles, to Hyperbolus, and Cleophon, leaders of the extreme democracy, who insisted on war to the death with Sparta; and, in a less degree, to Nicias and Theramenes, who were in favour of a more moderate constitution and peace. Only one of the great Athenians of the Peloponnesian war is allowed to escape: Alcibiades, the son of Cleinias, about whom, in spite of much that must have been very tempting in his position and character, Aristophanes is remarkably silent. And not the leading men only, but the institutions of the people, and even the people—the all-powerful sovereign Demos, —are brought forward for satire and ridicule. The absurdities of the law-courts form the subject of the "Wasps" of Aristophanes; the absurdities of the Demos form the subject of the "Knights." When there was nothing to be made of the men, the poets turned upon the women. Two of the plays of Aristophanes shew us Athens under the "regiment" of women; a third presents a picture of the women as they were, when left to themselves, and celebrating their sacred Thesmophoria.

On this side Attic comedy is not to be compared with the comedy of our own stage, but with the pamphlets of the age of Swift, or the *Rolliad*, the caricatures of Gillray and Rowlandson, and *Punch*. But the comparison is only partially true. Much greater licence was allowed at Athens than with us, owing partly to the state of society at the time, and partly to the fact that gross and licentious ribaldry was an accepted part of some religious rites in Greece. And doubtless a great part of the attacks were made and taken in no very serious spirit. So long as the persons assailed were in a strong position, they cared little for the extravagances of comic satire. Unmeasured abuse often brings its own antidote. We know that when Fox was hurling his denunciations upon North in the House of Commons, the recipient was generally asleep! So, too, with the city. So long as Athens felt her greatness secure, she was willing to let the comedians do their worst upon men and institutions. She was pleased with her own follies, as Justice Shallow was pleased with the wildness of his youth, and not the less pleased because "every third word was a lie." In times of distress and danger her temper changed. She became fretful and suspicious. Twice in the fifth century—in 440 B.C., when Samos was in revolt, and in 415 B.C., at the time when the great Sicilian expedition was being sent out, and the public mind was disturbed by the mutilation of the Hermæ—it was forbidden to satirise anyone by

name. The result in the second case may be seen in
the comedies of Aristophanes. In all the plays
brought out before this date he is political and personal; in the "Birds," which appeared in 414 B.C., he
never alludes directly to the events which were occupying the minds of all. After the fall of Athens,
in 404 B.C., the character of comedy entirely changed :
it became a comedy of manners; the allusions to
politics either disappeared or were carefully veiled.

The plays of Aristophanes are sometimes named
after the choruses which appear in them ; and among
these we find such fantastic titles as "Wasps,"
"Clouds," "Birds," and "Frogs." The practice did
not begin with him ; he tells us that his predecessor,
Magnes, availed himself of the same artifice to attract an audience, and from the fragments we can
see that the practice was universal in the older
comedy. The names were not without meaning; in
appearance and dress, so far as possible, the choruses
in these plays were what they were called. A paint-
ing on a vase has preserved to us a picture of men
dressed to represent birds, and though we have no
right to connect it with Aristophanes, the picture
probably represents some scene from a comedy.

But why, we ask, does the poet have recourse to
these strange disguises? We may answer the question by saying that comedy never forgot her origin.
In the village festivals all kinds of fantastic dresses
had been worn to attract attention and excite curiosity, as well as for the sake of concealment, and the
practice thus begun was continued when comedy
became a part of the state festivals. There was also

another reason. By bringing in a chorus of Birds or Clouds, the poets were able to look at human nature and society from an external and abnormal point of view, as they might appear to beings who did not share the delusions of mankind. Like the Fairies in " Midsummer Night's Dream," they could watch the stir and stress of life, and declare : " Lord ! what fools these mortals be ! " It is the same feeling which has prompted the introduction of animals into fables. The " great and sane and simple race of beasts," whose instincts never swerve from the appointed end, have always formed an excellent vehicle for the delivery of moral precepts and criticism. The comic poets claimed an even greater licence than the fabulists, for their fancy was not bounded by the animate world ; but amid all their extravagance there ran a vein of common-sense and sound criticism, often of vigorous personal remonstrance—especially in the form of chorus called a Parabasis, which could only be introduced under some sort of disguise.

Of the gross indecency of the old Attic comedy it is impossible to speak without reserve, and yet a few words of explanation, if not of palliation, must be said. However strange the statement may appear to us, it is nevertheless true, that this grossness is largely due to the nature of Greek religion. In its essence that religion was a worship of the powers which are at work in the universe, whatever they might be, without distinction of higher or lower, or the exclusion of animal forces in favour of moral. Not only were there rites of a grossly obscene nature in Greek temples,

but there were festivals in which the worshippers
claimed the privilege, in language and in symbolism,
of being naked and not ashamed. This strange departure from the ordinary manners and customs of
life was found among women no less than men;
what the worship of Dionysus was to the one, the
worship of Demeter was to the other. In our eyes
it forms a repellent feature in Greek civilisation, and
it was repellent to the Greeks themselves at a later
age. Aristotle and Plutarch condemn it; in their
time the open and outrageous indecency of Cratinus
and Aristophanes had been exchanged for veiled
suggestions and innuendoes. The change may have
been in the interest of good manners; but whether
it was in the interest of pure morals is more doubtful, and at any rate we must not be misled into
harsh judgments on the morality of the age of
Pericles. These are matters in which one age cannot understand another. In spite of the drunken-
ness which prevailed at the Dionysia, the Greeks
were a sober nation; and though we have no evidence on which to found a good opinion of the
private life of the Athenians, we are at least in
possession of two facts which prove the high value
placed, in theory, at any rate, on good conduct: No
nation was ever more careful than they of the moral
and physical education of youth; none watched
more strictly to prevent the slightest insult to
women of the household.

Philosophy was not the only gift of the Asiatic
Greeks to their kinsmen on the peninsula. The

same spirit of enquiry which led them to investigate the causes of natural phenomena induced them also to examine and record the past history of Greek cities and the customs of neighbouring barbarians. By the beginning of the fifth century Hecatæus of Miletus had written a description of the earth; maps had been drawn; lists had been made of priestesses and officers; genealogies had been compiled and worked into a foundation for chronology; legends had been compared and assimilated; traditions of the founding of cities had been committed to writing. A prose literature made its appearance beside the various forms of poetry, which had hitherto been the only literature of Greece, and, as was natural in an age of such mental activity, it spread rapidly. The sense of style was awakened—a sense which could not fail to be stimulated by the importance of rhetoric in civic life and the attention paid by the sophists to expression. By the middle of the century Herodotus had begun the composition of the immortal work, which forms the foundation of our knowledge of the history of antiquity; and at the beginning of the Peloponnesian war Thucydides was preparing to record the struggle which he thought the greatest of all wars; though his history, which he did not live to complete, was not published till after the end of it.

We have already seen that Sophocles and Euripides, though contemporaries in age, were widely separated in thought and feeling. The same distinction may be observed between Herodotus and Thucydides, though it is shown in a different way.

Herodotus is essentially the historian of Hellas;
Thucydides is the historian of Athens: the first is
penetrated with the feeling of the Persian war; the
second, with the feeling of the Peloponnesian war.
Both were great admirers of Athens and of Pericles;
but one looks at them from without, the other, as it
were, from within. The spirit of criticism, which is
all in all to Thucydides, is faintly felt by Herodotus.
He repeats what he has heard, even when he does
not believe it; he asserts what he believes, even
when it is against all evidence. He is wrong when
he is at the greatest pains to be scientific, as in his
account of the Nile; and right when he is merely
guessing, as in his account of the Caspian, which he
asserts to be a "sea by itself," *i.e.*, closed at the
northern end. His measurements are wrong, for he
makes the Euxine twice as long as it really is; his
numbers are wrong, for he calculates the length of
life on a year of 375 days! He describes the pyra-
mids of Memphis, but says nothing of the Sphinx;
he travelled to Thebes, but passed by the splendid
buildings of the Ramessids without a word. His interest in history was not the interest which a modern
historian would have. Of the countries which he
knew best he tells us least, and what he does tell
is often of very little historical value. He might
have said a great deal about the Greek cities in
Asia, as they existed in his own day, when they
were claimed as subjects by Athens and Persia, or
about the constitution of Sparta; among the "episodes which his work affects," these would have found
a fitting place. Instead of these we have accounts of re-

mote and unknown nations, foreign criticisms on Greek myths, or popular stories about the domestic complications of the Spartan kings, or legends of the burning of Crœsus and the invasion of Scythia ; and it is not till he settles down to the invasion of Greece by the Persians that he pursues his theme in a settled order, and with some attempt at chronology. The history of Thucydides is the reverse of all this. He opens his work with a preface in which he establishes his view that the Peloponnesian war was the greatest ever known in Greece, and dwells on the importance of wealth in warfare, knowing that Athens entered on the struggle incomparably richer than her opponents. Then he traces the causes of the war, and, after a digression, in which he relates the origin and growth of the Athenian power, he enters on his subject, never to leave it again. His narrative is annalistic in form, each year being divided into two parts, a summer and a winter ; he took the greatest personal trouble not only to find out what men said, for Herodotus did that, but to find out the precise truth of what they said, having the greatest mistrust of poets whose business it was to exaggerate, and of " logographers," who composed less with a view to the lasting value of their work than to the immediate impression made by it. But, with all this devotion to accuracy, he does not approach the task in the spirit of a modern historian. He tells us little of the internal politics of Athens during the earlier part of the tremendous struggle. Of some of the popular leaders who played a considerable part in the drama, such as Lysicles and Hyperbolus, he hardly says a word; the comedians and the sophists, Sophocles and Socrates, are never so much as mentioned. It is the war, and nothing but the war, on which he has fixed his attention. Attica was laid waste, but we hear nothing of the revolution in property which this must have caused; the education of the Athenian youth was influenced by sophists and philosophers, but Thucydides never condescends to say whether the issue of the war was or was not in any degree due to the decay of the fibre of the Athenian nation.

The work of Herodotus is epic in its plan and highly religious in feeling. The episodes which carry him almost over the whole known world may be compared with the episodes which carry Odysseus to Calypso's isle and to Scheria; the strong, swift stream of narrative, which runs through the later books of the " Odyssey," may have furnished a hint to the historian in the management of the closing part of his story. Throughout the whole he is tracing the doom which overtakes human pride and insolence; Crœsus, Polycrates, and Xerxes are all examples of the favourite theme, that the paths of pride lead to destruction. It is in vain that men are warned of the danger. Crœsus is warned by Solon; Xerxes by Artabanus; Polycrates by Amasis, but without effect. There is no way of saving a man from the anger which is in store for him.

Thucydides, as we have said, is annalistic,—attempting by this means to secure strictness in chronology even at the expense of the connexion of events,—and he is anything rather than religious.

He speaks in contempt of signs and wonders and prophets, for any crisis will bring its crop of such; he never alludes to any theories of divine envy or human pride; he wishes to record things merely as they are, believing that human life moves in cycles, and that the past may form a guide to the future. Yet we may notice that even he cannot wholly free himself from the idea that the plague was the work of Apollo, the god who was pledged to aid the Spartans.

In spite of all their differences, Herodotus and Thucydides are alike in one point : they are both more dramatic than any modern historian would venture to be. Not only do they introduce speeches into their works on occasions, when perhaps no speeches were made, and relate conversations which could not have been preserved,—this is especially the case with Herodotus, who can tell us what Atossa said to Darius in the silence of the royal bed-chamber—but the speeches are obviously in some cases composed with a view to the situation ; they are not a record of what was actually said at any time. This is going further than a modern writer would venture to do, but this is not all. In some cases it seems very probable that Herodotus did not hesitate to ascribe to others opinions which were really his own—at any rate it is very difficult to understand what interest the Egyptian priests could have taken in the story of Helen,—and Thucydides has been accused, not without some shew of reason, of making rhetorical comments on the Corcyrean sedition. Whatever the truth of this criticism, we shall, in any case, find it difficult to deny that the nature and use of historical evidence was imperfectly understood by Greek historians. Yet the two great works will never be displaced from the position which they hold at the head of descriptive and philosophical history, for Herodotus has never been surpassed in the art of telling a story, nor Thucydides in his insight into the motives of human action.

Pericles was not content that Athens should be the centre of the highest art and literature of Greece; he resolved that, so far as possible, the people should share in all the pleasure which art and literature could give. In regard to the great artistic triumphs of Pheidias and his fellow-workers, the end was easily attained; the beautiful Parthenon was there for all who chose to see; and once in every four years, at the festival of the great Panathenæa, all Athens went in procession through the gateway to the temple. The plays at the Dionysia could not be so easily thrown open. The theatre in which they were acted was leased to a manager, who charged a certain sum for entrance to cover his expenses. The sum was not high—about threepence a day during the festival,—but even this trifle was more than many of the Athenians could afford to spend. Pericles met the difficulty by distributing to each of the poorest class, out of the public funds, the amount which would enable him to pay the fee charged for entrance. This was the celebrated " Theoricon," or sum given for attendance on amusements. In the time of Pericles it was given to the very poor and only at the Dionysia, but afterwards the word was used to cover the division of the surplus funds of the state among the citizens.

DANCER.
From the marble relief discovered in the
Theatre of Dionysus.

CHAPTER XVIII.

THE ATHENS OF PERICLES: MANNERS AND SOCIETY—CONCLUSION.

Slavery at Athens—Athenian women—Pericles;
his appearance and manners—His character.

HE monuments of Athens remain, though in ruins, to attest the splendour of the art which adorned the city in the days of Pericles; the noble works of literature, which delighted the Athenian of his day, can be read by us in a form not very different from that in which they first appeared. But when we turn to matters of a more ephemeral nature, and attempt to realise the manners and society of the time, our evidence is far more precarious. It is always difficult to judge of an age by the literature which it produces; ideals mislead us in one direction, and caricatures in another; or we mistake the part for the whole in our ignorance of the extent to which literature penetrated; or, to take another point of view, in our ignorance of the area from which ideas and characters are drawn. We know, for instance, that all Athens congregated in the theatre of Dionysus to hear the new tragedies at the Spring Festival, but we cannot tell how many of the audience entered into the spirit of Æschylus and Sophocles. The eager interest in knowledge, which we find among the young men who figure in the dialogues of Plato and Xenophon, must have been confined to a few; and when we ask what was the general level of intelligence and culture at Athens in the best days of the city, it is very difficult to give an answer.

The most obvious point of difference in Greek civilisation, when we compare it with our own, is the existence of slavery. There were slaves everywhere; in every workshop and every household; on the farms and in the mines; the police were slaves, the clerks in public offices were slaves. This feature at once places a wide distinction between the democracy of Athens and the democracies of modern times. The questions which are now among the most prominent, such as the relations of labour and capital, the growth of population, or the extension of the franchise, were hardly raised at Athens; their place was taken by others, not less important to the welfare of the society, but widely different: the defence of the masters against their slaves; the admission of the evidence of slaves in courts of law; the rules and sanctions of manumission. On these subjects much might be said which would not be to the credit of Greek civilisation. If we remember that twenty thousand slaves deserted to the Peloponnesians at a time when the Public Assembly at Athens never numbered five thousand citizens, we can understand that there was reason to dread the

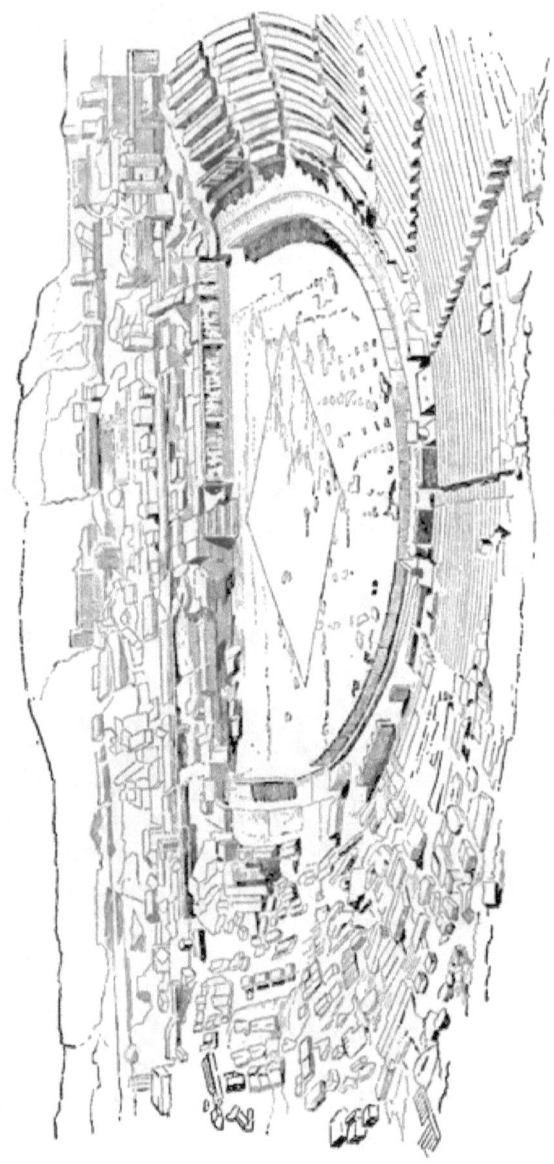

THEATRE OF DIONYSUS—HYMETTUS IN THE DISTANCE.

(*Curtius and Kaupert.*)

combination of slaves against masters; and under
such circumstances the measures taken for repression
were not likely to err on the side of mercy. We
also know that the evidence of slaves was never
taken except under torture, more or less severe.
On the other hand, it would not be difficult to collect instances of kind and humane treatment of
slaves by their masters, or of devotion on the part
of slaves. It is also obvious that the existence of
female slaves placed a number of questions, which
are among the most difficult of our day, in quite a
different light; and without attempting to decide
whether the evil was greater or less, it is at least
certain that a slave, who was always an article of
value, in one way or another, was never so utterly
abandoned to her fate as the outcast of modern
society. Her death, at any rate, could be traced and
avenged. But these are wide and intricate results
of slavery, on which we cannot enter here. Looking at the matter from a more special point of view,
we may ask: What was the effect of slavery on the
Athenian democracy?

As a first and obvious effect it allowed the citizen
an amount of leisure which without it would have
been impossible. While the slave was at work, the
master was in the Ecclesia, or in the law-courts, or
in the market-place, or in one of the numerous
porticoes. Without the opportunities thus afforded,
the Periclean constitution could not have existed.
Had the poorer part of the population been compelled to spend their days in laborious occupations,
the rich must have remained the governing body of

the city, but the existence of slavery, united with
payment for service in the Council and the law-
courts, placed a majority of the citizens in the
position of men who had both the means and the
leisure to devote their time to the state.

Such an arrangement not only led to the development of an extreme democracy, but it also gave a
new turn to the old conflict between rich and poor.
In countries where the franchise depends on wealth,
or the poor live on wages paid them by the rich,
democracy may degenerate into socialism. But this
is less likely to be the case in a state where all the
citizens are equal, and few, if any, are employed in
the service of others. In Athens, at any rate democracy never took a socialistic form. A man who
possessed a large fortune was expected to contribute
largely to the state ; he was burdened with heavy
contributions to the maintenance of the fleet ; out
of his pocket came the money necessary for the
choruses, which took part in the Dionysia and other
festivals of the city. So long as he paid these sums
—and many citizens not only paid them, but seized
the opportunity to make a display of their liberality,
—he was permitted to enjoy his fortune, however
large. Pettifoggers might attack him, it is true, but
they could be beaten off by their own weapons—as
Socrates advised his rich friend Crito to keep a tame
sycophant who would defend him from others of his
kind ! The jurors might bear hardly upon him in
their administration of the law, for that evil, as we
have said, was inseparable from the institution of
the law-courts, but the democracy never attempted

anything like a confiscation of property, even under
the severest pressure. Such measures appear for the
first time in the acts of the "Thirty Tyrants." The
same protection was extended even to those who,
though not citizens of Athens, were residents in the
city, the "resident aliens," or metœci. These men
paid certain taxes, and liberal gifts were expected
from them, but no attempt was made to interfere
with their just gains, so long as these were made in
a manner which did not impair the wellbeing of the
city. Most of the metœci were traders, and, in fact,
the trade of Athens was largely in their hands; as a
class they were probably richer than a large number
of the citizens; their property, and even their lives,
were at the mercy of the Athenian jurors; yet we
never hear that they were oppressed. The fact that
they were politically in a subordinate position satisfied
the ambition of the citizens, whose vanity was much
in excess of their cupidity. That an alien or even a
slave was better clad and better fed than the citizen
provoked no jealousy. The citizen was the only
free man in the city. He lived as he pleased, master
of his time and of his actions, and, what was more
delightful still, master of the time and actions of
others. The poorest citizen, in theory, at least, was
the equal of the richest, and when he held up his
hand in the Assembly, or dropped his pebble in the
juror's box, he felt not only that he was the ruler of
a mighty empire, but that the rich who came forward
as officers of the state were in a manner his servants.
This consciousness of a superiority went far to balance the bitterness of feeling between classes. If the

poor man felt that the rich received more than his share of the good things of the city, he could at least say his say without reserve. He was not the servant of another, dependent on his will and purse. It is in this spirit that Dicæopolis expresses himself towards one of the Athenian generals:

Lamachus.
　　Is this the sort of language for a beggar
　　To use to a commander such as me?
Dicæopolis.
　　A beggar am I?
Lam.　　　　　　Why what else are you?
Dic.　I 'll tell ye! An honest man : that 's what I am,
　　A citizen that has served his time in the army,
　　As a footsoldier, fairly, not like you,
　　Pilfering and drawing pay, with a pack of foreigners.
　　　　　　　　　　　　　　　　　　—Frere.

Slavery had also another effect. Like every government the government of Athens had to contend with extremes of intelligence and ignorance. On the one hand was the citizen, who, belonging, let us say, to the circle of Pericles, was not only trained in the best education of the time, but knew the relations which prevailed between Athens and foreign states, and the past history of his city ; on the other was the dull peasant whose talk was wholly of oxen. But owing to the presence of slaves these extremes were probably less marked at Athens than in modern states. Every citizen could, if he chose, attend the meetings of the Assembly, where he would hear a good deal of discussion and acquire at least an outline of the facts; he could sit as a juror in a lawcourt and have his wits sharpened by distinguishing between the lies and counterlies which were prevalent there. Twice in the year he could listen to comedies ; once, at least to the masterpieces of the great tragedians, and though books were scarce, every citizen had been to some kind of school, and could at least read and write. It is probable that the average intelligence of an Athenian audience was not less than the average intelligence of artisans in a modern city, and their knowledge of affairs was certainly greater. It is true that they had no newspapers, but on the other hand they had few books and no religious dogma, so that the affairs of the city, and no doubt the affairs of the citizens also, occupied a far larger share of attention with them than with us, and as few hours of the day were spent in labour, they had a great deal more leisure to bestow upon their city and their neighbours than the modern artisan.

From Aristophanes we can borrow pictures of Athenian life which in spite of exaggeration bring before us some leading traits of character. His sympathies are largely with the farming class, on whom the war brought such suffering. We have already made the acquaintance of Dicæopolis, the hero of the "Acharnians." While the authorities are busy forming alliances with Persia and Thrace, Dicæopolis—in the play—ventures on a private peace with Sparta, and the reign of peace begins, at least in his household. He revisits his country home, where he celebrates the rural festival of Dionysus with the abundance and freedom of old days.

Dic. Oh blessed Bacchus, what a joy it is
      To go thus unmolested, undisturbed,
      My wife, my children, and my family,
      With our accustom'd, joyful ceremony,
      To celebrate thy festival in my farm.
      —Well, here 's success to the truce of thirty years!
Wife. Mind your behaviour, child ; carry the basket
      In a modest, proper manner ; look demure
      And grave— * * * Come, move on.
      Mind your gold trinkets, they 'll be stolen else.
Dic. Follow behind there, Xanthias, with the pole,
      And I 'll strike up the bacchanalian chant.
      —Wife, you must be spectator ; go within
      And mount the housetop to behold us pass.
                  —Frere.

Then he proceeds to establish a market, in which the products of Megara and Bœotia, both contraband during the war, are brought to him. Fish and fowl are cooked for his table, while the miserable soldier has nothing but an onion and salt fish. The enjoyments of Dicæopolis are gross and material enough, but there is an air of honesty and straightforwardness about him which contrasts—or at least is represented as contrasting—very strongly with the meanness and greed of politicians and informers. Another character of the same kind is Trygæus in the " Peace," who triumphantly brings down Peace from the gods to Attica, and in his own person illustrates very vividly the blessings of her return.

How sweet it is to see the new-sown corn-field fresh and even,
With blades just springing from the soil that only ask a shower from
    Heaven.
There, while kindly rains are falling, indolently to rejoice,
Till some worthy neighbour, calling, cheers you with his hearty voice :
" Well, with weather such as this, let us hear Trygæus tell us
What should you and I be doing? You 're the king of all good
    fellows.

Since it pleases Heaven to prosper your endeavours, friend, and
    mine,
Let us have a merry meeting, with some friendly talk and wine.
In the vineyard there 's your lout, hoeing in the slop and mud ;
Send the wench to call him out, this weather he can do no good.
Dame, take down two pints of meal, and do some fritters in your
    way ;
Boil some grain to stir it in, and let us have those figs, I say.
Send a servant to my house—any one that you can spare—
[There he 'll find a brace of linnets, and beside them] pies of
    hare.*
There should be four of them in all, if the cat has left them right ;
We heard her racketing and tearing round the larder all last night.
Boy, bring three of them to us :—take the other to my father :
Cut some myrtle for our garlands, sprigs in flower, or blossom rather,
Give a shout upon the way to Charinades our neighbour
To join our drinking bout to-day, since Heaven is pleased to bless
    our labour."

                                —Frere.

In the " Clouds " we have a man of a similar stamp
married to a lady of the highest rank. On his side
there is nothing but coarseness and thrift ; on hers,
finery and extravagance. The son born to this ill-
assorted pair takes after his mother, involving his
father deeply in debt by his extravagance in horse-
flesh and carriages. To be rid of his creditors
Strepsiades is anxious that his son should learn the
new doctrine by which the "worse is made the better
cause." The son will not hear of it. He associate
with Socrates and the god-forsaken Chærephon ! he
would lose his complexion, become pale instead of
sunburnt, and what would his companions say to
him then ? Strepsiades then offers himself as a
pupil, but he is so old and stupid that nothing can
be made of him. To save the house from ruin the

    * Line 14 was left imperfect by the translator.

son is at length induced to give way and study the new learning, which he does with such effect that he beats his father out of the door!

Other pictures bring before us the informers, who made it their business to detect any goods introduced into Athens contrary to law; and the hardly less miserable hierophants, who quickly appeared on the scene whenever any sacrifice was going on, for a sacrifice meant a dinner to all concerned. Another feature of Athenian life constantly occurring in the comedies is the faith in omens and oracles. Oracles are quoted on every occasion, and for any purpose. Here is a scene from the "Knights" of Aristophanes:

Demos. But what are these?—all?
Cleon.   Oracles.
Demos.   What all?
Cleon. Ah, you're surprised, it seems, at the quantity!
That's nothing: I've a trunk full of 'em at home—
Sausage-Seller.
And I've a garret, and out-house both brimful.
Demos. Let's give them a look—Whose oracles are these?
Cleon. Bakis's mine are.
Demos. to S.-S.   Well! and whose are yours?
S.-S. Mine are from Glanis, Bakis's elder brother.
Demos. And what are they all about?
Cleon.   About the Athenians,
About the island of Pylos, about myself—
About yourself—about all kinds of things.
Demos. And what are yours about?
S.-S.   About the Athenians,
About pease-pudding and porridge, about the Spartans,
About the war, about the pilchard fishery,
About the state of things in general,
About short weights and measures in the market,
About all things and persons whatsoever,
About yourself and me. Bid him go whistle.
                                        —*Frere.*

The wrath of Aristophanes is more especially bitter against the men who have come forward as political leaders: Cleon the tanner, Lysicles the cattle-dealer, and Hyperbolus the lamp-maker. As a type of the degradation to which the city was sinking, he introduces the Sausage-Seller, who in ignorance and impudence outstrips the rest. The fellow can barely read or write, but his future eminence was predicted even in his boyhood, from the readiness with which he could steal and lie.

Cleon. Answer me truly!
What was your early school? Where did you learn
The rudiments of letters and of music?

S.-S. Where hogs are singed and scalded in the shambles,
There was I pummelled to a proper tune.

Cleon. Hah! say'st thou so? thy prophecy begins
To bite me to the soul with deep foreboding.
Yet tell me again—What was your course of practice
In feats of strength and skill at the Palæstra?

S.-S. Stealing and starving, perjuring and swearing.

Cleon. O mighty Apollo, your decree condemns me!
Say what was your employment afterwards?

S.-S. I practised as a Sausage-Seller chiefly,
Occasionally as pimp, and errand boy.

Cleon. Oh misery. I am lost and gone.

—Frere.

These pictures are, of course, exaggerations, yet the contrast of country and city, the degeneration of education and politics, were facts. In the better days, before the war broke out, Athens was a beautiful and well cultivated territory. There were excellent houses and homesteads in the villages, and round them settled a contented and thriving population. In the city, on the other hand, there was a considerable number of persons who, while existing in a very low degree of comfort, claimed for themselves almost the foremost place in the state. They were restless and dissatisfied, full of suspicions of every one who undertook public office, and anxious to make the most out of the advantages which the empire offered. The richer citizens were helpless against them, and when Pericles died the power passed into the hands of their nominees. For with the war came the ruin of Attica, the confinement of the people in the city, the impoverishment and final destruction of all whose income depended on land. The change was an inevitable accompaniment of the war as planned by Pericles, and it was fatal to the state. Athens rose again after her fall; Attica was once more cultivated and prosperous, but the old spirit never revived. The great names of the fourth century are quite different from those of the fifth, a change which implies that the old families had disappeared; and the feeling which animated public men was different too.

We have already spoken of the presence of sophists at Athens. Under any circumstances they would have made their appearance in a great city, which was the centre of Greek thought and intellect, but the growing importance of public speaking for those who took a part in the affairs of the city made them especially welcome. Among the younger men of the richer classes, who wished to be somebody in the city, their influence was very great, and it seems to have penetrated into the common education of the time. In the "Clouds," Aristophanes pits the

new education, with its immorality, its ruthless logic
and impudence, against the old quiet, seemly, reverent training of the Attic youth ; in the "Acharnians"
he contrasts the young man who could speak with
the old warriors who had done great things in the
past. The influence, though intellectually stimulat-
ing, was not a good influence ; it put private interests
above public, and taught the disciples to look at
everything in reference to themselves. The action
of Pericles towards the Areopagus had long ago
destroyed the spirit of reverence for the ancient
institutions of public life; sophistry went farther
and destroyed it in private life. If the people were
becoming more and more impatient of restraint,
until at length they insisted on doing "what they
pleased," regardless of the checks provided by the
constitution, the young Athenians became impatient
of the general decorum which the old education
imposed upon them. Such freedom was especially
dangerous in Greece. The old sanctions which
religion and moral law had supplied were poor at
the best, and it was useless to quote them when the
young retorted by appeals to the grosser side of
Greek mythology, or even denied the existence of
the gods altogether.

Along with this evil went another. In a very
striking passage Thucydides has shown us how,
under the crushing influence of the war, political
considerations began to outweigh all others. "The
seal of good faith was not divine law, but fellowship
in crime. If an enemy, when he was in the ascendant, offered fair words, the opposite party received

23

them not in a generous spirit, but by a jealous watchfulness of his actions. Revenge was dearer than self-preservation. Any agreements sworn by either party, when they could do nothing else, were binding so long as both were powerless. But he who, on a favourable opportunity, first took courage and struck at his enemy when he saw him off his guard, had greater pleasure in a perfidious than he would have had in an open act of revenge; he congratulated himself that he had taken the safer course, and also that he had overreached his enemy and gained the prize of superior ability."* Such feelings would co-operate with the new views of life in bringing about an extirpation of the old patriotism which united an honest love of country with the best traditions of domestic life and personal conduct. The spirit of the best men was corrupted, and the spirit of the worst was not good for much at any time. The sons of the men who had fought with Cimon and Aristides became intriguers with Antiphon and Theramenes, and when the game fell into their hands they came forward as the Thirty Tyrants. Their opponents — the democratical party—were first led by Pericles, then by Cleon, then by Hyperbolus, and the like, until at length they found themselves the prey of the Spartan commander, without empire, without revenues, and without ships.

The tone of society at Athens was peculiarly masculine. Men lived little at home, and much in

---

* Thuc., iii., 82. Jowett.

PORTICO OF THE ERECHTHEUM.

From a Photograph.

the market-place or the porticoes, or the barbers'
shops, or wherever they found it convenient to congregate. Yet there, as elsewhere, the women were
one half of the whole, and, in spite of the seclusion
in which they lived, a very important half. Plutarch tells us how Themistocles spoke of his little
son as the most influential person in Athens ; " for,"
he said, " the child rules his mother, his mother rules
me, I rule the Athenians, and the Athenians the
Greeks." The greater is our disappointment at the
few records which have survived of the women of
Athens during the fifth century. The ribaldry of
Aristophanes is of course no evidence of the domestic
life of the time. Nearer the truth is the pretty picture
which Xenophon has given in the "Œconomicus"
of the married life of an Athenian gentleman, but
such a picture, even if it is not ideal, only gives us
the idyllic side of life ; it tells us nothing of the
sterner aspect ; and there were times when the aspect
must have been stern indeed. In the darkest periods
of the century, after the overthrow of the great
Egyptian expedition, at the time of the plague, and
after the Sicilian expedition, there can have been
few houses at Athens in which there was not one
dead. What was the effect of this constant bereavement on the minds and feelings of the women?
Were they hardened into a stupor, or were they
rendered hysterical and wild, or were they merely
indifferent ?

We cannot tell. The only occasions on which we
get a glimpse of the Athenian women are the festivals and the funerals. From her early childhood a

pretty girl might share in the rites and ceremonies
of the city; when she grew older she took part in
the Panathenaic procession; older still, she worshipped with other Athenian matrons at the Thesmophoria, and to her lot it fell to discharge the last
duties to the dead. Through these ceremonies she
was allowed to feel that she had a part in civic life.
"It is right," says the chorus in the "Lysistrata" of
Aristophanes, "that we women should give good
advice to the city which has nursed us in splendour
and softness. At seven years of age I carried the
sacred chest of Athena; at ten I was mill-woman
to our Lady; then, clad in saffron dress, I was
a bear at the Brauronia, and once again, with a
string of figs round my neck, I bore a basket in a
procession."

There were other occasions on which a larger scope
was given to personal feelings. At the worship of
Adonis, which became common at Athens during the
Peloponnesian war, emotions long repressed found
relief in wild lamentations; and in the orgiastic festival of Dionysus—though this was Theban rather
than Athenian—the outpourings of hysterical passion
were carried to an extreme which seems almost
incredible.

It is common to speak of society at Athens in the
time of Pericles as highly intellectual and grossly immoral. We can point to great names, and we can
point to great vices. But on closer examination we
shall find that it is easy to exaggerate. There were
great names in France before the Revolution—
greater than any since,—yet the mass of the people

SEPULCHRAL MONUMENT.
From the original (as restored) in the Louvre.
After Clarac—Musee de Sculpture.

(*Müller.*)

were sunk far below their present level of intelligence; the vices of the court of Charles II. are notorious, but we can draw no conclusions from them about the state of the people. So far as can be ascertained, the Athenians were extremely careful of their children and their women, and this care cannot have failed to exercise a great influence on the men, for most Athenians had a wife and children. There, as everywhere, there were men who refused to live the life of the ordinary citizen, and gave themselves up to dissolute habits. Their excesses may have been more uncontrolled than with us, for there were no adequate arrangements at Athens for keeping order in the streets; they were certainly more known, owing to the greater publicity of life. Yet if we remember that the streets in Athens were narrow and crooked, that there were deserted houses where bad characters could congregate, and that there were no lamps of any kind, we shall not deny that the Athens of Pericles contrasts favourably with what we know of the state of London a hundred years ago. And if the satire of Aristophanes is more open in its attacks on vice, it does not exhibit a deeper acquaintance with iniquity than the satire of Swift or Mandeville.

Such was Athens in the age of Pericles. Let us try, in conclusion, to estimate the work which he did for his city and for the world.

The democracy of Athens was carried by Pericles to its highest stage of development; when he substituted the law-courts for the Areopagus, and allowed pay to the jurors, he removed the last traces of the aristocratic constitution. By the new arrangement he enlisted an immense body of citizens on the side of law, with the result that there was perhaps no city where the law was more strictly maintained than at Athens. Whatever the law was, it was supreme; even the omnipotent Demos could not touch it without a formal repeal, a process which could only take place at a particular time and with elaborate formalities. This supremacy of the law was chiefly maintained by the distinction drawn between decrees or acts of the sovereign assembly, and laws or ordinances, and though this distinction is not due to Pericles, the "indictment for illegality," which kept it alive, was probably his work. The aim of Pericles was to create a sovereign people, but to regulate their sovereignty by fixed laws. This result he could only attain by instituting a body of jurors, or possible jurors, so large that they were sure to command a majority in the Assembly, if any question touching the sovereignty of law arose. And here the evil of the system came in. The arrangements of the courts were so cumbersome and imperfect that they did as much harm in administering the law as they did good in upholding it. They brought together a number of men who, without being themselves responsible to any one, were constantly pronouncing upon the lives and fortunes of their fellow citizens. And from the very circumstances of the case, these men were drawn from the class of needy and useless citizens, who could least of all be expected to forget themselves and their own interests.

To Pericles is also due the final development of the Athenian empire. With the suppression of the revolts of Eubœa and Samos the equality which prevailed among the original members of the Delian confederacy became a mere fiction. The league was now an empire, existing for Athens only, and controlled entirely by her. She was the centre of the circle ; the guardian goddess of the city was the guardian goddess of the league. It may be said in defence of this high-handed proceeding that Pericles merely sought to put unity in the place of isolation, and build up a great national power out of a number of cities, which would otherwise have been perpetually at war with each other. He saw clearly that the want of unity was the great defect of Hellas, and he determined, if possible, to remedy the defect. Such aims were in themselves more than legitimate. No statesman could have rendered a greater service to his country than the formation of a league, which should combine the scattered forces into one focus. But here again Pericles adopted means which failed to bring about the desired result. His hostility to Sparta was fatal to any attempt to unite Greece, while his constant efforts to win the control of the Corinthian Gulf brought on him the bitter hatred of Corinth, by far the most enterprising member of the Peloponnesian confederacy.

The truth is that he regarded the matter far too exclusively from an Athenian point of view. If Greece could be united under the headship of Athens, he would accept the position ; if not, Greece

must be subject to Athens. Whether any means
could have been found in the existing state of Greek
feeling, by which the various cities, Dorian and
Ionian, within Peloponnesus and without, could have
been brought into a single confederation, is very
doubtful; the love of "autonomy" was too inveterate to admit of the smallest infraction of civic
rights. But, in any case, the methods adopted by
Pericles were not likely to find favour. The cities
naturally resented the tyrannical force which compelled them to furnish troops for wars declared without their consent, and to carry their disputes for
settlement before a jury which looked on them as
subjects of Athens. It is true that they brought
their tribute to Athens at the Dionysia, when they
could admire the splendour of the city and enjoy the
plays in the theatre, but these delights were a poor
compensation for the degradation which the enforced
payment of tribute seemed to entail. When Pericles
spoke of Athens as the "School of Hellas," he confounded the theories of the lecture-room with the
common-sense of politics. A few of the allies were
attracted by the splendours of the dominant city,
but if these were intended to create a feeling of
attachment in the subjects, they were pretty certain
to fail of their object.

It was otherwise with the Athenian people. They
doubtless were proud of their city and proud of her
position as head of the empire. The "great name of
Athens" was a spell wherewith to charm them. The
older party, who would gladly have seen Athens less
imperial, if only she could have kept on terms with

Sparta, were silenced after 444 B.C., and for twelve or
fourteen years Pericles was supreme.   In this period
he succeeded in instilling the imperial policy so
deeply into the hearts of the people, that when the
struggle came, they were willing to fight to the death
rather than relinquish it.   In this, the crude, material
side of the matter, the Athenians were willing disciples.   But the higher motives, which guided the
policy of Pericles, were little appreciated by the
masses.   The sights presented to the populace at
the Panathenæa and Dionysia were indeed magnifi-
cent, and at such times the whole city might seem to
be united in great acts of worship.   But dearer far to
the inhabitants of Attica, than these great displays,
were the little local festivals in the country; the
jovial hospitality of neighbours, the delights of
spring-time and harvest; the "rest on the violet-bed
by the well."   The enjoyments of the average Athenian were those of the average man ; he did not take
that delight in higher art and literature, which caused
Pericles to give them so large a share in his theory of
politics.   In this matter the leader mistook his followers ; he had too little sympathy with what was
commonplace in them, and failed to apprehend how
closely what was soundest in civic life at Athens was
connected with the rather limited—not to say mean
—desires and aims of the Athenian people.   In seeking to carry them away from their old views by the
spectacle of something higher and more intellectual,
he aggravated some of their failings.   What the
Athenians needed above all things was balance and
weight.   Even at the best their institutions and be-

liefs were supported by sanctions which would not
bear logical examination. It was a great mistake to
weaken the force of such sanctions as were established, for it was very unlikely that anything more
intellectual would have greater force. The beauty
of the city, the great name of Athens, might flatter
the selfishness of the Athenians, but they could never
become the source of a national morality.

Still more disastrous for the future of his country
was the personal government which Pericles established. In his determination to be the foremost man
in the city, he left no room for a second. He repressed the growth of those who in the course of
nature would be required to take his place. Under
his shadow no fresh shoots sprang. He taught the
people to follow a leader, and left no one behind to
lead them; he destroyed their independence—or at
least the mutual play of opposite forces,—and when
he died came "the deluge." There was no one who
could succeed him. A democracy without great
men is a dangerous form of democracy, unless it be
steadied by a very strict constitution. It is at the
mercy of every wave of feeling—of every unprinci-
pled orator. When Pericles rose to power it would
have been possible to frame a Pan-Hellenic union, in
which Sparta and Athens would have been the leading states; and such a dualism would have been the
best guarantee for the rights of the smaller cities.
When he died there was no policy left but war with
Sparta, and conquest in the West. And not only so,
but there was no politician who could adjust the relations of domestic war and foreign conquest. The

Athenians passed from one to the other, as they were addressed by Cleon or Alcibiades. We cannot wonder that the men who lived in those days of trouble spoke bitterly of Pericles, holding him accountable for the miseries which fell upon Athens. Other statesmen had bequeathed good laws, as Solon and Clisthenes, or the memory of great achievements, as Themistocles or Cimon, but the only changes which Pericles had introduced were thought, not without reason, to be changes for the worse; and he left his country involved in a ruinous war.

But though Greece hated him, and Athens spoke of him with mingled feelings, the debt which the world owes to Pericles is immense. Without him and his personal government; without the money which he lavished on shows and spectacles, on temples and statues; without the sophists and philosophers whom he sheltered, we should have been the poorer by the loss of half our intellectual life. And in his political aims, however unfortunate the results, we can trace the outlines of a purpose which must always be the guiding light of the greatest statesmen: the wish to give to every citizen in and through the state, not only the blessings of peace and prosperity, but the still greater blessing of unimpeded action in all noble aspirations; to awaken in him such a devotion to his state as shall prove an unerring guide in conduct; to train his intellectual and moral powers, not with the lessons of a school, but by the experience of life; to develop an equal balance between the individual and the citizen; to make duty a delight, and service an honour; to remove the sting

from poverty and the charm from wealth; and to
recognise benefits to the community as the only
ground of civic distinction. Such a purpose was
perhaps a distant ideal, even at Athens, and it is far
more distant now; but near or far away, it is from
such ideals that the spark is sent which kindles the
flame of our highest efforts.

A few details have come down to us of the personal appearance and manners of Pericles. In his
looks, and still more in his voice, he so closely
resembled Pisistratus that for some time he was
afraid to come forward in political life, lest he
should be suspected of cherishing the designs which
made the name of the tyrant hateful to every
Athenian. His head, which was of unusual size and
shape, was a common theme of merriment with the
comedians; they compared it to a kind of bean,
called *schinus*, and exercised their wits in all kinds
of allusions to the heavy head of the new Olympian.
To conceal the defect, Pericles was accustomed,
when in public, to wear a helmet, a practice which,
as we have said, provoked Cratinus into declaring
that he went "about with the Odeum on his head."
The suspicions which his appearance excited were
not diminished by his education and manners. His
tutor in "music," which at Athens included most
of the intellectual part of education, as opposed to
the physical, was Damon, the "friend of tyrants"
and a "consummate sophist," who, under cover of
his art, was thought to cherish designs against the
democracy. Whether this view was correct or

not, Damon was ostracised from Athens. Another teacher was Zeno, from whom Pericles learned the art of disputation as it was practised in the Eleatic school.

More important still was his connexion with Anaxagoras (p. 158). In the society of this eminent man he not only acquired a knowledge and an elevation of thought which raised him above the superstitions of his time, but the influence extended to his language and demeanour. As an orator, Pericles was stately and dignified, carefully avoiding anything familiar or common in his language; calm and quiet in his delivery, and by these very qualities producing a deep impression on his audience. His movements were at all times sedate; his dress was careful and becoming; he was rarely seen to smile, and nothing could provoke him to anger. When an impudent scoundrel, who had pursued him all day long with abuse and threats, followed him even to his door, he merely gave orders to his servants to see the fellow home through the dusk of the evening. He never moved in society, and was rarely seen in any street in the city but that which led from the public offices to his own home. He lived apart, dividing his time between the friendships of his intimate circle and the cares of state. Such reserve was a novel feature in an Athenian statesman, and different interpretations were placed upon it. To some it was mere arrogance and pride; he was the Olympian who governed Athens with his nod; others regarded it as a cloak for private vices, and told the worst stories of the Periclean household. For himself he held that familiarity bred contempt; a man so greatly occupied in public business must beware of making himself too cheap. Like the state galley, he must only appear when his presence was required.

His power was far greater than that of any other man of his time. Yet he never abused it for mean or malicious purposes. In his last utterance, as we have said, he declared that no Athenian had ever put on mourning owing to any act of his. With these words before him, Plutarch, no mean judge of Greek and Roman character, pronounces sentence on the great Athenian. The Roman selected for comparison with Pericles in Plutarch's series is Fabius Maximus, the opponent of Hannibal—

Unus qui nobis cunctando restituit rem.

In graciousness and clemency, in the forbearance and patience with which they endured the attacks of foolish and ignorant enemies, the Roman and the Grecian were fairly matched. "But not less admirable than his clemency was the loftiness of spirit which prompted Pericles to utter that last noble speech, giving the foremost place among his triumphs to the self-restraint which had governed his exercise of supreme authority. Such a saying changes the epithet Olympian—attached to his name by a rash and thoughtless crowd—into a worthy and becoming title.　For if indeed Olympus be a place of radiant calm,

> Where falls not hail, or rain, or any snow,
> Nor ever wind blows loudly,

a life so unruffled by the storms of state, so spotless amid the temptations of unbounded power, may be called in the truest sense Olympian and divine." *

* Plut. " Pericles."

COIN OF ATHENS, WITH ACROPOLIS AND
STATUE OF ATHENA (LATE).

INDEX.

Heroes of the Nations.

EDITED BY

EVELYN ABBOTT M.A., FELLOW OF BALLIOL COLLEGE, OXFORD.

A SERIES of biographical studies of the lives and work of a number of representative historical characters about whom have gathered the great traditions of the Nations to which they belonged, and who have been accepted, in many instances, as types of the several National ideals. With the life of each typical character will be presented a picture of the National conditions surrounding him during his career.

The narratives are the work of writers who are recognized authorities on their several subjects, and, while thoroughly trustworthy as history, will present picturesque and dramatic "stories" of the Men and of the events connected with them.

To the Life of each "Hero" will be given one duodecimo volume, handsomely printed in large type, provided with maps and adequately illustrated according to the special requirements of the several subjects. The volumes will be sold separately as follows:

Cloth extra	$1 50
Half morocco, uncut edges, gilt top . . .	1 75
Large paper, limited to 250 numbered copies for subscribers to the series. These may be obtained in sheets folded, or in cloth, uncut edges	3 50

The first group of the Series will comprise twelve volumes, as follows:

G. P. PUTNAM'S SONS

NEW YORK
27 AND 29 WEST TWENTY-THIRD STREET

LONDON
27 KING WILLIAM STREET, STRAND

The Story of the Nations.

MESSRS. G. P. PUTNAM'S SONS take pleasure in announcing that they have in course of publication, in co-operation with Mr. T. Fisher Unwin, of London, a series of historical studies, intended to present in a graphic manner the stories of the different nations that have attained prominence in history.

In the story form the current of each national life is distinctly indicated, and its picturesque and noteworthy periods and episodes are presented for the reader in their philosophical relation to each other as well as to universal history.

It is the plan of the writers of the different volumes to enter into the real life of the peoples, and to bring them before the reader as they actually lived, labored, and struggled—as they studied and wrote, and as they amused themselves. In carrying out this plan, the myths, with which the history of all lands begins, will not be overlooked, though these will be carefully distinguished from the actual history, so far as the labors of the accepted historical authorities have resulted in definite conclusions.

The subjects of the different volumes have been planned to cover connecting and, as far as possible, consecutive epochs or periods, so that the set when completed will present in a comprehensive narrative the chief events in the great STORY OF THE NATIONS; but it is, of course, not always practicable to issue the several volumes in their chronological order.

The " Stories " are printed in good readable type, and in handsome 12mo form. They are adequately illustrated and furnished with maps and indexes. They are sold separately at a price of $1.50 each.

The following volumes are now ready (April, 1890):

THE STORY OF GREECE. Prof. JAS. A. HARRISON.
    "   "   " ROME. ARTHUR GILMAN.
    "   "   " THE JEWS. Prof. JAMES K. HOSMER.
    "   "   " CHALDEA. Z. A. RAGOZIN.
    "   "   " GERMANY. S. BARING-GOULD.
    "   "   " NORWAY. HJALMAR H. BOYESEN.
    "   "   ' " SPAIN. Rev. E. E. and SUSAN HALE.
    "   "   " HUNGARY. Prof. A. VÁMBÉRY.
    "   "   " CARTHAGE. Prof. ALFRED J. CHURCH.
    "   "   " THE SARACENS. ARTHUR GILMAN.
    "   "   " THE MOORS IN SPAIN. STANLEY LANE-POOLE.
    "   "   " THE NORMANS. SARAH ORNE JEWETT.
    "   "   " PERSIA. S. G. W. BENJAMIN.
    "   "   " ANCIENT EGYPT. Prof. GEO. RAWLINSON.
    "   "   " ALEXANDER'S EMPIRE. Prof. J. P. MAHAFFY.
    "   "   " ASSYRIA. Z. A. RAGOZIN.
    "   "   " THE GOTHS. HENRY BRADLEY.
    "   "   " IRELAND. Hon. EMILY LAWLESS.
    "   "   " TURKEY. STANLEY LANE-POOLE.
    "   "   " MEDIA, BABYLON, AND PERSIA. Z. A. RAGOZIN.
    "   "   " MEDIÆVAL FRANCE. Prof. GUSTAV MASSON.
    "   "   " HOLLAND. Prof. J. THOROLD ROGERS.
    "   "   " MEXICO. SUSAN HALE.
    "   "   " PHŒNICIA. Prof. GEO. RAWLINSON.
    "   "   " THE HANSA TOWNS. HELEN ZIMMERN.
    "   "   " EARLY BRITAIN. Prof. ALFRED J. CHURCH.
    "   "   " THE BARBARY CORSAIRS. STANLEY LANE-POOLE.
    "   "   " RUSSIA. W. R. MORFILL.
    "   "   " THE JEWS UNDER ROME. W. D. MORRISON.
    "   "   " SCOTLAND. JOHN MACKINTOSH.

Now in Press for immediate issue:

THE STORY OF SWITZERLAND. R. STEAD and Mrs. ARNOLD HUG.
    "   "   " VEDIC INDIA. Z. A. RAGOZIN.
    "   "   " THE THIRTEEN COLONIES. HELEN A. SMITH.
    "   "   " MODERN FRANCE. EMILY CRAWFORD.
    "   "   " CANADA. A. R. MACFARLANE.

G. P. PUTNAM'S SONS   T. FISHER UNWIN
NEW YORK   LONDON

www.ingramcontent.com/pod-product-compliance
Lightning Source LLC
Chambersburg PA
CBHW022013110726
47901CB00006B/1511